CONTENTS

Preface

This book is primarily aimed at scientists and engineers who find they have a requirement to program in Fortran. The book should help those who are unable to attend a convenient course or those who are looking for a book to support what they are learning in an introduction to programming. We have therefore started the book with two chapters which give the first-time programmer a good idea of what programming in general is all about. This has been followed with a more detailed description of the Fortran language and its use. These subsequent chapters will also be useful to the more experienced reader wanting an introduction to the Fortran 90 language.

The major features of the language have been organised into separate chapters so the book should form a good reference and *aide memoire* to the language long after the initial learning phase is complete. The text, examples, and answers to the exercises set at the end of each chapter, will be useful to those with a real problem to solve who are asking the question "How do I do that in Fortran?". The book is suitable for use as the basis of a training course in Fortran programming. Some guidelines for using the book in this way are given at the end of this preface.

It is clear that even non-professional programmers need to be concerned about the issues of writing programs that are portable between different computers. Many computer users now have access to machines at work and at home. Some will have access to more than one machine at work, and it is more than likely that these will be of different types. For instance many scientists and engineers will have access to high-performance computers which use multiple processors working in parallel. Since access to such machines is expensive much of the initial program development will be done on desktop uni-processor PCs or workstations. As a result programs will need to be ported between these very different machine architectures. In writing this book therefore we have paid considerable attention to introducing Fortran in a way which aids portability and have relegated features which can hinder portability to a later chapter on "features to be avoided".

As anyone who has spent more than a couple of years writing programs will testify, it is rare indeed for any program to be used once and then thrown away. Most programs are modified and re-used many times to solve similar but slightly different problems. It is sometimes said, only half as a joke that there are very few original programs - all the rest are said to be produced by modification and amendment of these. It is also a truism that all but the simplest programs contain undetected bugs. Such bugs can remain dormant for years but can also at some time cause a program to malfunction when working on a new combination of data. There is therefore the continuing need for programs to be re-read and modified (sometimes by people who did not write the original code). Whatever the reasons for modifying programs it is a fact that the process of carrying out such changes is notorious for introducing new bugs. To minimise such problems, it is essential that a reasonably disciplined approach to programming is followed and so we have paid some considerable attention to methods which aid readability and maintainability of programs.

Fortran is the oldest of the established "high-level" languages, having been invented by a group in IBM during the late 1950s. The language became so popular in the early 1960s that other vendors started to produce their own versions and this led to a growing divergence of dialects. It was recognised that such divergence was not in the interests of either the computer users or the computer vendors and so Fortran became the first language to be officially standardised in 1966. This meant that Fortran became more widely implemented than any other language. By the early 1970s virtually every computer, mini or mainframe, was supplied with a standard-conforming Fortran 66 language processing system. It was therefore possible to write programs in Fortran on any one system and be reasonably confident that these could be moved fairly easily to work on any other system. This applied to systems from different manufacturers and to different systems supplied by the same manufacturer. This, and the fact that Fortran programs could be processed very efficiently, led to Fortran being the most heavily-used programming language for non-commercial applications. (Cobol was designed slightly later than Fortran, specifically for commercial computing such as company payroll, financial record keeping, etc. It, too, was standardised in the late 1960s and this, together with the fact that the majority of computers in use are involved in the commercial field, has made it by far the most heavily-used programming language).

The standard definition of Fortran was updated in the late 1970's and a new standard, ANSI X3.9-1978, was published by the American National Standards Institute. This standard was subsequently (in 1980) adopted by the International Standards Organisation (ISO) as an International Standard (IS 1539 : 1980). It is commonly known as Fortran 77 (since the final draft was actually completed in 1977) and is the version of the language now in widespread use.

The venerable nature of Fortran and the rather conservative character of the 1977 standard revision left Fortran 77 with a number of old-fashioned facilities that might be termed deficiencies, or at least infelicities. The standards bodies therefore set out in the early 1980s to revise the standard and to modernise Fortran to incorporate many of the developments of language design demonstrated in other effective but less heavily used languages such as Algol (60 and 68), Pascal, APL, C, and Ada. This process took almost twelve years and many, many hours of hard work by people on committees in several different countries. The ANSI committee X3J3 and the ISO working group with the memorable designation ISO/IEC JTC1/SC22/WG5 were the primary bodies responsible. The language defined by this revised standard, which was finally published by ISO in August 1991, is called Fortran 90. The authors of this book were both active members of these various committees and very much involved with the design of many of the new facilities in Fortran 90.

Fortran 90 is a major development of the language but nevertheless it includes all of Fortran 77 as a strict subset and so any standard conforming Fortran 77 program will continue to be a valid Fortran 90 program. However Fortran 90 allows programs to be expressed in ways that are more suited to a modern computing environment and has rendered obsolete many of the mechanisms that were appropriate in Fortran 77. In this book we have tried to present an approach to programming which uses the new features of Fortran 90 to good effect and which will result in portable, efficient, safe and maintainable code. The book is not intended to be a complete description of every possible feature of the language. A significant number of features that the authors believe to be obsolete or undesirable and essentially redundant, have been either relegated to a special chapter on such facilities or left out altogether. However, the language that remains is rich, powerful, modern and highly expressive. Any reasonable program (not setting out to perform rather tricky and inherently unsafe operations) can be written using the recommended subset of Fortran 90. In fact the subset of Fortran 90 covered, and the style of programming used, is significantly more powerful than that available in most other modern programming languages.

The book can be considered to be in two parts. The first two chapters are a brief informal introduction to the main ideas and concepts which form the fundamental basis of programming. The aim here is to get the reader as rapidly as possible to the point of being able to read, write, and understand complete programming examples, albeit simple ones. The remaining chapters cover selected features of Fortran 90 programming in more detail. As indicated previously, the book is not meant to be a complete "language reference". The reader who requires a definitive and complete statement of Fortran 90 is recommended to consult the official standard definition, and the Fortran language manual(s) for his particular processing system(s). Anyone who is seriously intending to write any significant amount of Fortran will, eventually, have to consult the latter and the former is the essential definitive statement of what is a standard-conforming and hence potentially portable program.

Although Fortran is traditionally the programming language of the highly numerate physical scientist and engineer, we have tried to make this book digestible to the rather less mathematically sophisticated reader. Therefore examples have been chosen which assume only the sort of mathematical knowledge that is likely to be common to any reasonably numerate secondary school graduate; in particular it is not assumed that the reader is an expert in matrix algebra or the calculus.

The beginner is recommended to read the book from the beginning, paying particular attention to understanding the basic concepts and ideas in Chapters 1 and 2. The reader who already has some knowledge of programming, and perhaps Fortran 77, and who is interested only in the specifics of Fortran 90, can skim quickly through these early chapters, and move more directly to the appropriate sections later in the book.

A selection of exercises has been included at the end of each chapter which provide the prospective programmer with the opportunity to practice some of the ideas covered. Example solutions to these exercises are included in Appendix B. However, in many years of teaching programming and programming in Fortran in particular, the authors have observed that the quickest way to learn to program is for students to solve a real problem which is of genuine interest to them. Those readers who wish to do this are recommended to read quickly through to about Chapter 8. This should provide a good general view of the essential shape and structure of Fortran 90. The reader should then start trying to build pieces of program to solve parts of his or her problem, probably starting with a module setting up the main data and procedures required and test programs to try them out. In doing this reference back to various Chapters for detailed information on the particular programming facilities will become necessary, and then actually trying them on a machine will very rapidly cement the concepts and skills of programming.

If used in support of a training course, the first two chapters can be used as the basis of a quick introduction to programming. Simplified subsets of chapters 3 through 8 (taken from the first part of each chapter) can then be introduced (with practicals) and then these areas returned to in more detail as the programming knowledge of the student grows. We would not recommend attempting to introduce the concepts of pointers and targets too early, but we **would** try to get students thinking in terms of modules containing "packages" of data and procedures as early as practicable. We believe these latter concepts will be essential for the user solving practical problems in Fortran 90 who wishes to develop a good programming style.

JSM & JLS
May '93

Acknowledgements

In writing this book we have inevitably drawn significantly on work that has been done at our workplace, the Computing Services Department at the University of Liverpool. Many of the examples used in the book have been adapted from a Fortran course which has been developed over many years by several present and past members of staff of the department and we should like to acknowledge this.

We should like to thank our colleague, Mary Thorp, for reading the manuscript and for making many useful comments on the contents.

Finally we should like to thank our wives Mary and Linda for their patience and support and for maintaining their sanity whilst we embarked on this our second book.

Chapter 1

Programming Fundamentals

We are starting this chapter, and indeed the book, with a basic introduction to computer programs and to some of the fundamental concepts that lie behind their development. To understand what a program is it is useful to refer to a simple model of how a typical computer works.

1.1 A simple computer

As shown in Figure 1.1, a computer consists of a processor, often called the *central processor unit* or cpu for short, and a *memory* which can be thought of as a large number of "pigeon holes" or locations in which data values can be stored. The cpu can perform various operations on values by placing the values in special internal locations called *registers* and then operating on these registers. The cpu can also pass information between the memory and the outside world. Information that is transferred in to the memory is called *input* and information that is transferred out is called *output*.

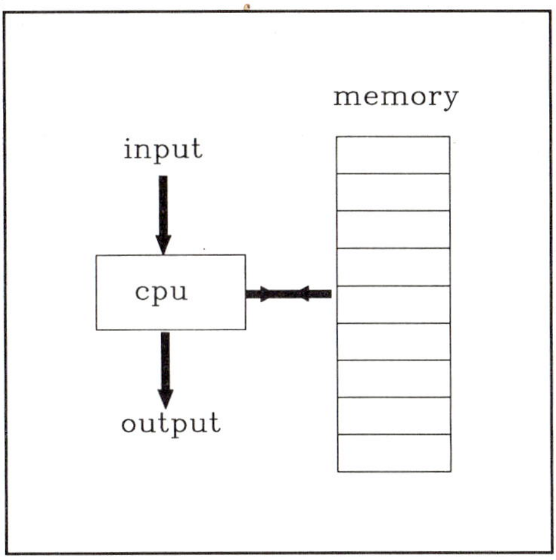

Figure 1.1: A simple computer

A cpu actually executes instructions that are coded as binary numbers, groups of 0s and 1s which represent machine instructions. Such instructions might look like:

```
011100100001001
011101000001010
000110100000000
100000100001011
```

which could represent instructions like,

```
(load contents of location 9 into register 1),
(load contents of location 10 into register 2),
(add contents of registers 1 and 2, leave the result in 1),
```

```
(store contents of register 1 in location 11).
```

A set of instructions like this which defines a task for a computer is called a program. Fortunately though, in order to write programs, it is not necessary to know the details of the most basic instructions described above. Programming languages like Fortran are available which allow programmers to use English-like words and mathematics-like expressions to code their problems. Programs written in Fortran are translated by special programs called *compilers* into machine instructions such as those illustrated above which can then be run on a computer. Languages like Fortran are called *procedural* since they require that solutions be expressed as tasks or procedures for the computer to carry out.

1.2 The development of a simple sequential program

Suppose we wanted to write a program to convert a time in hours, minutes and seconds to one in seconds only. In order to do this we must turn the problem into a series of steps which, when carried out, provide the solution to the problem. Such a series of steps is called an *algorithm* and can be compared to the instructions in a cooking recipe which would be carried out by a chef. A suitable set of instructions for our conversion problem might be:

```
1.  Multiply the number of hours by 60 and add the minutes.
2.  Multiply the result of step 1 by 60 and add the seconds.
```

These two instructions, if carried out by a reasonably intelligent human being, would be sufficient to produce the correct result. Unfortunately they are not sufficiently precise to be directly translatable into Fortran 90 for execution by a computer. There are no explicit definitions of the values on which the instructions are to operate although it is implicit that these are values for the number of hours, the number of minutes and the number of seconds. This is rather like leaving out the list of ingredients and quantities in a cooking recipe and leaving the person who is using it to infer from the instructions what should be used. It is assumed that the result of step 1 above will be remembered without anything being said explicitly as to how. Nothing has been said either as to how the input values are to be established, and no indication has been given as to how the output is to be reported. All of these deficiencies must be put right when we start thinking in terms of a program to be executed by a computer.

A more detailed set of instructions which would be suitable for converting into a Fortran program would be as follows:

```
1.  Start of program.
2.  Reserve three pigeon holes to store whole number values
    and give these names hours, mins, and secs.
3.  Take three values passed in from outside and store these
    in the pigeon holes named hours, mins, and secs.
4.  Multiply the contents of the hours pigeon hole by 60 and
    add the contents of the mins pigeon hole.  Store the
    result back in the pigeon hole mins replacing the value
    already there.
5.  Multiply the contents of mins by 60 and add the contents
    of secs, store the result in secs replacing the existing
    value.
6.  Write out the caption
        Time in secs =
    followed by the value stored in secs and pass this out to
    some suitable external device.
7.  End of program instructions so stop.
```

We can see that the two instructions in our original algorithm have now become instructions 4 and 5 in the new set of instructions. Notice that the extra instructions required result from the fact that a computer is not intelligent in the way humans are. It will do only what it is told to do, no more and no less. It needs to be told pedantically where the program instructions start and finish, to name and reserve pigeon holes where necessary, when to wait for us to give it the values, and when to pass out the result.

In fact each of the seven instructions of the above algorithm translates directly into a corresponding Fortran 90 statement which would tell a real computer to perform the corresponding step in the program. The Fortran 90 program would be as shown below.

```
PROGRAM example1
  INTEGER :: hours,mins,secs
  READ(UNIT=*,FMT=*) hours,mins,secs
  mins = hours*60 + mins
  secs = mins*60 + secs
  WRITE(UNIT=*,FMT=*) 'Time in seconds =',secs
END
```

This shows the Fortran 90 source text of the program, as it would be created by the programmer and stored in a file[1]. Each line in this program is called a statement and each statement is an instruction to the computer to perform a particular action.

---

[1] Note that a file is a collection of information permanently stored in a computer usually on a magnetic disc. Such a collection is given a name by which it can be located and used.

The first statement:

```
PROGRAM example1
```

is merely a heading which notifies the compiler that a program called `example1` follows. Note that the use of upper and lower case letters in `PROGRAM` and `example1` has no significance. We have used the different cases merely to enhance readability. Our normal practice is to use upper case for keywords of the Fortran language and to use lower case for names chosen by the programmer. More detail on the way Fortran 90 programs may be expressed is given in Chapter 3.

The last statement:

```
END
```

notifies the compiler that there are no more program statements. It also tells the machine that the program execution has finished and that it should return control of the computer to the operating system[2]. The `END` statement must appear as the last statement in all programs.

The second statement:

```
INTEGER :: hours,mins,secs
```

instructs the compiler to reserve space to store three integer, or whole number, values and to call these locations `hours`, `mins` and `secs`. These names can be used to refer to these locations and their contents in the rest of the program. Since the values stored in these locations may change during the execution of the program they are normally called *variables*.

Statements like the `INTEGER` statement above are called *declarations* and are analogous to the list of ingredients in a cooking recipe. The remaining statements in the program are all instructions to perform actions when the final translated program runs. These are analogous to the processing instructions in a recipe.

The statements between the `PROGRAM` and `END` statements are executed one after the other. When there are no more statements (i.e. when the `END` is reached) the program stops. The `END` statement causes instructions to be

[2] The operating system is an overall control program which manages the computer hardware and sorts out such questions as the physical placing of files on disc, the control of keyboard and display devices, and the running of other programs, including user programs.

inserted into the translated program to finish the execution and to return control of the computer to the operating system.

The statement,

```
READ(UNIT=*,FMT=*) hours,mins,secs
```

causes the program to read three integer values that will be typed in from the keyboard. These values are to be stored in the storage locations named `hours`, `mins` and `secs`. In general a `READ` statement in Fortran 90 tells the computer to read data from an input device. Exactly where the data values are to come from is indicated by a unit specifier. This is the first item in the parentheses, following the keyword `UNIT=`. In this case we have set the unit specifier to `*`. This indicates we wish to read from the default input unit which is normally the keyboard being used by the person running the program. The second `*` in the parentheses, following the `FMT=` keyword, indicates that the input values will be of the kind required to fill the storage locations named in the list that follows and that these will be typed with each value separated from the next by at least one space, comma, or end of line. The parentheses are followed by the list of the names of the storage locations, or variables, which are to be filled by the values read in. When the program gets to this statement it will wait for the person running the program to type three whole numbers on the keyboard. These will be interpreted by the program as the number of hours, minutes and seconds in the time to be converted.

The next statement,

```
mins = hours*60 + mins
```

tells the computer to retrieve the value stored in the `hours` pigeon hole, multiply it by sixty and then add the value stored in the location named `mins`. The resulting value is then to be stored in the `mins` location, replacing the value already there. In programming the multiply operation must always be indicated explicitly, and the symbol `*` is used for this purpose. It is also important to notice that the equals sign is used in Fortran programming with a meaning that is different from its use in mathematics. In mathematics "=" normally means "is equal to", in programming "=" means "make equal to". Interpreted as a mathematical equation the statement above would imply that `hours` was equal to zero. This is clearly not what was intended.

The statement,

```
secs = mins*60 + secs
```

is essentially the same as the one before except that it works with different locations to calculate the final `secs` value.

The last of the statements, before the `END`,

```
WRITE(UNIT=*,FMT=*) 'Time in seconds=',secs
```

transfers the final result to the display screen. The `WRITE` statement is similar to the `READ` statement in that the first item in the parentheses, following the `UNIT=` keyword, specifies the unit to which the data will be transferred. Again we have used an asterisk, `*`, in this role to indicate the system default unit which is normally the display screen. The second asterisk in the parentheses indicates that the results are to be output in a standard way, that a system default format is to be used to determine how the results will be positioned on the screen. The text between the quote symbols is output exactly as shown, starting on a new line of the display screen. It is followed by the integer value that is stored in the variable `secs`, separated by a few spaces from the text itself.

The important point to note in this simple example is that when the computer executes this program it performs the actions indicated by each statement in sequence, i.e. in the order in which the statements appear in the program. The same program statements in a different order would usually be a completely different program and would produce quite different results.

1.2.1 Running the program

Once a program such as the one described above has been typed into the computer, usually using a text editor of some sort, and stored in a file, it needs to be compiled. As was mentioned earlier, a compiler is a program which takes as input the source code of a Fortran program and translates it into machine language. During the compilation process it is quite common for errors to be detected. These *compilation errors* arise if the detailed rules of the Fortran language are not satisfied. It is often necessary to have several runs of the compiler before a program is successfully compiled.

After successful compilation the compiler will have normally created a translated version of the program and stored this in a file. This translated version is usually called the *object code version*. However, before the program can be run, a further step called *linking* is necessary. Many of the common, sometimes complex actions involved in fully executing Fortran instructions are implemented by pre-written pieces of program that are stored in a library. The linking process inserts these pieces of program in the appropriate places in the object code to produce a fully-executable program, often called a *binary program*, that is also stored in a file. This file is in the correct form to be loaded into the computer and executed. The compilation and linking process is summarised schematically in Figure 1.2.

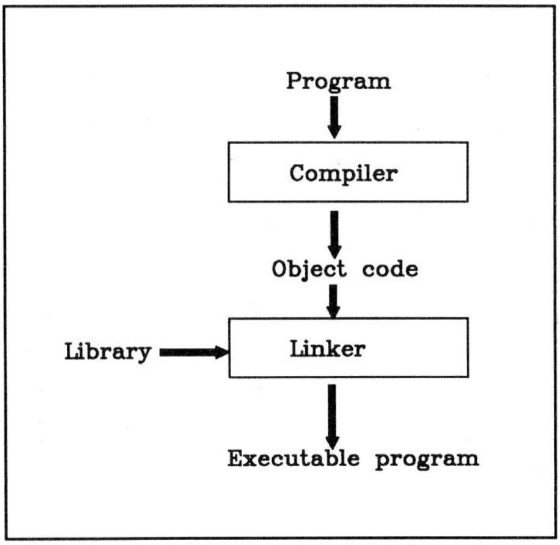

Figure 1.2: Compiling and linking

When our example above is executed it will wait for us to type the hours, minutes and seconds values. We might type

```
2,46,14
```

and when the enter key is pressed to indicate the end of the input line, the program will proceed to perform the requested calculation and would very quickly display

```
Time in seconds =   9974
```

Of course, this is what would happen if we had written the program correctly. It is commonly the case, however, for there to be errors in programs which cannot be detected by a compiler. These only become evident when a program is run and are often called *execution errors*. For instance, an attempt to divide a number by zero is obviously an error and the computer will normally stop executing the program and print out a suitable message to the user. Much more serious are errors that cause the production of wrong results only for certain values of input data. Such errors (often called *bugs*) can be caused by faulty programming or by poor algorithm design. They can be partially but not completely prevented by testing programs on data which produce known results. There are many well-known stories of cases where bridges have fallen down and where space probes have failed which can be attributed to bugs in computer programs that have gone undetected during development.

1.3 Conditional execution

The simple example presented in the previous section was useful for illustrating some basic ideas. However most real-life tasks require decisions to be made based on knowledge that has been acquired during the execution of the task. These decisions determine what action is to be taken next as the task is carried out. We have all heard of the story of the pensioner who is threatened by the bailiffs for non-payment of a computer-produced electricity bill for a few pennies or even for a zero amount. Such a mistake would usually be caused by a programmer forgetting to take account of the fact that a bill could possibly be ridiculously small or even zero. A simplified statement of the algorithm used for printing out bills could have been,

```
1.   Calculate bill
2.   Print invoice
```

whereas it probably should have been,

```
1.   Calculate the bill
2.   If the bill is greater than some fixed minimum then print
     invoice otherwise add the bill to customer's account and
     do not print invoice.
```

The second algorithm is much more sensible since it only produces a bill if there is a reasonable amount to be paid. If the bill is small, the amount is not lost but is added to the next bill the customer pays. Of course the calculation of the bill in the first instruction has to be changed so that any small amounts "left behind" from previous program runs are added to the new bill.

The two instructions "print invoice" and "add the bill to the customers account..." in statement 2 above are said to be conditionally executed. Either one or the other is executed depending on whether a certain condition holds. The first instruction is executed if the bill is greater than a fixed minimum, the second is executed if the bill is not greater than a fixed minimum.

We shall now illustrate these ideas by developing a program to convert a given number of seconds to the equivalent time in hours, minutes and seconds. This, of course, is the inverse of the problem solved by the first example program. We shall make the program a little more elaborate than the first example by making it prompt the user for the appropriate input when it is required. This is preferable to having a program just wait for no obvious reason. The prompt can be included by making the program write out a message just before it is going to require the number of seconds to be read in.

The conversion calculation itself can be done by dividing the number of seconds by 60. The quotient is the number of minutes, the remainder is the final number of seconds. A similar calculation will convert the minutes into hours and minutes. Finally we would like our program to write out the result in the form of a number followed by the word `hours`, a number followed by the word `minutes` and a number followed by the word `seconds`. If however the input number of seconds is less than one hour, it would be better if we omitted the hours part altogether rather than write out a zero number of hours. We can write a description of what our program has to do as follows:

```
1.  Start of program.
2.  Reserve memory locations to store the number of
    hours,minutes, and seconds.
3.  Write a prompt to the display to request the input.
4.  Read the value typed on the display and store in seconds
    location.
5.  Convert the value from seconds to hours, minutes, and
    seconds and store the results in the appropriate memory
    locations.
6.  If the number of hours is zero then
        Write out the minutes and seconds only
    otherwise
        Write out the hours, minutes, and seconds.
7.  End of program
```

A significant feature of the above example is that the algorithm still consists of a set of instructions which are carried out one after another. Instruction 6, which tells us to do one of two different things depending on the value we have calculated for `hours`, is slightly more elaborate than the instructions we met in the program of the previous section but it is still only one statement in the sequential flow of the algorithm.

The following program expresses the above instructions in Fortran 90.

```
PROGRAM seconds_to_hours_mins_secs
!---------------------------------------------------------!
! convert time in seconds to hours, minutes and seconds   !
!---------------------------------------------------------!
  INTEGER :: hours,mins,secs

! write a prompt and read the seconds value
  WRITE(UNIT=*,FMT=*) ' Type the number of seconds'
  READ(UNIT=*,FMT=*) secs
```

```
! convert seconds to hours, minutes and seconds
  mins = secs/60
  secs = secs - mins*60
  hours = mins/60
  mins = mins - hours*60

! decide which way to output results
  IF( hours == 0 )THEN
    WRITE(UNIT=*,FMT=*) 'Time =',mins,' minutes', &
                              secs,' seconds'
  ELSE
    WRITE(UNIT=*,FMT=*)'Time=',hours,'hours', &
                             mins,'minutes', &
                             secs,' seconds'
  ENDIF
ENDPROGRAM seconds_to_hours_mins_secs
```

When this program is compiled, linked and run with an input value of 9974 seconds, it would produce the following display.

```
Type the number of seconds?
9974
Time = 2 hours 46 minutes 14 seconds
```

If run with an input of 245 it would produce.

```
Type the number of seconds?
245
Time = 4 minutes 5 seconds
```

The first value we typed (shown emboldened) for the number of seconds was larger than 3600 and so the program produced a non-zero number of hours. For the second run we have used a small number of seconds, less than an hour, and the program has now typed out the result in the alternate form with the hours part omitted.
The two different forms of output required by statement 6 of the algorithm are selected by the statements,

```
IF( hours == 0 )THEN
  WRITE(UNIT=*,FMT=*) 'Time =',mins,' minutes', &
                            secs,' seconds'
ELSE
  WRITE(UNIT=*,FMT=*) 'Time =',hours,' hours', &
                            mins,' minutes', &
                            secs,' seconds
ENDIF
```

These statements can be read as, "if hours is equal to zero then do the first write statement otherwise (else) do the second write statement". The phrase "hours is equal to zero" is an expression written in plain English which is either true or false. Its equivalent in Fortran 90, `hours == 0`, is called a logical expression and is also either true or false. The `IF()THEN...ELSE...ENDIF` group of statements, often called an `IF` *construct*, thus tests the truth of a logical expression. If it is true the statement(s) following the `THEN` are executed, and execution then continues with the statement following the `ENDIF`. If the logical expression is false, the statement(s) following the `ELSE` are executed and execution then continues with the statement after the `ENDIF`.

Some other new elements of Fortran which require further explanation have also been introduced in this example. These are the described below.

1.3.1 Comments

The characters following a `!` character on any line in a Fortran 90 program are treated as commentary. Comments do not instruct the computer to do anything but are included in programs to explain to human readers what the program is trying to do. It is good practice to include comments in programs to explain non-obvious groups of statements. It is surprising how quickly the original intention of a piece of program is forgotten and how quickly the code becomes obscure even to very experienced programmers. If someone other than the author needs to read a program to modify it or correct it, comments are invaluable.

1.3.2 Continuation lines

If a statement is too long to fit on a line or if, for reasons of layout, it is preferable to spread a single statement over two or more lines then continuation can be indicated by appending a & character to the line to be continued. The `WRITE` statements in the above program have been continued in this way.

1.3.3 Integer arithmetic

To understand integer arithmetic as it is defined in Fortran 90 we need only cast our minds back to how we are taught arithmetic at school. Before we are taught decimal fractions we learn that if one number is divided by another the answer is a whole number (the quotient) and a remainder. For example 7 divided by 2 gives "3 remainder 1". In Fortran 90 the result of dividing 7 by 2 is just 3. That is, the quotient is the result of integer division, the remainder is ignored.

By dividing the number of seconds by 60 in the program we get the whole number of minutes as a result. To get the remainder we must then multiply the result by 60 and take it away from the original number of seconds. This is achieved in the statements

```
mins = secs/60
secs = secs - mins*60
```

1.4 Repeated execution

The huge success of computers has stemmed primarily from their ability to handle highly repetitive tasks with great speed and accuracy. Computers are regularly used to perform the same calculation over and over again with different data, without getting tired and without making mistakes. In such cases it is clear that if each set of data was processed using different program instructions the task of writing the program would take much longer than simply doing the task by hand. In fact the computer is made to execute the same instructions over and over again in a *loop*. The instructions are written once and the computer re-executes them with different data. This is how the programmer, by doing a relatively small amount of work, can make the computer do a great deal.

To illustrate the concept of a loop in a programming context, consider the program developed in the first section. If we had a large number of times that needed conversion, for instance a set of readings from some piece of measuring equipment, then such a program would be useful if it could be modified to repeat the conversion for each time. What we want is to make the program repeat the execution of its existing statements for the read-calculate-write part of the program until we have dealt with all the times we have to convert.

The algorithmic description of the program would be:

```
1.  Start of program
2.  Reserve memory locations for three whole number values
    named hours, mins, and secs.
3.  Repeat the following until all values are processed:
        read in the data
        convert to seconds
        write out the results
4.  End of program
```

This defines in general terms what we are setting out to do and it also defines the overall structure of the program that we must produce. It leaves till later the job of sorting out the details of what is to be done in the repeated block of instructions of statement 3. The next stage in the development of the program is to refine, or elaborate, instruction 3. We have to read the time, convert it, and print the result and we have to carry on doing this until we have dealt with all the necessary values. An important question is, how are we going to tell the computer that all the necessary values have been processed and that it should stop repeating the loop? One very commonly-used method is to give an item of input data a value which it would not normally take. The program can then be made to check for this value as an indication that this is the end of the data to be processed. In our example we use a negative number for the value of the hours. Our loop instructions could thus be written as,

```
3.0      Start of loop
3.1      Write prompt to request input of data.
3.2      Read three values storing them in the locations named
         hours, mins, and secs.
3.3      If the value in hours is negative, terminate the loop
         and continue with the next main instruction.
3.4      Multiply the contents of hours by 60 and add the
         contents of mins, store the result back in mins.
3.5      Multiply the contents of mins by 60 and add the
         contents of secs, store the result in secs.
3.6      Write out the caption 'Time in secs =' followed by
         the value stored in secs.
3.7      End of loop.
```

We have numbered the above instructions as 3.x to indicate that they are all part of the main level loop instruction 3.

We can now translate the complete specification of the program, instructions 1 to 3, into Fortran 90 statements as,

```
PROGRAM calsec
!-------------------------------------------------------!
! Converts times in hours, minutes, seconds to seconds  !
! The program is stopped by a negative number of hours  !
!-------------------------------------------------------!
! Reserve three locations for whole number values
  INTEGER :: hours,mins,secs
  DO      ! start of read-convert-write loop
    READ(UNIT=*,FMT=*) 'Input hours, minutes, and seconds?'
    READ(UNIT=*,FMT=*) hours,mins,secs
    IF( hours < 0 ) EXIT   ! finish loop if hours negative
    mins = hours*60 + mins
    secs = mins*60 + secs
    WRITE(UNIT=*,FMT=*) ' Time in seconds =',secs
  ENDDO  ! end of read-convert-write loop
ENDPROGRAM calsec
```

We have used comments to indicate the start and finish of the block of statements that are the translation of the loop into Fortran. The program has become much more complex, but it is a significantly more useful program than the example in the first section. The main additions are the statements for constructing what is called a "conditional exit" loop. These statements are the `DO` and `ENDDO` statements that serve to mark, or to delimit the sequence of statements that are to be repeated each time round the loop and the `IF(condition)EXIT` statement which is executed each time round the loop. If the condition is false the remaining statements in the loop are executed, but if the condition is true an exit from the loop is made and the program continues with the statement following the `ENDDO`. The `IF` statement used in the program is a special short-hand form which can be used when the `ELSE` part of a general `IF` construct is not needed and the `THEN` part is a single statement. In this particular case the single statement is `EXIT`, the instruction to exit from the loop.
When run, the program might produce output like,

```
Input hours, minutes, and seconds?
1,10,5
Time in secs = 4205
Input hours, minutes, and seconds?
0,1,5
Time in secs = 65
...
Input hours, minutes, and seconds?
-1,0,0
```

The program will continue to prompt for data as it goes round the loop until the negative number, -1, is typed. At this point the `EXIT` statement is executed and the loop will terminate. The next statement encountered will be the `END` and so the program will also terminate.

1.5 Summing up

In this Chapter we have used simple examples to introduce some concepts that are the basis of programming in a language like Fortran. We have shown programs that illustrate three basic patterns (often called *control structures*) of Fortran statements that are used to write programs. These are,

1. A simple sequence

2. A conditional choice of sequences

3. A repeated sequence or loop

In fact it can be proved that all algorithms, and hence programs, can be expressed using just these three structures. In practical programming, however, it is often convenient to use several other structures and these will be described later in Chapter 5.

1.6 Exercises

All the exercises accompanying this chapter can be done by modifying one or other of the examples used earlier in this chapter.

1. Write out the steps of an algorithm to convert a given number of years and weeks into the equivalent number of days.
   (ignore any effects due to leap years)

2. Translate this algorithm into a Fortran program to perform this conversion, choosing suitable names for the variables used to store the values involved. Assume that the number of years and weeks will be read from the keyboard and that the number of days will be written to the display screen.

3. Write out the steps of an algorithm to convert a given number of days to weeks and days and convert this algorithm into a suitable Fortran program.

4. Modify the algorithm of question 3 to make it handle an arbitrary number of input values. Convert it into a suitable Fortran program.

Chapter 2

Sub-dividing the Problem

Most tasks that are to be programmed for computers are at first expressed in a general way. For example:

```
Produce a monthly pay cheque for all employees in an
organisation.

Calculate how a bridge structure will behave under traffic
load and during high cross winds

Control the speed and direction of a spacecraft landing on
the moon

Write a program to play chess
```

Such problems can be daunting when first posed since, when expressed in this general way, they obviously hide a great deal of complexity. In order to program such problems we need to convert them to instructions in algorithmic form. For instance in the first case above we could expand the initial specification as,

```
For each employee in the organisation do the following:
    determine the employee's details
    calculate the basic pay
    calculate stoppages
    calculate overtime
    calculate take-home pay
    print the pay slip and cheque
```

This breakdown identifies several sub-tasks which must be carried out. The sub-task to calculate the stoppages can itself be broken down into,

```
    calculate superannuation
    calculate National Insurance contribution
    calculate tax payable
```

For complex problems this *successive refinement* process can be repeated until each subtask is simple enough to be directly programmable. This approach to problem solving is widely used in programming. It is a way of implementing the so-called *top-down* method of designing programming solutions to problems. The skill of designing good solutions to complex problems involves taking into account all the possible permutations and combinations of input data that might arise and creating programming solutions which are understandable and maintainable (i.e. alterable) by people who may not have been involved in the original design process. This is why a careful disciplined approach to programming is essential.

The successive refinement method naturally leads to programs that are designed in terms of more or less discrete units which can be treated largely in isolation. Each subtask in the overall problem solution is defined with its own job to do, and its own inputs and outputs by which it is linked into the overall problem solution. The approach has the additional advantage that it often produces subtasks which are relevant to other problems and can hence be re-used in other contexts. Thus, some of the subtasks identified in a new problem may already have been programmed as a result of previous work.

The style of problem solution described above is well supported in Fortran by the subprogram facility which will be described briefly in the rest of this chapter. In fact Fortran supports two different types of subprogram, jointly known as procedures. These are the subroutine and the function. The subroutine is a procedure that performs the actions required by a subtask in a program. The function is a procedure that calculates and returns a value as a result and is useful when such a result is required as part of some calculation in a program.

2.1 Subroutines

The best way of introducing subroutines is via a concrete example. Consider writing a program which must read in the cost of a purchase and the amount of money handed over by a customer and work out how the change is to be given, i.e. how many coins of each denomination are needed to make up the correct change. The program will be constructed as if it was to be run from a keyboard/display, but it could equally well be running in a microprocessor-controlled cash register in which it would be used to help control the release of the correct number of coins from an attached change dispenser. The keyboard/display program can be considered as a test harness for verifying the subroutine before installing it in the real situation.

We shall assume in our case that a person sitting at a keyboard will type in the total price and the amount handed over by the customer. To avoid unnecessary complications in the program we shall also assume that both amounts typed are in pence. The program will then be required to display the number of pounds, 50p, 20p, 10p, 5p, 2p, and 1p coins needed in the correct change. The object of the program is to give the correct change with the smallest number of coins. When possible therefore a large denomination coin will be used rather than an equivalent value in smaller denomination coins. For instance, if the change was to be £1.53 then it would be dispensed as a £1 coin with a 50p, a 2p, and a 1p coin.

An algorithmic description of the task required would look like:

```
1.   Read the price of the goods.
2.   Read the amount tendered by the customer.
3.   Calculate the change.
4.   Convert the change into coins.
5.   Display the number of coins needed to make up the change.
```

Clearly with this algorithm we shall need to reserve space for variables to hold the price, the amount, and the numbers of each type of coin. The most significant part of this algorithm will be the conversion of the change into coins. If this part of the algorithm is seen as a separate procedure, its input would be the amount of change to be dispensed and its outputs would be the numbers of coins in each denomination. To make this clear let us re-write step 4 in a slightly different way. Thus,

```
4.   Pass the value of the change to the change conversion
     procedure and receive back the numbers of coins in each
     denomination.
```

What we have done here is to recognise that the requirements of the step are best implemented as a subtask. We have expressed the step as invoking a procedure which receives the change as its input and returns the number of coins in each denomination as its outputs. The algorithm, with step 4 modified in this way, is now directly translatable into Fortran 90 using the subroutine facility.

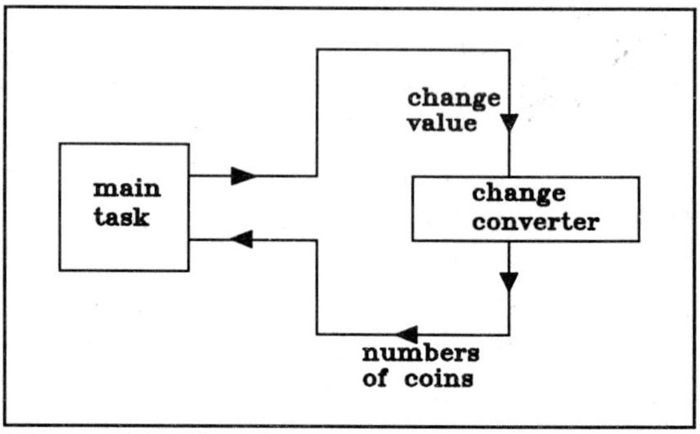

Figure 2.1: The change converter sub-task

The expression of the algorithm in a Fortran 90 program would be as shown below,

```
PROGRAM to_calculate_change
!-------------------------------------------------------!
! Calculate the change required for a particular sale    !
! price given the amount handed over by the customer.     !
! The change is calculated so that there are a minimum    !
! number of coins in each denomination.                   !
!                                                         !
! np, n50, etc. denote the number of pounds, number of 50 !
! pence pieces etc. in the change.                        !
!-------------------------------------------------------!
  INTEGER :: change,price,amount,np,n50,n20,n10,n5,n2,n1
  WRITE(UNIT=*,FMT=*) 'Type Price?'
  READ(UNIT=*,FMT=*) price
  WRITE(UNIT=*,FMT=*) 'Type amount?'
  READ(UNIT=*,FMT=*) amount
  !  Calculate the change
  change = amount-price
  !  Call subroutine to calculate change distribution
  CALL change_calculator(change,np,n50,n20,n10,n5,n2,n1)
  !  Write out the results
  WRITE(UNIT=*,FMT=*) ' Change=',np,':pounds ',n50,':50 ',&
        n20,':20 ',n10,':10 ',n5,':5 ',n2,':2 ',n1,':1 '
END
```

Instead of including the statements to calculate the distribution of coins in the program we include a call to a subroutine to do this job. When the main program execution reaches the statement,

```
CALL change_calculator(change,np,n50,n20,n10,n5,n2,n1)
```

control is transferred to the statements of the subroutine named `change_calculator`. This subroutine uses the value of the `change`, calculates the required number of coins, and returns the results `np, n50, n20,` etc. The subroutine itself is a rather longer version of the calculation part of the seconds to hours, minutes and seconds program we used as an earlier example.

The program as it stands of course will not run correctly since we have not yet supplied the subroutine. To do this we now refine step 4 of our algorithm to obtain,

```
Given the change as a number of pence,
1.  Calculate the number of pounds, np, by dividing by 100.
2.  Calculate the remainder by subtracting 100 times np from
    the change.
3.  Calculate the number of 50p's in the remainder by
    dividing by 50.
4.  Calculate the remainder.
5.  ... etc.
```

In Fortran 90 this would be written as shown on the following page,

```
SUBROUTINE change_calculation(change,np,n50,n20,n10,n5,n2,n1)
!------------------------------------------------------------!
! Calculate the best distribution of coins for the change !
!------------------------------------------------------------!
  !--Argument declaration
  INTEGER,INTENT(IN) :: change
  INTEGER,INTENT(OUT) :: np,n50,n20,n10,n5,n2,n1
  !--Local data declaration
  INTEGER :: remainder
  !--Store change in local work variable remainder
  remainder = change
  !--Calculate pounds
  np=remainder/100
  remainder=remainder-np*100
  !--Calculate 50p's
  n50=remainder/50
  remainder=remainder-n50*50
  !--Calculate 20p'S

  ... and so on

END
```

The subroutine starts with a `SUBROUTINE` statement which tells the compiler that this is the start of a piece of program which is to be compiled as a subroutine. The `SUBROUTINE` statement also specifies the subroutine name and a list of items enclosed in parentheses. These items are called *arguments* and they are used to pass information to and from the program which calls the subroutine. These arguments are declared as variables in the subprogram. When the subroutine is called from the main program, the `CALL` statement specifies the main program variables that are to be associated with these arguments. The `INTENT` for each argument is used to specify which values are passed to which arguments on input and which main program variables will receive the results on output.

An additional variable, `remainder`, which is required to store the intermediate values of the change in the subroutine itself is also declared. The subroutine takes a copy of the value held in the variable `change` and stores it in the variable `remainder`. This again may seem unnecessary but if we had used the variable `change` in the subroutine to store the remainder at each stage of the calculation, then on return from the subroutine we would have lost the original value of the change; it would have been overwritten by the last value its associated variable had in the subroutine.

Since we have declared this argument to have `INTENT(IN)` this would not be permitted.

The number of pounds is calculated by division of the change (now held in remainder) by 100. The remaining change is calculated and the number of 50p coins found by division by 50. This is repeated for all the coin denominations in decreasing order of value until there is only the odd penny left. As each number is calculated it is assigned to the appropriate argument variable.

The `END` statement in the subroutine, as for the main program, signifies that there are no more statements to be executed. When execution reaches the `END` statement control is therefore returned to the calling program and execution continues with the statement after the `CALL`.

The change program can be entered into the computer by combining the statements of the main program and the subroutine in one file created by the editor in the usual way. The subroutine statements would simply follow after the `END` statement of the main program. The program would be compiled, linked and run exactly as for the case when the file contained only the single main program. It would be possible, and in some cases it is desirable, for the subroutine to be created in a separate file. In this case the compiler will have to be run twice, once for the main program and once for the subroutine. Then when the linker is run to create the executable program the linker will need to be told where to find both the main program object code and the subroutine object code.

2.2 Function subprograms

For the very common special case where the required result of a subprogram is the value of a single variable[1] which is to be used as part of an expression, it is normal to use a function subprogram instead of a subroutine. For example, suppose as part of a problem we needed to find the largest of three values. Such a subtask could be used in any program that required to find, say, the best of three trial values. An algorithm for this subtask could be:

```
Given three values to be compared and a location to hold the
resulting largest value:
1.  Compare the first and second values, set the possible
    result to the larger.
```

[1] The restriction to a single variable does not mean a single value. As we shall see later a variable may be a single value or it may be a whole set of values.

```
2.   Compare the possible result with the third value, set the
     result to the larger.
```

A possible function subprogram to implement this could be,

```
FUNCTION largest_of(first,second,third)
!----------------------------------------------------!
! Returns the largest of the three argument values !
!----------------------------------------------------!
  INTEGER,INTENT(IN) :: first,second,third
  INTEGER :: largest_of
  IF(first > second)THEN
    largest_of = first
  ELSE
    largest_of = second
  ENDIF
  IF(third > largest_of)THEN
    largest_of = third
  ENDIF
END
```

Note the use of the underscore in the name `largest_of`. Underscores are commonly used where it is convenient to divide names into separate explanatory components. The function above differs from a subroutine in a number of respects. First, as one would expect, a function subprogram starts with a `FUNCTION` statement. This gives the name of the function which is followed, as for the subroutine, by a list of arguments. The second difference is less obvious but very important. The function name, in addition to the argument variables, is now also declared as a variable in the body of the function. However, unlike the argument variables the function name variable is not declared with a specified intent. The function name variable is required to allow the result of a function subprogram to be returned to the program which invokes it. This is done by assigning a value to this function-name variable before the subprogram ends. The function result is the value this variable has when control returns to the program which invoked it.

As an example of the use of the above function, consider a program that reads the results of three trials and adds the largest to a total. The loop that reads successive values could be terminated by a negative value for the result of the first trial. The program could be written to output the final total along with the number of trial sets processed. The algorithm might be:

```
Reserve space for three trial values, trial1, trial2, trial3,
the total, and the count of the number of sets.
```

```
1.  set total and count to zero
2.  start loop
    2.1     prompt and read three trial values
    2.2     if first trial value is negative exit from loop
    2.3     add one to count
    2.4     add largest of trial values to total
    end loop
3.  display total and count
4.  end of program
```

The Fortran 90 program for this could be,

```
PROGRAM best_of_three
!-------------------------------------------------------------!
! Totals the best of three trials until a negative first      !
! trial is read from the VDU. Counts the sets of trials       !
! and displays results                                        !
!-------------------------------------------------------------!
  INTEGER :: trial1,trial2,trial3,total,count
  !  Initialise total and count
  total = 0
  count = 0
  DO ! Start of loop
    WRITE(UNIT=*,FMT=*) 'Type three trial values?'
    READ(UNIT=*,FMT=*) trial1,trial2,trial3
    IF( trial1 < 0 ) EXIT
    count = count + 1
    total = total + largest_of(trial1,trial2,trial3)
  ENDDO ! End of loop
  WRITE(UNIT=*,FMT=*) 'Number of trial sets = ',count, &
              '  best of 3 Total= ',total
END
```

The significant feature of this example is the way in which the function `largest_of` is invoked, or referenced. The function is referenced by simply including its name followed by the required arguments in an expression where the result value will be required. In the above case this is the value to be added to the total. When this statement is executed the function is invoked with the argument `first` set to `trial1`, `second` to `trial2`, and `third` to `trial3`. The statements in the function are executed copying the largest of the three values into `largest_of` and this value is passed back to the main program, where it is added to the value stored in `total`.

In fact although this example is a nice simple one to illustrate the basic principle, it is not a function one would actually need to write. The requirement of finding the largest of a set of values is so common that a function to do this is defined and supplied as part of the Fortran 90 language. Such a function is called an *intrinsic* function because it is an intrinsic part of the Fortran language. In this case the appropriate intrinsic function to use is named `MAX`. So we could have written the statement to increment the total as:

```
total = total + MAX(trial1,trial2,trial3)
```

and not bothered to write our own function `largest_of`.

Fortran 90 defines a number of intrinsic functions to perform many of the common general tasks that occur in programming. (The full list is given in Appendix A). The specific intrinsic functions used in any program are linked into the executable version of the program from the standard Fortran library when the linker is run.

2.3 Summing up

In this Chapter we have developed several ideas which are important when considering the solution of problems on computers. These are:

1. Problems must be specified carefully and precisely.
2. Top-down design based on successive refinement of more general problem specifications is a useful way of breaking down complexity.
3. Successive refinement naturally identifies discrete subtasks.
4. Programming of sub-tasks is supported in Fortran 90 by subroutine and function subprograms, collectively known as procedures.

2.4 Exercises

1. Design an algorithm to read and print the smallest value of a set of three.

2. Extend this algorithm to handle any number of such sets, and to calculate the average of the minimum values.

3. Write Fortran 90 programs, using the statements already covered, to implement these algorithms.

4. Design an algorithm to find the middle value of a set of three. (Hint, the simplest way to do this is to sort the three values into order)

5. Write a Fortran 90 function subprogram to perform this task.

Chapter 3

Fortran Source Form

The reader who has reached this point and understood most of what has been presented should have a good idea of what a program is and how it instructs a computer to perform its various tasks. He, or she, should also be able to read simple Fortran programs and be able to understand roughly what they are trying to do. Unfortunately reading a program and writing one are very different. Human beings are very adept at interpreting the intent of language even when the precise grammatical rules are broken and only some of the vocabulary is totally familiar. We are all quite capable of understanding a foreign speaker who does the most dreadful things to our native tongue. Computers unfortunately are not so accommodating and flexible. To write a program in a programming language which can be successfully interpreted by a machine, translated and then executed correctly, we must write it absolutely and precisely according to the rules of that language. The correct alphabet must be used, only the vocabulary known to the computer is allowed, and the grammar rules of the language must be strictly observed.

The most basic rules in any programming language are those which govern the source form. These rules determine exactly how statements in a program are entered into the computer and how they are displayed. The source form rules are analogous to those fundamentals of natural language which define the alphabet used to express the words in the language, the punctuation symbols to be used, how sentences are to be written (left to right, up and down, right to left), etc. These are the rules we are going to describe in this chapter.

Fortran 90 has two basically incompatible source forms, an old form compatible with that used in Fortran 77, and a new form more suited to the modern computing environment. The old form used a very strictly defined layout of program statements on lines. This was well suited to the expression of programs when the main method of entering programs into a computer was by the use of stacks of cards with holes punched in them to represent the characters of the program statements. Such punched card systems also worked with a very restricted set of characters; only upper-case letters, for example, were allowed. The new form is designed to be easier to prepare and to read using the sort of keyboard/display that is now ubiquitous. This new form uses a much wider character set and it allows much greater freedom in laying out statements on a line. It is this new form that we are going to describe here since this is the form we would expect any new programmer to employ. The old form is described briefly in Chapter 13 together with with a number of other obsolete features. That chapter is included as an aid for readers who need to be able to read and understand old programs.

3.1 Character set

The statements of a Fortran 90 program are expressed using a carefully defined restricted character set. This character set has been chosen so that it is available on almost every machine currently in use. The Fortran 90 character set can be reproduced by virtually every display, printer or other input/output device which uses characters. It consists of the set of alphanumeric characters and a limited set of punctuation marks and other special symbols. The alphanumeric characters are the upper case letters, `A-Z`, the lower case letters, `a-z`, the digits, `0-9`, and the underscore character, _. The allowed punctuation and other special symbols are shown in the following table.

Symbol	Description
	space/blank
=	equal
+	plus
-	minus/hyphen
*	asterisk/multiply
/	slash/divide
(	left parenthesis
)	right parenthesis
,	comma
.	period/decimal point
'	apostrophe/single quote
"	double quote
:	colon
;	semicolon
!	exclamation
&	ampersand
%	percent
<	less than
>	greater than
$	dollar
?	question mark

The last two, `$` and `?`, do not have any special meaning in the language.

Most modern computer systems are able to process a somewhat wider character set than this. However, this set is chosen so that it will be available on virtually every computing system in every country in the world. The characters found on any particular machine in excess of these are very likely to either not exist on some other machine or have very different graphic representation. For example, what is frequently represented as left square bracket in some countries could well be the character 'a' with an accent in others. Restricting Fortran to the set of characters shown above makes it possible for a program written on one machine to be read on another, even when the machines are in use in different countries.

When used to write the name of a variable, like `hours`, or a language keyword, like `INTEGER`, it does not matter which case is used. Fortran ignores case differences except in character string values such as we used to write out captions in the earlier examples. The keywords, such as `INTEGER`, `WRITE`, `END`, etc., could equally be written as `integer`, `write`, `end`, or even `InteGeR`, etc. The different cases can therefore be used to improve the readability of the program.

3.1.1 Spaces or blanks

A particular feature of Fortran 90 is the way it interprets spaces, or blanks, in statements. Consecutive spaces/blanks have the same meaning as one blank. Blanks are not allowed in language keywords. For instance, `INT EGER` is not the same as `INTEGER`. Neither are blanks allowed in names defined by the programmer. The name `hours` could not be written as `ho urs`; not that any one would be likely to do so. However, it might be tempting to write the name of the function in the previous chapter as `largest of` instead of `largest_of`. This would be illegal and so it is common practice to use underscores to break up long names with several descriptive components.

Keywords and names may not be run together without spaces or some other "punctuation" to separate them. Thus,

```
INTEGERI,J,K
```

would be illegal and not equivalent to

```
INTEGER I,J,K
```

since, in the first case, the words in the statement would be `INTEGERI`, `J` and `K`, whilst in the second case they would be `INTEGER`, `I`, `J` and `K`. There are no Fortran statements that start with `INTEGERI` so the first statement is invalid. The second statement is, however, correct Fortran. In Chapters 1 and 2 we deliberately chose to use a double colon instead of just a space to separate the keyword `INTEGER` from the list of variable names it declares. In fact the `::` is optional when only the type of the variable list is being declared and there are no other attributes. However, when more than one attribute is specified in a single statement such as,

```
INTEGER, INTENT(IN) :: first, second, third
```

the `::` is mandatory and so we believe it is good practice to use it even when only one attribute is involved. In general the `::` makes the statements more readable.

Apart from observing the above rules, spaces can be used liberally to increase the readability of programs. Thus the following statements,

```
    C=A+B
```

and

```
    C = A + B
```

are equivalent. The additional blanks in the second simply add insignificant layout spacing between these words that are already separated by "punctuation".

To sum up, the rules governing the use of blanks are largely common sense. Blanks should not be placed in the middle of keywords or names, and these need to be separated from each other by a blank or a some other separator. Otherwise blanks may be used freely to lay out a program in order to make it more readable. Judicious use of blanks and sensible use of upper and lower case can often significantly clarify more complicated constructs or statements, and some systematic convention for this use can make it very much easier to read and hence to write correct programs.

3.2 Lines and statements

A Fortran program is entered from a keyboard and stored in the machine as a sequence of lines. Each line is in turn a sequence of characters, the characters being drawn from the Fortran character set. By and large each line is a single Fortran statement, a single instruction to perform some program function. A Fortran line uses up to 132 character positions on the line. Most modern computers have displays which can show lines of 80 or 132 characters, but since 80 is much more common than 132 it is a good idea to keep lines to this length.

3.2.1 Statement layout

Statements can start anywhere on a line. If the first characters of a statement are numeric, they are considered to be a statement label. The label, if present, must be separated from the statement proper by at least one space, and the label must not contain embedded spaces.

```
10 c = a + b
```

is a valid statement labelled `10`, but neither

```
10c = a + b
```

nor

```
 1 0 c = a + b
```

are valid. A label must be a numeric string between `1` and `99999`.

3.2.2 Comments

On any line a `!` character indicates that all subsequent characters up to the end of the line are commentary. Such commentary is ignored by the compiler. Comments are part of the program source but are intended for the human reader and not for the machine. Most compilers can produce a file called a "listing" which is suitable for printing or for display. It will contain the source of the program and information about what the compiler has done with it. Although the compiler otherwise ignores comments it does include them in the listing file. They can therefore, in conjunction with other information provided by the compiler, be invaluable in helping to sort out the intention of the program and in determining where it has gone wrong, if it has.

A comment can contain any of the characters available on the computer being used. A comment is not restricted to use the Fortran character set. A program containing comments using characters outside this set may still be portable but the comments may look somewhat odd if the program is moved to another system with a different extended set of characters.

We have already seen several examples of comments in the previous chapters. Some further illustrative examples of comment statements are,

```
! THIS IS A COMMENT
!*** THIS IS ANOTHER COMMENT ***
! {{\|Any character is allowed in a comment e.g. :,*,&,%,$
!
```

```
! Previous comment is blank
!  D = C * F
C = A + B ! add input variables to produce output
          ! additional comment for previous statement
```

The last but two comment may look like an ordinary Fortran statement but the `!` in character position 1 makes it a comment and therefore it would not be translated by the compiler. The last but one comment has been placed "in line" with the statement it explains.

Before leaving this section it is worth noting that a statement that is completely blank is treated like a comment. So it is equivalent to the statement which has a `!` in any position but is blank otherwise.

3.2.3 Continuation

If a statement is too long to fit on a single line it may be continued onto the following line. Statements may be continued from one line to the next by placing an `&` character at the end of any line that is to be continued. For example the lines,

```
10 WRITE(UNIT=*,FMT=*) 'THIS IS A LONG STATEMENT', &
RESULT
```

are equivalent to,

```
10 WRITE(UNIT=*,FMT=*) 'THIS IS A LONG STATEMENT', RESULT
```

The above statement could also be written as

```
10 WRITE&
(UNIT=*,&
FMT=*) &
'THIS IS A LONG STATEMENT', &
RESULT
```

although this perhaps is carrying things too far.

Fortran 90 statements can be spread across up to 40 lines. This allows for one initial line and up to 39 continuation lines. Some compilers may well permit more but it is risky to take advantage of this if the program is meant to be portable. In practice the safe maximum of 39 continuation lines is sufficient for most purposes.

Names and keywords such as `hours`, `INTEGER`, `READ`, etc. may not be broken across line boundaries any more than they are allowed to be broken up by spaces. Long character constants (i.e. text enclosed in quotes) can, however, be broken across multiple lines. This is done by ending a line on which there is a character constant to be continued with an `&` and starting the continuation line also with a `&`. For example,

```
'This is a long constant continued from line to line&
&by use of the continuation mark at both the end of the&
&continued line and at the start of the continuation line'
```

3.2.4 Multiple statement lines

More than one statement can be included on a line provided the statements are separated by `;` characters. This is a facility which should be used with circumspection. Over use of multi-statement lines can make a program unreadable. However there are times when it can be very useful. For example,

```
IF( denominator == 0 )THEN; CALL fault_handler
ELSE
 ...
 main normal process block
 ...
ENDIF
```

is a quite neat way of expressing such a structure. Also several short statements put on a single line as in

```
a = 3; b = 4; c = 5
```

can usefully reduce the 'spread' of a program down the screen or page.

3.3 Names

The Fortran language defines a number of names, or keywords, such as `WRITE`, `INTEGER`, `MAX`, etc. The spelling of these names is defined by the language. There are a number of entities that must be named by the programmer, such as variables, subprograms, etc. These names must be chosen to obey a few simple rules. A name can consist of up to 31 alphanumeric characters (letters or digits) plus underscore. The first character in any name must be a letter. In names, upper and lower case letters are equivalent. Thus `DEPTH`, `Depth` and `depth` refer to the same entity. The following are valid Fortran names,

```
A, AA, aaa, Tax, INCOME, Num1, NUM2, NUM333, N12MO5,
atmospheric_pressure, Line_Colour
```

The following are invalid names,

```
1A
```
(does not begin with a letter)
```
A_name_made_up_of_more_than_31_letters
```
(too long, 38 characters)
```
Depth:0
```
(contains an illegal character ":")
```
A-3
```
(would be interpreted as subtract `3` from `A`)
```
B.5.
```
(illegal characters ".")
```
,I
```
(starts with illegal character)

It is helpful to use meaningful names in a consistent way wherever possible. For instance, suppose we were writing a program to draw graphs on a plotter (a peripheral device designed to draw lines of various colours rather than to print text). A useful scheme might be to use the first part of a name to denote a particular geometric item and the second part to denote a property of that item. When talking about lines, arcs, and text of different colours we could use `line_colour, arc_colour, text_colour.` Line and arc width would become `line_width` and `arc_width`, and text height and width would become `text_height` and `text_width`. Such names are clearly meaningful in the context of this particular application and their use would subsequently make it much easier to read and understand any program written using this convention.

3.4 Summing up

In this chapter we have looked at the detailed source-form, or statement layout rules of the Fortran 90 language. The Fortran 90 source form is fairly straightforward and basically logical. The main special features are the explicit continuation rules and the use of `!` to indicate the start of commentary. Apart from these the rules are as would be expected in any language; words of the language do not have embedded spaces or line-ends, and words are separated from each other by punctuation (special characters) or by spaces.

It is however important to ensure that this freedom is not abused. Erratically laid out programs; particularly those that cram as much program as possible per line using continuous multiple statements and continuation at random, are very difficult to read and are therefore very error prone.

Well laid-out readable programs are not guaranteed to be error free, but are much more likely to be correct than ones that have no systematic style.

3.5 Exercises

1. Which of the following are valid Fortran characters,

```
X, c, £, $, %, *, ", ', @
```

2. Indicate which of the following statements are invalid and why.

```
a)   INTEGER1,B, C
b)   READ(UNIT=*,FMT=*)I1,I2,I3
c)   READ(UNIT=*,FMT=*)I1 I2 I3
d)   d = a+b-c
e)   d = a + b - c
```

3. The following Fortran statements all contain errors. Write versions of these correcting the mistake.

```
a)   A = B + C +
                 D
b)   Write(UNIT=*,FMT=*) SUM, ! the sum of B,C,D
c)   INTEGERA,B,C
```

4. The following program is correct but has been very badly set out. Rearrange it so that it means the same thing but is more readable.

```
 PROGRAM MAIN;INTEGER::degreesfahrenheit&
,degreescentigrade;READ(UNIT=*,FMT=*)&
degreesfahrenheit;degreescentigrade&
=5*(degreesfahrenheit-32)/9;WRITE(uniT=&
 *,fMT=*)degreesCENtiGrAde;END
```

5. Which of the following are invalid Fortran names and why?

```
A  AaA  Nmae  Time  tiMe  T1Me Filename.Ext Filename_Ext
```

Chapter 4

Data Types and Basic Calculation

In Chapters 1 & 2 we were very careful to talk only about whole numbers, or integers, and not just numbers. All our early examples were designed so that only integer values were needed. This was done to simplify the introductory examples. In fact, Fortran provides facilities for manipulating data of many different types. The most basic of these types are defined to be an intrinsic part of the language, and as we shall see in a later chapter there are facilities for the user to define additional types specific to a given program.

The most important of the intrinsic types are[1],

`INTEGER`	for exact whole numbers.
`REAL`	for approximate, possibly fractional numbers.
`CHARACTER`	for strings of one or more characters.
`LOGICAL`	for objects which may have the values true or false.

Constants and variables of the various data types can be combined, by the appropriate operators, to form expressions. These expressions are evaluated when the program is executed. Expressions are the way in which the program instructs the computer to perform calculations. A program distinguishes the different types of data so that the appropriate operations are used when evaluating expressions. The operations we might wish to perform with numbers are quite different from those we might wish to perform with characters or truth values. The two numeric types also have different operations. The differences here stem from the very different ways real values and integer values are represented in a computer. Integers are always stored to be exact and so the arithmetic performed with integers is exact. Real values, on the other hand, are not stored exactly. They are stored correct to a certain number of significant figures of accuracy. Therefore arithmetic performed on real values is not exact but is limited to the same sort of accuracy. It is important for a program to distinguish between the different sorts of numbers it is dealing with so that the correct operations can be used.

---

[1] There are other intrinsic types such as COMPLEX and DOUBLE PRECISION but these are only required for a minority of programming tasks in fairly specialist areas. These additional types are described briefly in Chapter 12.

The results of a calculation can be stored for future use by assigning the value to a variable. This is done by an assignment statement whose general form is,

```
<variable name> = <expression>
```

where `<variable name>` is the name of a variable of any of the Fortran data types and `<expression>` is an expression formed by combining variable names and constants using operators and/or functions. The sets of operators and the rules of how expressions may be written and evaluated are determined by the types of the operands involved. The type is therefore a very critical attribute of any data value. In the rest of this chapter we are going to look at each of these data types and how they can be manipulated. Since the two numeric types are quite closely related we shall consider them more or less together.

4.1 Numeric types

Values of the integer type are essentially the same as those of mathematical whole numbers except that there is a limited range of values that can be represented in a computer because of the finite storage available. Integer values are restricted to lie in a finite range which will depend on the particular computer being used. Ranges are typically,

-32768 to +32767 (-2^{16} to $2^{16}-1$)

or

-2147483648 to +2147483647 (-2^{32} to $2^{32}-1$)

depending on the nature of the machine.

Integers are used for many different purposes in programming. For instance to keep a count of the number of times a loop has been executed, to record the number of cases in a sample of data, the position of an item in a list, the location of a character in a string, and so on. Integers are also used when it is important that the data and the results calculated with that data are exact. Money transactions such as payrolls or company accounts, if written in Fortran, would most likely use the integer data type for the storage and calculation of all monetary quantities.

Real values are approximate and possibly fractional. They are used for most calculations where quantities that can vary continuously are manipulated, such as the strength of a bridge and the degree of bending caused by traffic load; the speed of a rocket; the density of a moving fluid, and so on.

Again, as with integers, because there is only a finite amount of storage available, real values are restricted to a finite range. Because of the way real numbers are represented the ranges are typically much greater than for integers. The smallest range in common usage is of the order of

10^{-38} to 10^{+38}

and a range as high as

10^{-4932} to 10^{+4932}

can be found on some machines. Calculations which generate numbers outside the permissible ranges, for either numeric type will cause errors.

4.1.1 Numeric constants

We have already come across the occurrence of integer constants in statements such as

```
minutes = minutes + 60 * hours
```

The number `60` in this statement is an example of an integer constant.

Integer constants consist of an optional sign followed by a simple string of digits with no decimal point. The compiler will interpret the string of digits as a decimal whole number. It will convert the value to whatever format is used to represent integer values internally in the computer. This value will then be used as required in the execution of the program. Other examples of integer constants are

```
0  1  -1  3568  +20  -999
```

Real constant values can be written in a way very similar to integer constants. The major difference is that real constants contain a decimal point. Real constants may be written in one of two ways, a *fixed point* form or a *floating point* form. The fixed point form is the more familiar of the two forms. Examples are,

```
1.3  -5.67  -12345.6789  +12.678
```

That is, the normal decimal number notation is used.

Floating point form is closely related to the scientific notation used for writing large or small magnitude values. This form expresses numbers in the form of a real constant with an attached power of 10. Thus the number 156.34, which is also expressible as,

1.5634×10^2

can be written in Fortran as the real constant

```
1.5634E+2
```

The "E" stands for "multiplied by 10 to the power of". The same value could equally well be written as any of

```
0.15634E3   0.015634E4   15.634E1   15634.0E-2
```

This is why the term "floating point" is used to describe this form of constant. The internal representation of real values is actually very similar to this except the decimal number system is not commonly used. Usually a binary representation is used with a power of two exponent instead of a power of ten.

As for integers, the appearance of a real constant of either form will cause the compiler to convert the value represented by the string of digits and the power of ten, if any, into the internal storage form for a REAL value. Unlike integers the value represented will not normally be exactly the same as that indicated by the decimal string. During the conversion process the value will be approximated so that it will fit into the available storage.

It should be noted that there is no difference between fixed-point and floating-point constants in so far as calculations are concerned. The difference is merely in the way they are written down. Both are real numbers. Unless the values are very large or very small it is usually more convenient to write them in fixed point form.

4.1.2 Numeric variables

Variables that are to be used for data of type integer are declared by an `INTEGER` type statement, of which a number of examples have been given in the earlier chapters. For example,

```
INTEGER :: count, num_of_students, income, mark
```

declares that the names `count`, `num_of_students`, `income`, and `mark` are for objects of type integer. They are variables since their value can change during the execution of the program.

Real variables can be declared in a similar manner. A statement like,

```
REAL :: width, depth, height
```

creates three real variables. Real quantities may be used in very much the same ways as we have already seen for integer quantities.

4.1.3 Implicit declaration of numeric variables

It is not strictly necessary in Fortran to use a type statement to declare names for variables. Fortran allows programmers to take advantage of an implicit naming convention which specifies that by default, variables not explicitly declared and whose names begin with the letters I,J,K,L,M, or N, will be assumed to be of type integer. Similarly names beginning with any of the other letters of the alphabet (i.e. A-H and O-Z) are assumed to be for real variables, unless they are specified explicitly in a type statement.

In spite of the convenience of this "implicit declaration" convention, we recommend that all variables are declared explicitly. The use of the implicit declaration of variables is known to be the origin of by far the largest number of bugs in existing programs. The use of implicit declaration can lead to some extremely enigmatic programming errors. For instance when reading a program on the display or the printout, it is often difficult to distinguish the letter O and the digit 0. So the difference between a variable called `AO` and one called `A0` can be difficult to spot by eye. If a programmer inadvertently typed `A0` by mistake instead of `AO` the compiler would automatically create a real variable of name `A0`. Such an error could remain undetected during the development of a program and then eventually surface and cause some seriously incorrect results to occur, perhaps a long time after.

Fortran 90 allows the implicit typing facility to be turned off by including as the first statement in each program, or subprogram, a statement

```
IMPLICIT NONE
```

If this is done, all variables used in that program must be explicitly declared as we are suggesting. It will then be very easy to detect any accidental misspelling of variable names of the type described above.

4.1.4 Expressions and assignments for numeric data

The two statements

```
Sum = Term1 + Term2
Max = 2 * Min
```

both instruct the computer to evaluate the numeric expression on the right-hand side of the equals sign and to store the result in the variable specified on the left-hand side, replacing whatever value was there before.

The expressions in the examples above involve only addition (+) and multiplication (*) but Fortran allows numeric expressions of almost arbitrary complexity to be written. There are in fact five different arithmetic operations which can occur in numeric expressions. These are,

```
+     addition
-     subtraction
*     multiplication
/     division
**    exponentiation (i.e. raise to the power of)
```

Some examples of arithmetic expressions are,

```
A*B - C
A + C1 - D2
X + Y/7.0
2**I
A**B + C
```

Notice that multiplication is always indicated explicitly using the operator *. Unlike in algebra where "ab+c" would denote "a multiplied by b plus c", in Fortran this must be written as in the first example with the * operator shown explicitly. `AB + C` would be interpreted as "add the contents of the variable `AB` to the contents of variable `C`" which is quite different.

The meaning of some of the above examples might not be clear. For instance, is `X+Y/7.0` to be read as `(X+Y)/7.0`, or as `X+(Y/7.0)`? Does the last example mean "`A` raised to the power of the sum of `B` and `C`", or "`A` raised to the power of `B` and then add `C`"? In fact Fortran resolves these questions by defining an order of precedence for operators which determines the order in which the expression is to be evaluated. The order of precedence is very much as would be expected from algebra. Exponentiations (**) are carried out first, then multiplications and divisions, and finally additions and subtractions.

For example, since exponentiation has higher precedence than addition, the expression

```
A**B + C
```

is understood to be

```
(A**B) + C
```

Similarly

```
X+Y/7.0
```

is understood to be

```
X + (Y/7.0)
```

Notice, that just as we have used parentheses to make it clear how these expressions would be evaluated, Fortran allows parentheses to be used to force an order of evaluation. The rule is that any sub-expression enclosed between left and right parentheses is evaluated first. So if we wrote

```
(X+Y)/7.0
```

instead of the above we would force the addition to be done first.

Finally it should be noted that multiplication and division have equal precedence. The rule used when there are a number of multiplications and divisions in sequence is that expressions are evaluated from left to right. So `A/B*C` is understood to be `(A/B)*C` and not `A/(B*C)`. The same is true of sequences of additions and subtractions. The one exception to this rule is the ** operator.

```
A**B**C
```

is evaluated right to left, i.e. this would be interpreted as

```
A**(B**C)
```

If the form of an expression is such that it could be ambiguous when read by a human (an expression cannot be ambiguous to the computer), then it is best to use parentheses to make its meaning explicit and clear. The minus(-) operator can also be used as a monadic operator. For example,

```
C = -A + B
```

The minus sign is used in here in its monadic form, where it applies to the item it precedes, as opposed to its dyadic form, where it appears between two items of data. In this particular example the meaning is quite clear and the statement is, as would be expected, equivalent to

```
C = B - A
```

Fortran 90 defines the monadic minus and plus operators to have the same precedence as their dyadic counterpart. The statement

```
C = -A**2
```

is therefore equivalent to

```
C = -(A**2)
```

and not

```
C = (-A)**2
```

for which it might be mistaken.

4.1.5 Common problem areas

A common mistake made by inexperienced and experienced programmers is to mismatch the parentheses of relatively complicated expressions. A simple way of avoiding this problem is to always check expressions by counting parentheses to see whether the number of left-hand parentheses corresponds to the number of right-hand parentheses. This would show that the expression,

```
( ( (A+B)/2 + B**3)/(4*C+D) ) + E)
```

which is intended to evaluate the mathematical formula

$$\frac{\frac{a+b}{2}+b^3}{4c+d}+e$$

is incorrect since there are four left-hand brackets and five right-hand brackets. Note that this only checks whether the expression is syntactically correct and not whether it represents the expected formula. Compilers will normally flag the mismatching of parentheses as errors. Only the programmer can check to see where the missing parenthesis should go.

Expressions which consist solely of integer constants or variables such as

```
I*J/K
```

where `I, J, K` have been declared as integers, are evaluated to produce integer results. The value of the expression, if I = 3, J = 4 and K = 5 would be 2. The properties of integer arithmetic can be exploited to good effect in problems such as the change problem of Chapter 2. The critical point is that division of two integers produces an integer result by discarding any fractional part in the true result; the integer result is produced by truncation towards zero. However, this can be a source of unexpected error when integers are mixed with reals in expressions.

Sometimes it is necessary to write expressions which mix integer and real operands. This is quite permissible. The expression is always evaluated according to the ordering rules discussed above. Each time a dyadic operation is performed, the type of the two operands determines the type of the result. If both operands are integers the result is an integer. If either operand is real the result is real, and the operation will be performed as if the integer value was first converted into a real of the same value. This facility is a great convenience but it can cause problems in statements such as

```
A = I/J*B
```

This statement, because of the rules stated above, is equivalent to

```
A = (I/J)*B
```

With `B=12`, `I=3` and `J=4`, we would expect the result `A=9`. However, the sub-expression `(3/4)` is calculated first and since integer arithmetic discards any remainders the result of this part of the expression is zero. Therefore the result for `A` is zero whatever the value of `B`. This is clearly not what was intended.

The remedy is to use the proper conversion function to convert the integers to reals. The correct form of the statement would be written as

```
A = REAL(I)/REAL(J)*B
```

The `REAL` intrinsic function takes as an argument a single integer value and returns the equivalent value but as a real type.

Care must be exercised when assigning numeric values of mixed type. Most assignments will be such that the expression on the right of the equals will be of the same type as the variable on the left. In this case the result is simply copied into the variable. If the type of the variable is different from that of the expression result then the value is converted to the type of the variable before the assignment takes place. If the expression is real and the variable integer then any fractional part of the real value is discarded to produce the integer value. The rules are summarised as follows:

Type of variable	Type of expression	Result
Integer	Real	Real is truncated
Real	Integer	Integer is converted

By far the most common errors that arise in numeric calculation stem from the limits on range for both types and on precision for reals. For instance if two large values just slight less than the relevant upper limit are multiplied the result would be very much greater than the limit. Such a value cannot be represented and an attempt to perform such a calculation would cause an *overflow* error. If

```
1.0E+25 * 5.3E+28
```

were multiplied together, the correct result would be `5.3E+53`. This would be too large to store on a system with a range up to `1.0E+38`. Such an error is almost always an indication of a serious mistake in the program, so most systems will detect such errors and stop execution.

Similarly multiplying two very small numbers, e.g.,

```
1.0E-25 * 5.3E-28
```

would generate an *underflow* error, (i.e. the result is too small). In many cases, when an operation produces underflow, the result can simply be set to zero. However, since an underflow means that the relative accuracy of the result has been drastically reduced, there are some occasions when underflow can be almost as serious as overflow. By and large both should be avoided if possible.

The other problem is due to the finite precision of reals. In general any operations between real values that are correct to, say, 6 decimal digits will produce a result that is of roughly the same accuracy. However, there will normally be some additional inaccuracy generated by the operation which will normally only effect the value of the least significant digit. For instance, if we wished to multiply two values such as .63700 and .51700 on a 5 decimal machine, the true answer would be .329329. This answer would have to be represented to 5 significant figures as either .32932 or .32933 depending on whether the result is truncated, or rounded to the nearest representable value. In either case an additional small inaccuracy has been introduced.

Obviously after many thousands of operations these inaccuracies can build up and cause a serious loss of overall precision. This loss of precision is called round-off error and it is the accumulation of these round-off errors along with the propagation of the original data errors that determines the final accuracy of the real results.

Catastrophic accuracy loss often arises because two values that are almost equal are subtracted. In such situations the subtraction may cancel the leading digits thereby promoting errors very rapidly from low order digits to high order ones depending on the degree of cancellation. For example, suppose we had the values,

```
.123456 and .123446
```

which were approximated correct to plus or minus 1 in the sixth place by

```
.123457 and .123445
```

The true difference would be `.100000E-4` but the result of subtracting the approximations is `.120000E-4`. We now have an error in the second significant figure.

Much of the work of numerical software specialists is devoted to constructing algorithms, and programs, to solve various types of numerical problem in such a way as to minimise both the build up of round-off error and to avoid the occurrence of catastrophic cancellation errors.

4.1.6 Numeric intrinsic functions

In computing it is frequently necessary to evaluate special functions such as the square root of a number or the sine or cosine of an angle. Fortran 90 has built in facilities to enable such functions to be evaluated easily. For instance the statement

```
Y = SQRT(X)
```

would calculate the square root of the value `X` and assign the result to `Y`. `X` in this context is called the argument of the function `SQRT`. Arguments of standard functions may be constants, variable names, or arithmetic expressions. For example,

```
value = SQRT(var)
concentration = SQRT( 3.0 * X )
pi = 4 * ATAN(1.0)
```

Note that the last statement is a convenient way of getting an accurate value of pi since the arctangent of 1.0 is pi/4.

A full description of available intrinsic functions is given in Appendix A. Some of the more important arithmetic functions are shown in the table on the next page.

Table of the most commonly used numeric intrinsic functions

`SQRT(x)`	calculates the square root of x .
`SIN(x)`	calculates sine of x where x is in radians.
`COS(x)`	calculates cosine of x where x is in radians
`TAN(x)`	calculates tangent of x where x is in radians.
`EXP(x)`	calculates e raised to the power x
`LOG(x)`	calculates the natural logarithm of x
`ASIN(x)`	calculates the arcsine of x
`ACOS(x)`	calculates the arccosine of x
`ATAN(x)`	calculates arctangent of x as an angle in radians (the result will be between -pi/2 and +pi/2)
`REAL(I)`	converts the integer argument I to the equivalent real value

INT(x)	converts the real value x into an integer by truncating any fractional part
NINT(x)	nearest integer to a real number
ANINT(x)	nearest real whole number value to a real number
ABS(x)	returns the absolute value of its argument
MAX(x,y,z...)	returns the maximum value of its list of arguments
MIN(x,y,z...)	returns the minimum value of its list of arguments

4.2 The character type

The character data type is used when the objects to be manipulated are strings of characters. Characters are used when the data to be manipulated are words rather than numbers. These are typically for people's names, the descriptions of products, headings, or other annotations for computer generated reports, etc.

A character value, as far as Fortran is concerned, is a contiguous string or sequence of one or more characters. The characters in such a value are considered to be numbered from the left as 1,2,3... up to the last character, N, say, where N is the number of characters in the string. The number of characters in a character value is called its length.

4.2.1 Character constants

We have already informally introduced character constants. In earlier chapters we used character constants to write out captions for output displays. In statements such as

```
WRITE(UNIT=*,FMT=*) 'Time = ',mins,' Minutes',secs,' Seconds'
```

the characters appearing between apostrophes are in fact character constants. The constant,

```
'TIME^=^'
```

is a character string value of length 7 with character 1 being a T, character 2 being an I, character 3 being an M, and so on.

N.B. We have used a ^ to indicate a blank character since it is important to show exactly how many blanks are present. This is a convention we shall use whenever explicit indication of the number of blank characters is important.

Character constants are defined to be any string of characters enclosed between apostrophes (single quotes) or double quotes. The maximum number of characters allowed in a character constant depends on the particular compiler being used but is likely to be at least 256.

The following are further examples of character constants.

```
'THIS IS A CONSTANT CONTAINING UPPER CASE LETTERS ONLY'
"This is another showing UPPER and lower cases"
'This one contains a quote (") character'
"This one contains an apostrophe (') character"
'any character representable *^&~{} etc can be used'
"two eggs, one sunny side up, and one easy over"
```

N.B. if the apostrophe or quote character needs to be included, the other must be used as the string delimiter or they must be represented by two adjacent apostrophe or quote characters. These are counted as one character in determining the length of the string. The statement

```
WRITE(UNIT=*,FMT=*) "This one contains a quote ("")"
```

would cause the display

```
This one contains a quote (")
```

4.2.2 Character variables

Character variables can be declared in a similar way to integers and reals using a `CHARACTER` statement. Thus the statement

```
CHARACTER :: answer, sex
```

would declare two character variables, named `answer` and `sex`, each of which could hold a single character. The variable `answer` might be used to hold the reply, such as 'Y' or 'N', to a question . The variable `sex` could hold the values 'M' or 'F' to indicate male or female.

The `CHARACTER` statement also allows us to declare variables which refer to not just one character but to a string of characters. When we declare names for character variables we can also declare the length of the character string to which the names refer.

```
CHARACTER(LEN=10) :: name, dept, faculty
CHARACTER(LEN=32) :: address
```

The variables `name, dept, faculty` will hold strings of 10 characters. The variable `address` will hold 32 characters. The processor will, on encountering such statements, reserve the necessary space in memory to hold these numbers of characters.

We could have written the two statements above as a single statement

```
CHARACTER(LEN=10) :: name, dept, faculty, address*32
```

The `*32` following the name `address` provides a length just for the variable `address`. It overrides the `LEN=10` defined for the whole statement. In general a length for the whole statement is specified by including `LEN=` qualifier in parentheses after the `CHARACTER` keyword. This statement-wide character length, can be overridden by appending a `*len` qualifier to any variable name in the list. The default length of a character variable, i.e. the length of a character variable for which no length specification is explicitly given, is one.
Thus the statement,

```
CHARACTER :: A*5, B, C, D*10
```

will declare variables `B` and `C` to be of length 1, `A` to be of length 5, and `D` of length 10.

4.2.3 Character assignment and expressions

Characters may be assigned to character variables using statements similar to those for numeric types.

```
CHARACTER(LEN=6) :: forename, surname
surname = 'Morgan'
forename = 'Polly'
```

Notice that `'Polly'` consists of only five characters whereas `forename` can contain six. The rule followed is that the characters of `'Polly'` become the first five characters of `forename`. The extra character is set to blank. If on the other hand the number of characters in the string to be assigned to one of the variable was greater than six, the excess characters on the right would be simply truncated, only the left-most six would be assigned. For example,

```
surname = 'Schonfelder'
```

would result in the variable called `surname` containing the characters `'Schonf'` only.

In general a character assignment statement is very similar to an arithmetic assignment. It has a character variable on the left of an `=` and a character expression on the right. The expression is evaluated and the resulting character string value is copied into the variable. It is illegal to assign an arithmetic value to a character variable, or a character value to an arithmetic variable. Such assignments make no sense and are flagged as errors by the compiler.

Character values may be concatenated or joined together using the `//` (double slash) operator. Thus

```
CHARACTER(LEN=6) :: identity
identity = 'TH'//'OMAS'
```

sets `identity` to `'THOMAS'`.

```
CHARACTER :: part1*5, part2*4, name*12
part1 = 'Marma'
part2 = 'duke'
name = part1//part2
```

sets `name` to `'Marmaduke^^^'`

If the length of the expression string on the right-hand side of an assignment is greater than that declared for the variable on the left-hand side, the excess characters are truncated on the right. If the expression is shorter than the variable, the variable is padded out on the right with blanks. For example,

```
CHARACTER(LEN=5) :: location
location = 'Lab' // 'oratory'
```

would set `location` to `'Labor'` and

```
CHARACTER(LEN=12) :: location
location = 'Lab' // 'oratory'
```

would set `location` to `'Laboratory^^'`

4.2.4 Substrings

Substrings, which are contiguous parts of character strings, may be selected by specifying the starting and ending points of the substring within a character variable. For example if

```
Name = 'Marmaduke'
```

then `Name(6:9)` would contain the value `'duke'`. `Name(1:1)` would refer to `'M'`, and `Name(2:4)` refers to the characters `'arm'`, and so on. We could therefore write statements such as

```
CHARACTER :: name*20, xnam*10, surname*18, title*4
name   = 'Dame Edna Everage'
title = name(1:4)
xnam   = name(6:9)
surnam = name(11:)
```

Note, in this last substring, that the upper value for the substring is omitted. If this is done the upper bound of the substring is assumed to be the same as the full length of the character variable from which the substring is selected. If the lower substring bound is omitted a value of one is assumed and the substring starts at the left-most character of the variable.

The integers which are used to define the start and end of the substring can be constants, as shown above, or they may be variables. In fact they can be any arithmetic expression as long as the expression produces an integer result. The lower bound must be greater than or equal to one. The upper bound must be less than or equal to the length of the character value. It should be noted that the lower bound may be greater than the upper bound. In such a case a zero length string is the result. Such strings are of limited use but the fact that they are allowed makes programming some operations more straight forward.

The following program, which could form part of a larger program, reads in the date and the name of the person running the program and prints out a message incorporating this date.

```
PROGRAM message
!----------------------------------------------------------!
! declare character locations large enough to hold message !
! and date and allow up to 40 characters for the name      !
!----------------------------------------------------------!

  CHARACTER :: mess*32, date*14, name*40
  !  Set up the message leaving blanks for the insertion of
```

```
  !  the date
  mess = 'Program run on        by '
  !  Read in the date and name
  READ(UNIT=*,FMT=*) date, name
  !  Insert the date into the message at the appropriate
  !  position
  mess(16:29) = date
  !  Write out the message
  WRITE(UNIT=*,FMT=*) mess, name
ENDPROGRAM message
```

4.2.5 Character intrinsic functions

As for the numeric data types there are several useful character functions which are predefined by the language. These intrinsic functions allow a number of commonly required character manipulations to be performed easily which otherwise would be quite difficult to program. A full description of these functions can be found in Appendix A. In the following table we will list a few of the more important ones.

LEN(C)	returns the length of a character entity
INDEX(SUB,STR)	finds the location of a substring in another string
CHAR(C)	converts an integer into a character value
ICHAR(C)	converts a character into an integer
TRIM(C)	returns the argument with trailing blanks removed

The conversion between character and integer is based on the fact that the available set of characters is organised into some form of sequence, called the collating sequence. It is therefore possible to associate an integer with each character according to its position in this sequence. This is the integer that will be used in CHAR and ICHAR. Without knowing precisely how a particular machine represents characters it is not possible to say which integer value corresponds to which character, and the value may be different on different systems. However we can assume that the two functions will be consistent

```
ICHAR(CHAR(I)) is always equal to I and
CHAR(ICHAR(C)) is always equal to C
```

provided the character `C` is a character of length one and the integer `I` is not too large (typically 128 or 256).

4.2.6 Character comparisons

Character strings are compared by matching the characters one by one from left to right. If one of the character values is shorter than the other it is space-filled on the right in order to perform the comparison. The effect of the equality comparisons, `==` (is equal to) and `/=` (is not equal to), is obvious and is independent of the collating sequence of the character set on any machine. Examples are

```
IF( surname == 'Jones' )THEN
  WRITE(UNIT=*,FMT=*)'High probability of being Welsh'
ENDIF
```

The inequality comparisons, `<`, `<=`, `>=` and `>` depend on the precise ordering of characters used for the collating sequence on the particular machine. One character is considered to be less than another if it occurs earlier in the collating sequence of the machine. The Fortran 90 standard does not fully specify what the collating sequence should be, so inequality comparisons on characters may give different results on different machines.

The standard does specify that the space character must come before both the letters and the digits. It also requires that the letters must be in alphabetic order and the digits 0-9 must be in that order. However the digits may appear earlier or later in the collating sequence than the letters. The special characters may be in any order and could occur anywhere in the overall collating sequence. For this reason inequality comparisons with characters must be used with care if a program is meant to be used on more than one machine. For example the character string `'AAA'` will always be less than the string `'AAB'`, but on some systems `'AAA'` will be less than `'AA1'` on others it will be greater.

N.B. On all systems `'AA'` will always be less than `'AAA'`, because the shorter string is padded with blanks in order to make the comparison, and space is always earlier in the collating sequence than any letter or digit.

4.3 The logical type

Unlike integer, real and character data, the logical data type is not closely related to quantities that are familiar outside of the world of computer programming. Objects of the logical data type may have one of only two values, representing true or false. They are used for recording information where there are only two choices. For instance, if the sex of a hospital patient was male or female; whether a pen on a graph plotter was up or down (ready to draw or not), and so on. There are many situations where a simple choice is required and the logical data type is the Fortran mechanism for storing and manipulating such values.

4.3.1 Logical constants

Logical values, as we have said, can take one of the two values, true or false. These two values are written as constants in Fortran as,

`.TRUE.` and `.FALSE.`

and they are the only possible forms of logical constant.

4.3.2 Logical variables

Memory locations for holding logical values can be declared in `LOGICAL` statements. For example

```
LOGICAL :: Tall,Thin,Red
```

defines three logical variables.

4.3.3 Logical assignment and expressions

Assuming the above declaration logical values can be stored in these variables by assignment statements such as

```
tall = .TRUE.
thin = .FALSE.
red = .TRUE.
```

An attempt to put numeric or character values into a logical variable would be an error, and would probably be detected and flagged by the processor.

Since a logical variable can contain either the value `.TRUE.` or the value `.FALSE.` it can be used in an `IF` statement as illustrated by the following program fragment.

```
   LOGICAL :: red
   ...
   ...
   IF (red) THEN
     WRITE(UNIT=*,FMT=*) 'Stop'
   ELSE
     WRITE(UNIT=*,FMT=*) 'Go'
```

```
ENDIF
```

The sort of conditions we have already seen in `IF` statements can be used in logical assignment statements as the value of a logical expression to be assigned to a logical variable. For example a statement such as,

```
tall = height > 6.0
```

would set `tall` to `.TRUE.` if the real variable `height` was greater than `6.0` and would set it to `.FALSE.` otherwise.

4.3.4 Logical relational operators

The most common form of logical expression is a comparison of the value of two quantities. These may be two numeric values or two character values. It would not make sense to compare the values of a character with a number so this is prohibited. Such logical expressions have the form:

```
<expression> <relational operator> <expression>
```

The `<relational operator>` can be one of the following:

```
<   less than
<=  less than or equal to
>=  greater than or equal to
>   greater than
==  equal to
/=  not equal to
```

The logical expression is true if the value of the expression on the left stands in the relation indicated by the particular operator to the value of the expression on the right. Logical expressions of this form occur most frequently in `IF` statements. For example,

```
IF (income < 2500) THEN
  ...
ELSE
  ...
ENDIF
```

The value of the variable `income` is compared to the constant value `2500`. If the value of `income` is less than `2500`, the logical expression is true and the statements following the `THEN` are executed. If it is greater than or equal to `2500`, the expression is false, and the statements following the `ELSE`, if any, are executed.

The previous example illustrates the simplest possible form of a comparison, the comparison of a variable with a constant. This simple form occurs very frequently in programs. However much more complicated expressions are possible. Any numeric expression, or character expression, of whatever complexity that is needed may appear on either side of the relational operator. In such cases the expressions are fully evaluated before the comparison is made. The following examples illustrate the point.

```
IF( B**2 - 4*A*C >= 0.0 )THEN
  WRITE(UNIT=*,FMT=*)' Real roots'
ENDIF

IF( B**2 < 4*A*C )THEN
  WRITE(UNIT=*,FMT=*) ' Complex roots'
ENDIF
```

If the two expressions on either side of a relational operator are of different numeric type, the type of one of them is changed to match that of the other before the comparison is done. The rules of automatic numeric type changes as described earlier for arithmetic expressions are applied as if the difference between the two values on either side of the relational operator was being calculated. For example, suppose we had written the following comparison

```
   income < 2500.0
```

where `income` had been declared as an integer, then the value on the left is of type integer and that on the right is of type real. Before the values are compared the value on the left is converted from `INTEGER` to `REAL`.

4.3.5 Combining logical expressions

More complicated logical expressions may be constructed by combining simple logical values or expressions with the logical operators, `.AND.`, `.OR.`, and `.NOT.`. For example,

```
IF( x**2 > a .AND. z**3 < b)THEN
     ...
ELSE
     ...
ENDIF
```

An example using character comparisons could be

```
IF(surname == 'Jones' .OR. surname == 'Morgan' &
                .AND. forename == 'Dai')THEN
  WRITE(UNIT=*,FMT=*)'DEFINITELY WELSH'
ENDIF
```

Compound logical expressions linked by `.AND.` are true only if both the left sub-expression and the right sub-expression are true. Expressions that are linked by `.OR.` are true if either or both the sub-expressions are true.

It is possible to invert or negate the value of a logical expression by use of the `.NOT.` operator which negates the value of any logical expression which follows it. It yields true if the following expression is false and vice-versa. For example

```
 .NOT.( A > 0.0 )
```

yields the value `.TRUE.` if `A` is less than or equal to zero since `( A > 0.0 )` will then have the logical value `.FALSE.`

As in arithmetic expressions there is a natural order which is applied when evaluating logical expressions. In a complex logical expression any arithmetic or character sub-expressions are evaluated first, then the comparison operations are performed. The `.NOT.` operators, if any, are applied to reverse the truth values of the relations, or logical sub-expressions, to which they are attached. This is followed by evaluation of any `.AND.` operations and last of all the `.OR.` operations are performed. If there are any strings of repeated `.AND.`, or repeated `.OR.`, operations these are evaluated from left to right.

As in arithmetic expressions these normal rules of precedence can be modified by use of parentheses. Anything enclosed in parentheses is evaluated first.

It is surprisingly easy to form logical expressions whose meaning is difficult to unravel so it is recommended that logical expressions be kept as simple as possible and that parentheses are used liberally to make their meaning clear. For example the following simple logical expression requires considerable thought to work out exactly what it means.

```
    (A > 0 .AND. .NOT. B /= -1 .OR. C == 1)
```

where `A`, `B` and `C` have been declared previously as integers is equivalent to,

```
( ( (A > 0) .AND. (.NOT.(B <> -1)) ) .OR. (C == 1) )
```

If `A` is `5` , `B` is `3` and `C` is `0` the expression becomes

```
( ( (.TRUE.) .AND. (.NOT. (.TRUE) ) ) .OR. (.FALSE.) )
```

and then

```
( ( (.TRUE.) .AND. (   .FALSE   ) ) .OR. (.FALSE.) )
```

and then

```
( (    .FALSE.               ) .OR. (.FALSE.) )
```

and then

```
(  .FALSE. )
```

4.4 Named constants

It is possible to define named constants of any of the Fortran data types. This is done by specifying a `PARAMETER` attribute on the type declaration statement. For example,

```
REAL, PARAMETER :: pi = 3.14159
```

declares the name `pi` to refer to a real value and also defines this value to be the constant `3.14159`. Once defined, the name `pi` is fixed and can be used whenever the value of `3.14159` is needed, e.g.

```
circum = pi * diam
```

Named constants can be used in any context where a constant of the same type could also be used. They cannot appear in contexts where only a variable is valid such as on the left-hand side of an assignment statement, or as a list item in a `READ` statement.

Names of any type can be defined by referring to previously defined constant values. For example,

```
REAL,PARAMETER ::   pi=3.14135, &
                    pi_by_4 = pi/4, &
                    two_pi = 2*pi
```

The type-matching rules of assignments apply; a character valued expression may not be defined as the constant value for a name that is declared to be of any other type.

To make defining named character constants a little easier it is possible to declare the name with an indeterminate character string length. The actual length will then be assumed from the length of the constant character string that is assigned to the name. For example,

```
CHARACTER(LEN=*),PARAMETER ::  author='Dickens', &
                               publisher='Blackwells'
```

The * in place of the usual integral value for the length indicates that the lengths to be associated with these names are to be assumed from the values that they will end up referring to. In this case `author` ends up with a length of seven, and `publisher` with a length of ten. Note these two values could be calculated in the program, if need be, by use of the function `LEN`, e.g.,

```
INTEGER :: author_length
author_length = LEN(author)
```

would set the value of `author_length` to 7.

One of the benefits of having named constants is that it allows critical constants to be gathered together in one place. If for some reason a different value for the constant is required it can be changed in one place and the effect is transmitted throughout the program. For instance, suppose we had a program which used the value of `pi` in many places. We might have defined `pi` to three places of decimal with the statements

```
REAL,PARAMETER :: pi = 3.141
```

If later we wished to make the program more accurate we could simply change the above statement to

```
REAL,PARAMETER :: pi = 3.1415926
```

This would cause the new value to be used throughout the sub-program in which it was defined.

4.5 Initial values for variables

When a program is loaded the contents of declared variables are normally undefined. It is frequently useful to be able to define initial values for some variables. That is to define what value will be contained in specific variables when the program starts executing. Initial values for variables can be defined in a type statement declaring the variables. For example,

```
INTEGER   :: count=0,I=5,J=100
REAL      :: inc=1.0E-05, max=10.0E+05, min=-10.0E+05
CHARACTER :: light = 'Amber'
LOGICAL   :: red=.TRUE., blue=.FALSE., green=.FALSE.
```

4.5.1 Initialisation expressions

It is worth noting here that the general form of an assignment in a type statement is,

```
<object name> = <initialisation expression>
```

where <initialisation expression> can be any expression involving constants that can be evaluated when the program is compiled. Thus the following statements are all valid:

```
REAL, PARAMETER :: pi = 3.141592, piby4 = pi/4
CHARACTER(LEN=*), PARAMETER :: xname= 'John', &
                               sname ='Soap', &
                               fname= xname//sname
REAL :: radius = 3.5, circum = 2 * pi * radius
```

However, the second of the following statements would be **incorrect**:

```
REAL, PARAMETER :: pi = 3.141592, piby4 = pi/4
REAL :: radius, circum = 2 * pi * radius
```

since radius has not been initialised.

4.6 Derived types

Many algorithms can be more elegantly and concisely expressed if they can be written in terms of aggregate structures. The intrinsic data types for integers and real numbers, characters and logical quantities are not ideal in such circumstances and tend to obscure the original problem. For example, suppose we wished to model a city consisting of a number of houses. For each house, we might wish to record the number of people living there, the name of the owner, and the value of the house for property tax purposes, and so on. It would convenient to keep all the data for a single house together so it could be manipulated as a single compound entity. We can create such compound entities by first defining a new type of object. For example,

```
TYPE HOUSE
  CHARACTER(LEN=16) :: owner
  INTEGER           :: residents
  REAL              :: value
ENDTYPE HOUSE
```

Such a type is called a *derived type* since it is derived from the intrinsic types. In this case HOUSE is made up of three components - one of type character with length 16, one of type integer, and one of type real. These components have the names owner, residents and value, respectively. Note that, such a definition does not create any data-objects as such. It merely defines a template to be used when an object of this type is declared so that the correct space can be reserved at that time.

The statement,

```
type(HOUSE) :: biggest, corner, cheapest
```

declares biggest, corner and cheapest to be objects of type HOUSE. Such objects are called *structures*. The declaration introduces these names to the program in the normal manner but the type is now user-defined so the compiler must refer to the type definition for HOUSE in order to reserve the correct amount of storage space for values of these variables. In this case it must reserve space for 16 characters, an integer and a real. However, it should be noted that the processor is not required to allocate space in that order nor is it even necessary that the space be contiguous. The processor may optimise the way it allocates memory for such objects in any way it chooses.

It is possible, once a new type is defined, to use it in defining further new types. Thus if we define a new type POINT as

```
TYPE POINT
 REAL :: X,Y
END TYPE
```

then we can define a further type CIRCLE as

```
TYPE CIRCLE
 type(POINT) :: centre
 REAL        :: radius
END TYPE
```

Objects of type CIRCLE can then be declared as,

```
type(CIRCLE) :: c1,c2,c3
```

and so on.

4.6.1 Component selection

Individual components can be selected from a structure and manipulated. For example, if the biggest house in a street was to have the number of residents increased by one this could be done by a statement,

```
biggest%residents = biggest%residents + 1
```

The `%` symbol is used to indicate the selection of a component from a structure. In the case above the `residents` component is selected from the structure called `biggest`. The component, `biggest%residents`, is an object of type integer, as defined in the type definition and as such can be manipulated and can appear in expressions just like any other object of type integer.

The x-component of the centre of one of the circles declared above could be assigned a value thus,

```
c1%centre%X = 55.
```

In this case two levels of reference are required to access the required datum.

4.6.2 Assignment

Assignment between objects of derived type is defined as simply the operation of assigning each component of one object to the corresponding component of the other object. The statement,

```
biggest = corner
```

where `biggest` and `corner` are both of type `HOUSE` (defined earlier), is thus equivalent to the statements,

```
biggest%owner=corner%owner
biggest%residents=corner%residents
biggest%value=corner%value
```

Assignment is the only intrinsic operation defined for derived types.

4.6.3 Type constructors

A value of a derived type can be constructed using a "constructor". This has the form,

```
type-name(expression,expression,....)
```

For example,

```
cheapest = HOUSE("Jones",4,25000.0)
```

constructs a value of type `HOUSE` and assigns it to the variable `cheapest`. The constructor on the right of the = has a list of expressions, one for each component of the type. The values of these expressions are converted, if necessary, as if they were being assigned to variables of the type required by the components defined in the `HOUSE` type definition. A further example is,

```
type(CIRCLE) :: spot
spot = CIRCLE(POINT(10.,10.),60.)
```

which creates `spot` as a circle with centre at (10.,10.) with a radius of 60. Notice here that the `CIRCLE` structure which itself contains an object of type `POINT` has been expanded into a list of its ultimate intrinsic components. That is, `CIRCLE` is expanded to a `POINT` and a `REAL`, and then `POINT` is further expanded to two `REAL`s thus giving three `REAL`s.

4.6.4 Input/output

Objects of simple derived types can be included in input/output lists where they are interpreted as equivalent to a list of their ultimate intrinsic components, in the order in which they were defined in the relevant type definition. For example,

```
READ(UNIT=*,FMT=*) cheapest
```

would be exactly equivalent to

```
READ(UNIT=*,FMT=*)cheapest%owner,cheapest%residents,&
                  cheapest%value
```

and would expect to find 16 characters, an integer, and a real as the next three items in the input file.

4.6.5 Operations

We saw above how whole derived-type objects could be assigned to one another. As mentioned above the ability to reference compound objects in this way brings great benefits since it allows programs to be expressed in terms of objects which directly relate to the problem at hand. However, to solve real problems, we need more than just assignment. We need to define operations which may be used to manipulate derived type objects. These operations, unlike the operations for the intrinsic types (addition, multiplication, concatenation etc.), can only be specified by the programmer who defines the new derived types. A discussion of this very important aspect of Fortran 90 requires an understanding of procedures and is thus postponed until Chapter 8.

4.7 Statement ordering

We know from the earlier chapters that a program starts with a `PROGRAM` statement and ends with an `END` statement. We also know that executable statements such as assignment statements and `READ` and `WRITE` statements must be ordered in correct sequence so that the execution flow of the program is as needed to solve the required problem. It is not obvious, however, what order the declaration statements (`INTEGER, REAL, CHARACTER, LOGICAL`) should come in.

Fortran has some quite strict rules about the order of statements. Basically in any program or subprogram the following rules must be used:

1. The program heading statement must come first, (`PROGRAM, FUNCTION or SUBROUTINE`).

2. All the specification statements must precede the first executable statement.

3. The executable statements must follow in the order required by the logic of the program.

4. The program or subprogram must end with an `END` statement.

Within the set of specification statements there is relatively little ordering required. However, in general if one entity is used in the specification of another, it is normally required that it has been previously specified. In particular, types must be defined before objects of those types may be declared and named constants must be declared before they can be used in the declaration of other objects. That is, if a particular name is going to be used as part of an expression defining the value of another constant it must have been previously defined in the same or a previous type statement with the PARAMETER attribute. Otherwise specification statements may occur in any order that is convenient.

4.8 Exercises

1. What are the data types of the following constants?

```
-1   30   .500   6.35   2E-5   .123E+12   'Have a nice day'
'.5'   '   '   .TRUE.
```

2. What are the types and the values of the following expressions given that `A=1.5, B=2., C=3., I=4, J=5`?

```
A*B     A*I   A*C/B     (4/5)*J   J/I   I/J   I*J + 3/C
I/J*I   I/J*B   (I/J)*I   I/(J*I)
```

3. Write a program to read in two phrases and print them out as one sentence with a comma in between.

4. Write a program to determine the character position of the comma in the sentence of question 4.

5. In the following, what is the value of red_or_not?

```
LOGICAL :: red_or_not
CHARACTER(LEN=4) :: colour1 = 'Blue', colour2 = 'Red'
red_or_not = (colour2 == 'Red' .AND. colour2 == 'Blue')
```

6. Explain the difference between the named items called `colour` and `hue` declared in the two statements,

```
CHARACTER, PARAMETER :: colour='Blue'
and
CHARACTER :: hue= 'Blue'
```

7. Write a program to calculate the area between two concentric circles and print out the result. Deal with any special values of the radii.

8. Declare the items given in column 1 of the following table

Name	Status	Type	Initial value
time	variable	real	0.0
height	variable	real	5.6
pi	constant	real	3.41
name	variable	character	Rush
club	constant	character	Liverpool
stat	constant	logical	true
turns	variable	integer	500

9. Define a data-type that would be suitable for holding the student name and marks received for subjects: English, Mathematics, Science, French, and History. Declare variables of this type for three students called Tom, Dick and Harry. Set Harry's specifications to Harold Brown, part-time, with marks of 34 in English, 76 in Mathematics and 64 in Science. Write a Fortran statement which would test whether Harry and Tom had the same mark in English and print out a suitable message.

Chapter 5

Control Constructs

The control constructs of any programming language provide the means of changing the normal sequential order of execution of a program. We have already introduced the basic features of the most important control constructs, and the statements that are used to create them, in the first two chapters. In this Chapter we shall cover these in more detail and we shall introduce some additional features which make practical programming easier.

5.1 The conditional execution construct

This construct is written in Fortran 90 using the `IF()THEN`, `ELSE`, and `ENDIF` statements. As we saw earlier, the `IF` construct's basic form is,

```
IF(<logical_expression>)THEN
      .
      . then_block of statements
      .
ELSE
      .
      . else_block of statements
      .
ENDIF
```

The `IF...ENDIF` group of statements is often referred to as the `block-IF` construct and its meaning is fairly obvious. The `logical_expression` is evaluated to yield a result which is either true or false. If the logical expression is true, the `then-block` of statements is executed. If the logical expression is false, the `else-block` of statements is executed. Whichever block is executed, the program then continues by executing the statement following the `ENDIF`.

In the examples of Part 1 the statements of the `then-blocks` and the `else-blocks` were either simple assignment or input/output statements but in fact these blocks may include any executable Fortran statements including other control constructs. It should be stressed, however, that if a `then-block`, or an `else-block`, contains another control construct, such as another `block-IF`, the whole construct must be completely contained within the block in which it appears. We say that the inner control construct is *nested* within the outer one. Such nesting of control constructs can, in principle, be continued to any depth. As an example of this consider the following program fragment,

```
INTEGER              :: age
CHARACTER(LEN=20)    :: desc
CHARACTER(LEN=8)     :: status
      .
      .
IF(age>=18)THEN

  desc="ADULT"

  IF(status=="ALIEN")THEN !---
    desc(7:)="NON-VOTER"  !   |
  ELSE                    !   |- inner construct
    desc(7:)="VOTER"      !   |
  ENDIF                   !---

ELSE
  desc="CHILD"
ENDIF
      .
      .
```

Note that, the inner `block-IF` is completely contained within the `then-block` of the outer `block-IF`.

Statements in either the `then-block` or the `else-block` may be labelled (see section 3.2.1) but jumps to such labelled statements are permitted only from within the block containing them. Entry into a `block-IF` construct is allowed only via the initial `IF` statement. Transfer out of either the `then-block` or the `else-block` is permitted but only to a statement entirely outside of the whole block defined by the `IF...ENDIF` statements. A transfer from a statement in a `then-block` to a labelled statement in an `else-block` is not permitted.

5.1.1 Alternative forms of the `block-IF` construct

Although the `IF()THEN...ELSE...ENDIF` pattern is the normal form of the `block-IF` construct there are a number of alternative forms which are useful in particular cases. The first of these caters for the situation when there is a block of code to be executed if a certain condition holds but otherwise is to be skipped i.e., the `else-block` would do nothing. When this type of construction is required the `else-block` and the corresponding `ELSE` itself may be omitted entirely. The construct would then take the form,

```
IF(logical_expression)THEN
    .
    . then-block
    .
ENDIF
```

The `logical_expression` is evaluated and if it is true the `then-block` is executed and then execution continues with the code following the `ENDIF`. If the `logical_expression` is false the `then-block` is not executed. Execution merely continues directly with the first executable statement following the `ENDIF`.

As an example, suppose we wanted to modify a set of names we had stored so as to make the titles of all women 'Ms.' instead of some being 'Miss', some 'Mrs.' and some already 'Ms.'. Obviously we would not want to change the titles for those that were already in the desired form, nor would we want to change those with different titles - men, doctors, professors etc. We would want to shift the remaining characters of the name up to fill the space created because 'Ms.' is shorter than the titles it is replacing. Assuming that `name` has been declared as a character variable of length 20 and we have read the name into it, a fragment of code to handle this would be,

```
!--Change title IF Miss OR Mrs. TO Ms.
!--otherwise leave unchanged
IF( name(1:4)=="Miss" .OR. name(1:4)=="Mrs." )THEN
  name(1:3) = "Ms."
  name(4:) = name(5:)
ENDIF
```

A further special case of the `block-IF` construct, which we have already seen, arises when there is no `else-block` and the `then-block` is only a single statement. When this occurs it is possible to leave out the `ENDIF` and replace the `THEN` by the single statement. The construct becomes,

```
IF(logical-expression) statement
```

The statement following the right bracket is executed only when the `logical-expression` is true. The statement may be any executable statement but the only control statements allowed are the simple `GOTO`, the `EXIT`, and `CYCLE` statements (see later).
A further form of `block-IF` exists to cater for the situation when there are more than just two alternative blocks of code that must be executed depending on a related set of conditions. For instance, suppose in our

example with incomes we wished to process the data in one way if the income was more than one standard deviation less than the mean, in another way if the income was within one standard deviation of the mean and in a third way if the income was more than one standard deviation greater than the mean. This could be done using the normal `block-IF` as follows,

```
IF( income < income_mean-income_spread )THEN
  .
  . code for low incomes
  .
ELSE
 IF( income < income_mean+income_spread )THEN
   .
   . code for incomes near mean
   .
 ELSE
   .
   . code for large incomes
   .
 ENDIF
ENDIF
```

This situation is sufficiently common that a shorthand form of `block-IF` is included in the language to make it easier to write. This form is illustrated by the following piece of code which is equivalent to that above.

```
IF( income < income_mean-income_spread )THEN
  .
  . code for low incomes
  .
ELSEIF( income < income_mean+income_spread )THEN
  .
  . code for incomes near mean
  .
ELSE
  .
  . code for large incomes
  .
ENDIF
```

A new `ELSEIF()THEN` block has been included thus avoiding the need to use the nested form shown previously. As many `ELSEIF()THEN` blocks as are required may be used but there must be at least one initial `IF()THEN` block at the start of the construct and at most one `ELSE` block at the end. The `ELSE` block may be omitted if it is not required, in which case the last `ELSEIF` block is terminated by the `ENDIF` statement which terminates the entire construct. An initial `IF` must always be matched by a terminating

ENDIF. This form is particularly useful when the number of different alternative blocks and their associated conditions becomes large. Such cases are awkward to write in terms of multiple nested IF...ENDIF constructs. It can be quite difficult to ensure that the IF and ENDIF statements are correctly matched, particularly if some of the internal blocks consist of many statements.

It should be noted that the various conditions do not have to be mutually exclusive. The conditions are always tested in order and the first one that is true causes its associated block to be executed followed by transfer of control to the statement after the ENDIF. So a later ELSEIF condition will only be evaluated and tested provided all the earlier ones have yielded false.

When genuine nesting of block-IF constructs is required the use of an indentation convention is a very good way of making the block level of the enclosed statements visible. For instance a common convention of this type is to start all statements of a then-block and any else-block two characters to the right of the IF, ELSE, and ENDIF which delimit the blocks. If a nested block-IF is required its interior statements are then moved a further two characters, and so on. This makes the nesting of constructs visible and so aids the detection of nesting errors. Correct nesting will then be indicated by the final ENDIF appearing back at the main left margin.

5.2 Conditional-exit loops

A loop comprises a block of statements that are executed cyclically. When the end of the loop is reached the block is repeated from the start of the loop. Loops are differentiated by the way they are terminated. Obviously it would not be reasonable to continue cycling a loop forever. There must be some mechanism for a program to exit from a loop and carry on with the instructions following the End-of-loop. The general conditional-exit loop in Fortran 90 has the form

```
DO
   ----------------
  | pre exit test  |
  | loop statements|
   ----------------
IF( condition )EXIT
   ----------------
  | post exit test |
  | loop statements|
   ----------------
ENDDO
```

The block of statements making up the loop is delimited by `DO` and `ENDDO` statements. This block is executed as many times as is required. Each time through the loop, the `condition` is evaluated and the first time it is true the `EXIT` is performed and processing continues from the statement following the `ENDDO`.

The statements between the `DO` and its corresponding `ENDDO` must constitute a proper block. The statements may be labelled but no transfer of control to such a statement is permitted from outside the `loop-block`. The `loop-block` may contain other block constructs but they must be contained completely; that is they must be properly nested.

This type of conditional-exit loop is useful for dealing with situations when we want input data to control the number of times the loop is executed. This type of program was used in Chapter 1 and showed a very typical, if somewhat simple, example of a program designed to work from an interactive display.

5.2.1 Conditional cycling of loops

Situations often arise in practice when for some exceptional reason it is desirable to terminate a particular pass through a loop but to continue immediately with the next repetition or cycle. For instance, consider a program to process the results of a questionnaire. Such a program would typically handle one response at each pass through its main loop. In such cases it is quite common to have to deal with results for some respondents who have refused, or failed for some reason, to give an answer to a particular question. To signify this a special value is usually included in the data to represent the missing data item. When the program encounters such a value, the rest of this particular pass through the loop needs to be skipped, and the program should continue processing with the next iteration of the loop. This can be achieved in Fortran 90 by arranging that a `CYCLE` statement is executed at an appropriate point in the loop. For instance, suppose we were processing student examination results to produce a class average. If the exam question was optional and students who did not take the exam were to be recorded as having a zero mark, and the average to be calculated assumed to be based only on those students choosing to do the exam, that is only those with a positive mark. We are assuming that anyone actually choosing to do the exam will manage to get at least one mark. A program to perform this task will require the loop to be cycled if the mark is zero.

```
PROGRAM class_average_marks
!-----------------------------------------------------------!
! Total and count the number of marks in a set of exam      !
! results read from the terminal. Calculate and display     !
! the class average. A negative mark terminates the set.    !
! A zero mark indicates a student not choosing to take      !
! this option and not to be counted.                        !
!-----------------------------------------------------------!
  INTEGER :: no_of_students
  REAL    :: mark,total_marks
  !--Initialise no_of_students and total_marks to zero
  no_of_students = 0
  total_marks = 0.0
  DO                               !--start of loop
    READ(UNIT=*,FMT=*) mark
    IF( mark < 0.0 ) EXIT          !--terminate loop on reading
                                   !--a negative mark
    IF( INT(mark) == 0 ) CYCLE !--skip count and total for
                                   !--this student
    no_of_students = no_of_students + 1
    total_marks    = total_marks + mark
  ENDDO                            !--end of loop
  WRITE(UNIT=*,FMT=*) " Average Mark =", &
                      total_mark/no_of_students
END PROGRAM class_average_marks
```

Of course for a program which was reading its data from a terminal like this one, the human operator could easily filter out the zero values. However in practice this type of application usually works with data that has previously been stored in a file, in which case the program must do the filtering. Files are discussed in Chapter 10.

Two additional points about this program should be noted. First the test that is used to decide when to cycle uses the intrinsic function `INT` to obtain the integer value of `mark` before testing against zero. The obvious test would be,

```
IF( mark == 0.0 ) CYCLE
```

However it is often dangerous to try to control a program using a test which compares real values for absolute equality. Real values are approximate almost by definition (see the discussion in Chapter 4) and a value that is approximately zero would not produce `true` in a test like the one above. By taking the truncated integer value of `mark` and comparing with the integer value 0 we ensure that the comparison is exact.

5.2.2 Special forms of loop

In general conditional-exit loops may contain more than one exit or cycle condition and these conditions may appear anywhere within the loop body. In particular, the conditional exit may be at the top of the loop producing a so-called *do-while* style of loop, or at the bottom producing a so-called *repeat-until* style of loop. In fact the form,

```
DO ; IF( .NOT.( <condition> )) EXIT
  ...
ENDDO
```

may be written

```
DO WHILE( <condition> )
  ...
ENDDO
```

Which mode of expression is used is largely a matter of taste. We have a preference for using the general form in all cases so would recommend using the former more general form even where the latter is possible. Experience suggests that, in practice, rather few loops turn out to be ones that naturally test the exit condition at the very top. Most loops will be expressed most directly with the explicit exit and condition somewhere in the middle of the loop block, and so for those few occasions when `DO WHILE` is naturally applicable, continuing to use the general form would appear sensible.

5.2.3 Named loops

With multiply-nested loops it is not always obvious which loop is being referred to when an `EXIT` or `CYCLE` statement occurs in an inner loop. For example, in the following code,

```
DO  !--loop 1
  ...
  DO  !--loop 2
    ...
  IF( condition ) EXIT
    ...
  ENDDO
  ...
ENDDO
```

the `EXIT` statement could be referring to loop 1 or loop 2. In fact the rules of Fortran state that the `EXIT` refers to the inner loop, loop 2. There can be some real problems with this rule however. Suppose the program was a large one and the ... symbols corresponded to many hundreds of statements, including many other complete `DO-loops`. It would then be difficult to see just which loop was terminated by any particular `EXIT` statement. It would even be difficult to find the relevant `DO` and `ENDDO` statements. A second problem occurs if we do not just want to terminate the inner loop at this point but we also want to terminate the outer loop. Both of the above problems can be handled by the use of named loops and exits.

The following example shows how we can attach a construct name to a loop and then refer to the name in `EXIT` statements and `ENDDO` statements.

```
loop1: DO
   ...
   loop2: DO
      ...
   IF( condition ) EXIT loop1
      ...
   ENDDO loop2
   ...
ENDDO loop1
```

The names `loop1` and `loop2` serve to tie together the `DO`, its corresponding `ENDDO` and any `EXIT` or `CYCLE` that apply to the particular loop. Any loop can be given a name but, if it is, then the name must be used on the corresponding `ENDDO` and any `EXIT` or `CYCLE` within the named loop must specify which loop is being referred to. This naming of loops is of considerable benefit in allowing easier detection of errors. For this reason we recommend that loops be given names, unless the loops are particularly short and simple.

5.3 Indexed loops

It is quite common in programming to want to write a loop in which the number of repetitions is known or can be calculated before the loop is started. We might require a loop which was repeated a specified number of times. Fortran again uses the `DO...ENDDO` loop construct to create loops of this type, but now controls the loop by way of an index counter. For example, a loop that was to be repeated one hundred times could be expressed in Fortran as,

```
DO i = 1,100
    <loop statements>
ENDDO
```

The above construct can be interpreted as "Repeat, or DO, the following loop statements for the values of `i` ranging through 1,2,3,...,100. The statements of the loop are thus executed 100 times. The quantity `i` is called the *loop index.* This is why this sort of loop is usually called an indexed loop.

In its most general form the DO statement can be written as,

```
loop_name: DO index = start_value, end_value, increment
```

As we saw above the `loop_name` is the name which identifies the ENDDO terminal statement of the loop, and any `EXIT` or `CYCLE` statements that apply. The DO statement and its corresponding ENDDO statement delimit the block of statements which are to be executed as a loop. In the general DO statement the `index` is an integer variable, and the `start_value`, `end_value` and `increment` are expressions which yield integer values. These three quantities are usually referred to collectively as the loop parameters. The first simple example we showed above was a special case where the loop parameters were 1, 100 and 1 respectively. Thus, when an increment is 1 it may be omitted. For example,

```
DO i = 1,100,1
```

and

```
DO i = 1,100
```

are both valid and mean exactly the same thing.

The fact that `start_value`, `end_value` and `increment` can be expressions means for example that loops of the form

```
DO j = 1, n/2
```

or

```
DO ind = i*j, n**2-1, k
```

are also perfectly valid.

Before an indexed `DO-loop` is executed, an iteration count is established which determines how many times the loop will be repeated. The iteration count is given by,

$$iteration\_count = \left[\frac{end\_value - start\_value}{increment} \right]$$

The square braces indicate that the integer value of the enclosed expression is taken. The loop is then executed this number of times regardless of any subsequent changes in the values of variables that might have been involved in the loop parameter expressions.

Some examples of DO statements and their corresponding iteration counts are shown in the following table,

statement	**iteration count**
`DO i=5,27,3`	7
`DO j=1,30,2`	14
`DO k=30,1,-2`	14
`DO l=1,n`	n

When the loop has been executed the number of times required by the iteration count, execution continues with the statement following the corresponding ENDDO statement. It is important to note that, if at the start of the loop the iteration count is calculated to be zero, then the loop is not executed at all. Loops of this sort which are not executed are sometimes called *zero-trip* loops. Note also that loops can have negative increments so that the value of the index is decremented at each iteration of the loop until it is less than the end-value.

5.3.1 General rules of operation of DO-loops

The detailed rules of operation of the DO statement and the loop are as follows,

1. If there is no index definition on the initial DO statement the block contained between the initial DO and its corresponding ENDDO are repeated indefinitely until the loop is terminated by execution of a corresponding EXIT statement, or control is transferred out of the loop by other means (a GOTO statement).

2. If an index definition is included, the three expressions for the start value, the end value and the increment are evaluated. The iteration count is established and the index variable is set to the start_value.

3. If the iteration count is positive, the statements of the loop are executed.

4. After the last statement of the loop has been executed, the ENDDO reached, the value of the increment is added to the index, and the iteration count is reduced by one. If the iteration count is still positive the loop is executed again. If the iteration count is zero the loop is terminated and execution continues with the first executable statement following the ENDDO statement.

The `start`, `end`, and `increment` expressions are evaluated only once, when the DO statement is first executed. So if they depend on variables that are changed in the body of the loop these changes have no effect on the number of times the loop is executed or on the values taken by the index variable.

The index variable may be used freely within the loop but it may not have its value changed within the loop body. When a loop has been fully executed the index variable is still defined and has the first value in the sequence which is outside the range defined by the expressions. An index loop can also be terminated by the execution of an `EXIT` statement. If this occurs the index variable retains the value it had when the `EXIT` was executed.

Control may only enter a loop body by way of the DO statement. No transfer of control into a `DO-loop` from outside except by the execution of the initial DO statement is permitted. Transfer of control out of a `DO-loop` is however allowed. This is illustrated by the following example which introduces the Fortran GOTO statement. The GOTO statement is discussed further in a subsequent section. Its meaning here is obvious.

```
jump_out: DO i=1,100
  READ(UNIT=*,FMT=*) length, area
  IF( length <= 0.0 ) GOTO 999   ! error in data
  ...
ENDDO jump_out
 ...
 further code to be executed
 after loop terminates
 ...
```

```
999 WRITE(UNIT=*,FMT=*) " error in loop ",i,&
          " the data item length is negative."
  ...
```

5.4 The select-case construct

In practice problems often arise in which, at some point, one of several different paths through an algorithm must be chosen based on the value of a particular expression. Such a situation could be programmed using nested `IF...ENDIF` constructs. For five possible paths we could have the following structure.

```
IF ( <exp> == <val1> )THEN
 ...
 path1
 ...
ELSEIF( <exp> == <val2> )THEN
 ...
 path2
 ...
ELSEIF( <exp> == <val3> )THEN
 ...
 path3
 ...
ELSEIF( <exp> == <val4> )THEN
 ...
 path4
 ...
ELSE ! <exp> equal to none of the values
 ...
 path5
 ...
ENDIF
```

However the use of the `block-IF` in such cases has the disadvantage that all the conditions of the construct have to be tested in order until one is found to be true. This means that even if the condition that is satisfied appears last in a long list of `ELSEIF`s, all the prior `ELSEIF` conditions still have to be tested. If it is known in advance that the `ELSEIF` conditions are mutually exclusive, there is no need to go through this testing sequence. It is then more efficient and more comprehensible if the appropriate block of code is immediately selected from the possible alternatives. Fortran 90 contains a multi-way choice construct. It is called the `SELECT CASE` construct. The multiple branch structure above would be better expressed as,

```
SELECT CASE(exp)
CASE(val1)
```

```
  ...
  path1
  ...
CASE(val2)
  ...
  path2
  ...
CASE(val3)
  ...
  path3
  ...
CASE(val4)
  ...
  path4
  ...
CASE DEFAULT
  ...
  path5
  ...
ENDSELECT
```

The expression, `exp`, is evaluated. It must yield an integer or a character value. The block of code following the `CASE` which includes the value of the expression is then executed. If `exp` is different from any of the values explicitly listed on `CASE` statements, the block following `CASE DEFAULT` is executed. One and only one of the `CASE` blocks is executed.

Multi-way branching situations, such as that shown in the above program, occur quite frequently, particularly in interactive programs where a user is to be presented with a menu of choices of what to do next. In such cases (no pun intended) the use of a select-case construct is an efficient way of handling the selection of the required task. Often in these circumstances the blocks of code for each case are calls to subprograms to perform the particular tasks (see the later chapter on subprograms).

5.5 Use of GOTO statements

The simple `GOTO` is a powerful but undisciplined branching statement. It can be used to create jumps to almost anywhere in a program. It is therefore important to use them with considerable circumspection. The general form of the simple `GOTO` is:

```
GOTO <label>
```

where `<label>` is the label of an executable statement. When the `GOTO` statement is executed control is transferred to the statement with the specified label. A statement with this label must exist and it must be executable. As illustrated below, transfer of control backwards or forwards is allowed.

```
       Forward                 Backward
       ...                     ...
       GOTO 10              23 CONTINUE
       ...                     ...
       ...                     ...
    10 CONTINUE                GOTO 23
       ...                     ...
```

Notice that in the case of the forward jump, unless the statement following the `GOTO 10` is itself labelled, it can never be executed. Compilers sometimes flag such a case as a warning since it usually means the programmer has made a mistake in the coding.

Although labels can be attached to almost any executable statement, in this book we have deliberately chosen to attach labels only to `CONTINUE` statements, and to show `GOTO`s jumping only to points in programs marked by `CONTINUE` statements. The `CONTINUE` statement is a statement that does nothing except to act as a marker in this way. This self-imposed discipline makes the flow structure of a program stand out more clearly from the processing statements. It makes the code easier to read and makes its subsequent modification safer.

Undisciplined use of the `GOTO` statements can cause a program to become highly unstructured, with jumps forwards and backwards intersecting with each other producing so-called logical spaghetti. `GOTO`s should therefore be used with caution. `GOTO` statements can nevertheless be very useful when it is necessary to jump right out of a piece of program that is heavily nested. For instance, when an error condition is detected somewhere in a program, maybe many levels deep in nested loops, block-IFs and/or other constructs, it may be possible to test some assumption about the data on which the program is working. If this is found to be invalid (it could be that a variable which is going to be used as a divisor turns out to be zero, one that must appear in a square root is negative, a male patient is about to be assigned to a labour ward, etc.) there may be little that can be done but to abort that section of the program or even the whole program. To do this it is necessary to get out of the nest of constructs immediately so that the exceptional condition that has been detected can be dealt with. The `GOTO` is especially useful for this purpose.

It is hardly ever appropriate just to stop when an error condition is detected. This would tell the user nothing about what had happened. We would usually want to jump to some special error code which would pass on the information as to what error has been detected and where. This could be to another quite different piece of program which would sort out the problem. In extreme situations the error code would simply print a message flagging the error and terminate the program. The GOTO statement is a useful statement for performing the jump required in such situations. Consider the following piece of code:

```
outer: DO i = 1,n
  ...
  inner: DO j = 1,m
    ...
    CALL SUBR(arg1,arg2,...,argn,ifail)
    IF( ifail /= 0 ) GOTO 99
    ...
    ...
  ENDDO inner
  ...
ENDDO outer
...
...
99 CONTINUE
SELECT CASE(ifail)
  CASE(1) !--code for ifail = 1
  ...
  CASE(2) !--code for ifail = 2
  ...
  etc.
```

This shows a quite commonly used method for handling errors that are returned by subroutines. In this case the subroutine SUBR has a list of arguments the last of which is an error indicator `ifail`. Following the call to the subroutine a test is made to determine whether an error occurred or not. By convention a value of `ifail` equal to zero signifies that no error has occurred. Values of `ifail = 1,2,3,`etc. signify different kinds of error. In this typical case the call to the subroutine is inside two nested DO loops. When the subroutine fails we do not wish to continue processing so we jump right out of both loops to the statement labelled `99`. The select-case structure is then used to deal with the different values of ifail. It would, of course, be possible to use the select-case structure immediately after the call to the subroutine (still inside the loop). It is usually preferable, however, to escape altogether at this point since it makes the program much more readable and the main flow does not become cluttered up with a lot of error handling statements that are only significant in exceptional circumstances.

5.6 Blocked control constructs

In this chapter we have described the main control constructs. These can be used to build programs of any complexity. These are:

- The simple sequence
- The conditional execution of alternative sequences
  (`IF()THEN...ELSE...ENDIF`)
- The loop or repeated sequence, with either conditional exit, index control, or both
  (`DO...ENDDO` loops with or without index or `EXIT`)
- selected execution of one sequence out of a choice of many.
  (`SELECT CASE....ENDSELECT`)

An important point about these constructs is that they are built using the concept of a *block*. The essential feature of a block is that it is always executed by starting at the top, i.e. the first statement of the block. The flow of execution never causes the transfer of execution control into the middle of a block. Also after execution of the block the program continues with the next statement in sequence following the end of the construct. The basic constituent of each construct is the sequential block which in its simplest form is just a sequence of simple processing statements such as assignment, input/output, or call statements. However, if we allow any sequential block to contain within it any of the other control constructs we can write programs of arbitrary complexity.

A program built using the above constructs is always viewable as a sequential block. In all but the most trivial of programs this sequential block will be made up of control constructs of different types but, provided they are written as block constructs, these compound instructions will always appear from the outer block of the program as just another step in the basic sequence of the program.

In principle any degree of nesting is allowed. This means that we can have blocks within blocks within blocks, ad infinitum. However, since the whole point of using a disciplined approach to programming is to maintain logical clarity, we clearly do not want to go too far in this. In practice, if an algorithm requires a high degree of block nesting, it is usually a sign that increased modularisation of the solution technique is needed. In terms of programming this almost invariably means that the inner blocks of code should be put in subroutines.

5.7 Exercises

1. Write a program that prints out the set of positive integers and their cubes from 1 to some upper limit read in from the terminal.

2. Modify the above program so as to guard against a user providing an upper limit which is too large.
   (assume that 100 is as large as is reasonable)

3. Write a program to sum the first n positive integers where n is read in from the terminal.

4. Write a program to print out the solution to any number of quadratic equations.

$$ax^2 + bx + c = 0$$

   Remember, the roots of the above equation are given by

$$x = -b/2a + SQRT(\ b^2 - 4ac\ )/2a$$

   and

$$x = -b/2a - SQRT(\ b^2 - 4ac\ )/2a$$

5. What happens to your quadratic equation program if you input the coefficients,
   a = 2
   b = 1
   c = 2
   If you have not written your program to cope with such data then modify it so that it does.

6. Write a program that will read a sequence of colours input as names, 'red', 'green', 'blue', 'yellow', 'black', 'white' or something else. Stop the program if a colour 'blank' is read. Count the number of occurrences of each colour, including the unspecified colours and print out the totals for each colour before terminating the program.

7. Write Fortran statements to count how many of a set of ten integers typed in at the keyboard are multiples of five. Ignore any negative numbers.

8. How many times are the loops defined by the following statements executed:

    a) `DO I=2,N/2,3`
    b) `DO I=1,N,4`
    c) `DO 3,N**2,5`

    where `N=15`.

Chapter 6

Sets of Similar Data: Arrays

Most problems that occur in practice require more than simple variables for their solution. It is often necessary to handle sets of similar objects. For example: the set of observations in an experiment; the set of all positions on a chess board; the set of names for students in a class, and so on. A complete set of student marks might be collectively referred to by a teacher as "the marks", and the individual marks for each student might be identified as the first mark, the second mark, the third mark, etc. In Fortran such a notion would be represented by an *array*. An array, like other data objects has a name, but now the name refers to a whole set of objects rather than just a single value. Each individual object in the set is called an *element*. These elements are numbered and these numbers or *indices*, which determine the position(s) of an element within the set, can be used to refer to an individual element or to a subset of the elements. This is like referring to all the houses in a street by the street name and an individual house by a street name and its number within the street.

The array facility allows such sets to be accessed in a very flexible manner. The whole set can be accessed via the array name. Subsets of the array, called *sections*, can be selected and manipulated by using a range of the position numbers, and when necessary individual members, or elements, of an array can be referenced by using the name and its numbered position in the set. We might have an array named `ramsy_st` which represented the numbers of residents in each of the houses in Ramsy Street. The number of residents in the first house would be stored in `ramsy_st(1)`, the number in the second house would be stored in `ramsy_st(2)`, and so on.

Arrays may be one-dimensional, as in the example above, or they may also be multi-dimensional. For example, when dealing with student marks, each student may take five courses and there may be 35 students in the class. The set of all marks could be represented by a two-dimensional array called `mark`, with one index selecting the student running from 1 through 35 and another index selecting the course running from 1 through 5. This might use an array called `mark` to hold all 35x5 marks. Now an individual mark for an individual student would be selected by something like `mark(2,5)`.

In general the *dimensionality* of an array is the number of indices used to locate its elements. Arrays may be visualised as a column (one dimension), a rectangle (two dimensions), a box (three dimensions), and so on as shown in Figure 6.1. The first array has one index running from 1 through 5, the second has two indices, the first running from 1 through 5 and the second running from 1 through 4, and so on.

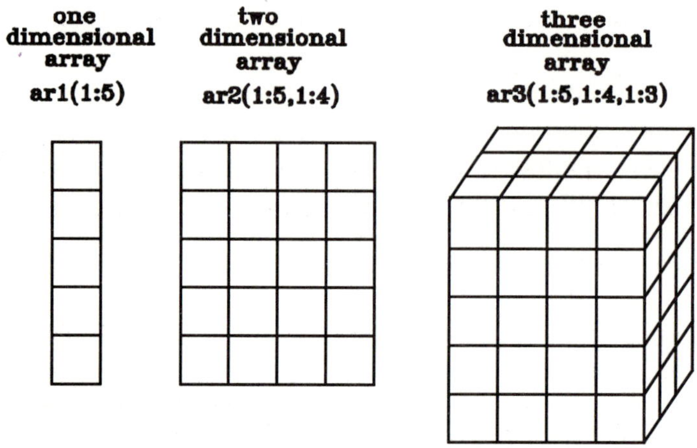

Figure 6.1: Arrays visualised

Fortran 90 defines a number of additional terms in order to make the description of its array handling facilities easier and more precise. In addition to those already introduced the following terms are important. The dimensionality of an array is termed its *rank*. Thus a one-dimensional array has rank 1, a two-dimensional array has rank 2 and so on. The *bounds* of the array are the upper and lower limits of the index in each dimension. The *extent*, or *size*, of an array in a particular dimension is defined by the number of elements in that dimension. The overall *size* of an array is the total number of elements it contains. Thus the overall size is the product of the extents. The *shape* of an array is determined by its rank and its extents in each dimension. Two arrays are said to be *conformable* if they have the same shape, that is if they have the same rank and the same extents in each dimension. Note that the bounds as such do not have to be the same for an arrays to be conformable; conformability depends on the difference in the bounds not on their absolute values.

6.1 Declaring arrays

As with simple objects, arrays have to be given names so they can be referenced in a program and the compiler has to be given instructions as to how much memory is needed to store the array. It has to be told what the arrays type is, its rank and bounds in each dimension. This is done by the appropriate additions to the type declaration statements. For example

```
INTEGER, DIMENSION(1:11) :: A
```

which would declare a rank one array called `A` to be of type integer. This array has lower and upper bounds of 1 and 11, and therefore also a size of 11. Similarly we could declare a real array with the statement

```
REAL, DIMENSION(-12:12) :: B
```

which would define the array named `B` to have 25 elements each of real type.

Array names obey the same rules as variable names. They can consist of up to 31 alphanumeric characters, including underscore, the first of which must be a letter. The variables are specified to be arrays by the inclusion of the `DIMENSION` attribute in their declaration. The rank is specified by the number of bound sets that are included in the *array-spec* within the parentheses. The bound sets have the form:

```
<lower bound>:<upper bound>
```

where the bounds can be any integer value. The upper bound will normally be greater than the lower bound, but a lower bound greater than the upper bound is permissible. In this case a *zero-sized* array is created.

Some further examples of array declarations are:

```
INTEGER, DIMENSION(0:99)   :: arr1, arr2, arr3
INTEGER, DIMENSION(1:12)    :: days_in_month
REAL, DIMENSION(1:350)      :: box_locations
CHARACTER(LEN=10), DIMENSION(1:250) :: names
CHARACTER(LEN=3), DIMENSION(1:12)   :: names_of_month
REAL, DIMENSION(-10:10,-10:10) :: coords
```

This form of declaration is especially useful where several arrays having the same bounds are to be declared. However, when several arrays are required of the same type but different bounds, it can become a little verbose to declare each one as a separate statement. Fortran has an alternative form of declaration for such cases as shown in the following examples,

```
INTEGER :: arr1(1:10), arr2(-10:10), arr3(1:150)
REAL    :: time(1:100), speed(0:200)
```

Here the array bound declaration can be attached to the array name being declared. The choice of which form to use is largely a question of style and convenience.

Arrays which have lower bounds of one are sufficiently common for there to be a short-hand way of declaring them. For example, declarations of the form

```
REAL, DIMENSION(100,100) :: val
INTEGER, DIMENSION(50)   :: counts
```

or

```
REAL    :: val(100,100)
INTEGER :: counts(50)
```

are quite valid and the missing lower bound is assumed to be one.

Higher dimensional arrays, with ranks of three, four, etc. up to seven are allowed although use of those above two is relatively rare. If higher rank arrays are to be used care needs to be exercised to ensure these are not made any bigger than they have to be. A rank seven array of extent only ten in each dimension would have 10 million elements. Objects of this size could very quickly use up the memory resources of the computer.

The terms given at the end of the last section can now be illustrated. Thus, given the following declarations:

```
REAL,DIMENSION(1:6)               :: C
REAL,DIMENSION(1:10,1:5)          :: A
REAL,DIMENSION(-9:0,0:4)          :: B
REAL,DIMENSION(1:100,1:50,-1:1)   :: D
REAL,DIMENSION(1:10,1:4)          :: E
```

we can say that C has rank 1, size 6, and bounds of 1 and 6. A and B both have rank 2 and extents of 10 and 5 in their two dimensions. Their size is thus 50. They both have the same shape which can be written as (10,5) and so they are conformable. Array D has rank 3, extents of 100, 50 and 3 in each of its dimensions. Its size is 15000 and its shape is given by (100,50,3). Notice that array E, although having the same rank as A and B, is not conformable with them since its shape is (10,4) not (10,5).

6.2 Array element references

The simplest way of manipulating arrays is by referring to individual elements. Array element references can be used in assignment statements and expressions and input/output statements in exactly the same way as simple scalar variables. The following shows a number of array element references,

```
INTEGER, DIMENSION(1:12)    :: days_in_month
CHARACTER(LEN=3), DIMENSION(1:12)    :: names_of_month
REAL, DIMENSION(-10:10,-10:10) :: coords
INTEGER :: current_month_days
CHARACTER(LEN=3) :: current_month

names_of_month(1) = "JAN"
days_in_month(1) = 31
j=12
current_month_days = days_in_month(j)
current_month = names_of_month(j)
coords(-5,6) = coords(-4,5) + coords(-6,7) + 2.5
```

The array reference is the array name followed by some integer values in parentheses, one for each dimension. These integer values are called the *subscripts*. For example, the `1` in `days_in_month(1)`, is a subscript. It selects the first element from the array. The usefulness of array references comes from the fact that an array index can be a variable quantity. It may be any integer expression whose value is calculated as the program runs. For example, `names_of_month(j)`, selects the `j`th element of the array. This facility means that array elements can be selected from an array in many different ways. For example,

```
INTEGER, DIMENSION(1:50) :: mark
DO I = 1, 50
   mark(I) = 2*I
END DO
```

sets the elements of Mark to 2, 4, 6, 8, etc. In this example we begin to see why the indexed DO-loop is such an important construct. Coupled with arrays, it provides a concise way of expressing large amounts of repetitive calculation. The example would be just as concise if thousands or even millions of locations were assigned values.

The subscript values in an array element reference may be any expression as long as the result is an integer and the value lies within the range of the bounds.

```
INTEGER,DIMENSION(1:80) :: series
DO K =1,40
  series(2*K) = 2*K-1
  series(2*K-1) = 2*K
ENDDO
```

This sets all the even numbered elements to the odd numbers and all the odd numbered elements to the even numbers.

6.2.1 Array element ordering

Except in special circumstances (see Chapter 13), Fortran does not specify anything about how the elements of arrays are stored in computer memory. There is no requirement that two elements of an array such as `A(1)` and `A(2)` are in adjacent memory locations, although in most implementations they will be. This is a deliberate feature of the language and it allows programs written in Fortran to be implemented efficiently on widely different computer architectures. For instance on some computer configurations it may be efficient to have different parts of the same array stored in memory attached to different processors. The Fortran language does not prevent implementers from doing this and therefore programs written carefully in Fortran are more likely to maintain their efficiency as new computer architectures become available.

There are certain situations, however, where it is necessary to define some order on the elements of arrays. In input/output statements there must be some implied order so that the data can be organised appropriately. Fortran 90 defines an *array element order* in such a way that all arrays, regardless of rank, can be thought of as linear sequences of elements. This is best illustrated by considering a special case.

Suppose we have a two-dimensional array called `A` declared as

```
REAL, DIMENSION(1:3,1:3) :: A
```

`A` has nine elements whose ordering can be illustrated as in Figure 6.2.

The array element order defines the relationship between the linear sequence shown in part (a) of the diagram and our usual conceptual picture of the square array as shown in part (b). Thus when the array `A` is declared an array element order is also defined as

```
A(1,1),A(2,1),A(3,1),A(2,1)A(2,2),A(2,3),A(3,1),A(3,2),A(3,3)
```

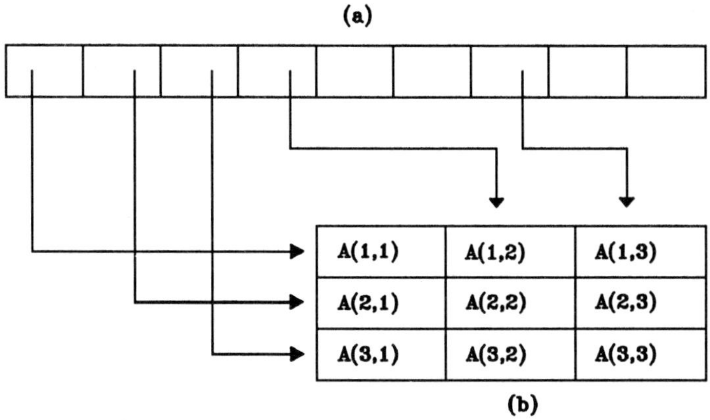

Figure 6.2: Array element order

Thus the array element order is such that the first subscript varies most rapidly. In the normal way of looking at things the array is stored in column order. This rule can be generalised in an obvious way to arrays of ranks greater than 2 by defining the array element order so that it is derived by varying the earlier subscripts most rapidly. Thus the array element order for the array `C` declared as

```
INTEGER, DIMENSION(1:2,1:2,1:2) :: C
```

is

```
C(1,1,1), C(2,1,1), C(1,2,1), C(2,2,1), C(1,1,2), C(2,1,2),
C(1,2,2), C(2,2,2)
```

For most of the computers in use today compilers store arrays in contiguous locations in real memory (i.e. locations that are adjacent) which correspond directly to the array element order. Many modern machines, including even the larger personal computers, extend the size of problem that can be handled by automatically using the disc storage as a temporary extension to the main electronic memory. This is done by dividing the program memory requirements into a number of fixed-size chunks of contiguous real memory, called pages. Only those pages actually in use, normally a small fraction of the total number required, are loaded into the main memory. The remainder is stored on disc. When a program needs to access a page not currently in memory the system automatically loads it from disc, possibly copying an already resident page from memory to disc to make room.

This means that in an example such as

```
DO J=1,5000
 DO I=1,5000
  A(I,J) = I * (J-1)
 ENDDO
ENDDO
```

by making the first index of A the inner loop index we are processing the adjacent items of data each time through the loop. This order of processing can be implemented more efficiently than if elements are accessed in non-consecutive order and so is to be preferred.

```
DO I=1,5000
 DO J=1,5000
  A(I,J) = I * (J-1)
 ENDDO
ENDDO
```

would be very much less efficient on a paged machine since every time it goes through the inner loop a new page would be accessed. However, if the program was run on a system that had many processors each with its own fast memory and only slow access to the memory on other processors there might be other quite different storage layouts that would be optimal and quite different optimal orders of evaluation.

6.2.2 Sorting: an array application

We shall now look at a more realistic application of arrays and array element references. To be specific let us look at the problem of sorting a list of numbers into ascending order of magnitude. We require the following steps:

```
1.  Read the numbers and store them in an array.
2.  Sort them into ascending order of magnitude.
3.  Print them out in sorted order.
```

The main problem here is of course step 2. What we need is an algorithm to do the sort which is suitable for conversion into a Fortran program.

The following is a simple method to understand which can often be useful. Imagine the numbers are stored in boxes or locations as shown below,

6	3	7	1	4

The object is to reorganise these numbers so that they are in ascending order. Consider the number in the first location. The process is to compare it with each of the numbers in the other locations in turn. If the number in the first location is greater than the number being considered then the two numbers are swapped. The new number is then compared with the next number and so on. For the case shown in the diagram, 6 is compared with 3 and a swap takes place to give the arrangement,

3	6	7	1	4

3 is then compared with 7, in which case no swap is necessary, and then with 1 and another swap takes place giving,

1	6	7	3	4

1 is then compared with 4 and no swap is necessary. The effect of all this is, of course, to bring the smallest number to the first location. This location could then be fixed and the method continued by considering the second then the third locations and so on in the same manner.

The sequence of changes produced by considering the second location would be,

```
            1      6      7      3      4
6 with 7    1      6      7      3      4     (no change)
6 with 3    1      3      7      6      4     (swap places)
3 with 4    1      3      7      6      4     (no change)
```

The above method of sorting is called the selection sort.

Let us now consider how we could express the above sorting algorithm for the general case where there are n locations to be sorted. We shall use the indices i and k to refer to the ith and kth locations.

The sorting algorithm can then be expressed in general terms as,

```
1.  Repeat the following for each location i = 1 to n - 1
```

```
    1.1     Repeat the following for each location k = i + 1
            to n
            1.1.1   If the value in location i is greater
                    than the value in location k then swap
                    them over
    1.2     End of Loop
2.  End of Loop
```

The above algorithm consists of one loop nested within another. The value of the index i is first set to 1 and then the index k runs from 2 to n. The index i is then set to 2 and k runs from 3 to n and so on. The lower limit of the inner loop depends on the index of the outer loop (k = i+1). Using this algorithm we could write the following Fortran 90 program to read a set of, say, ten numbers, sort them and output the list in ascending order of magnitude. The "Repeat..." loops are of course implemented using Fortran Do-loops.

```
PROGRAM sort10
!----------------------------------------------------------!
! Read ten numbers into an array, sort into ascending      !
! order and display the sorted list                        !
!----------------------------------------------------------!
INTEGER,DIMENSION(1:10) :: nums
INTEGER :: temp,I,K
!--Read in data
WRITE(UNIT=*,FMT=*) 'Type in ten values one line at a time'

DO I=1,10
  READ(UNIT=*,FMT=*) nums(I)
ENDDO
!--Sort the numbers into ascending order of magnitude
L1: DO I=1,9
  L2: DO K=I+1,10
    IF(nums(I) > nums(K)) THEN
      temp = nums(K)        ! Store in temporary location
      nums(K) = nums(I)     ! Swap the contents over
      nums(I) = temp
    ENDIF
  ENDDO L2
ENDDO L1
!--Write out the sorted list
DO I=1,10
  WRITE(UNIT=*,FMT=*) 'RANK ',I,' VALUE IS ',nums(I)
ENDDO
END PROGRAM sort10
```

The section of this program which swaps the contents of the locations requires a little further explanation. It uses a temporary or working variable `temp` to accomplish this. An easy trap to fall into when trying to swap two values is to write something like,

```
nums(K) =   nums(I)
nums(I) =   nums(K)
```

This would not have the desired effect. It would leave the two locations containing the same value! We need a temporary location to enable the swap to be done correctly as above.

6.3 Allocatable arrays

As it stands the above sort program could only be used to sort ten numbers. Let us consider how we might try to write it so that it could handle any number of items. We could obviously add a statement at the beginning of the program which read in the number of items (say `N_to_Sort`) to be sorted. This would allow the user of the program to specify `N_to_Sort` in his data. Suppose however the number of items to be sorted was greater than ten. The program would fail because we would not have allowed enough room to store all the numbers. This is a quite general problem in programming and Fortran 90 provides a simple facility to handle it. Instead of giving an array an explicit shape when it is declared as in

```
INTEGER, DIMENSION(1:10) :: nums
```

the programmer can give a *deferred* shape specification by declaring the array as

```
INTEGER, DIMENSION(:), ALLOCATABLE :: nums
```

By including `ALLOCATABLE` attribute in the above declaration, and declaring only the rank in the `DIMENSION` attribute, the compiler is being told to defer allocating space to this array until told to do so during the execution of the program. The array can then be allocated space at execution time with an `ALLOCATE` statement. For example,

```
ALLOCATE(nums(1:10))
```

or perhaps,

```
ALLOCATE(nums(-100:100))
```

if a little more space is required.

To illustrate the point fully, the sort program given previously can be re-written so that it can handle any number of items.

```
PROGRAM sort_any_number
!-------------------------------------------------------------!
! Read numbers into an array, sort into ascending order      !
! and display the sorted list                                 !
!-------------------------------------------------------------!
INTEGER,DIMENSION(:),ALLOCATABLE :: nums
INTEGER :: temp,I,K,n_to_sort
!--Ask the user how many numbers he wants to sort
WRITE(UNIT=*,FMT=*) &
     'Type in the number of integers to be sorted'
READ(UNIT=*,FMT=*) n_to_sort
!--Allocate memory for nums
ALLOCATE( nums(1:n_to_sort) )
WRITE(UNIT=*,FMT=*) 'Type in ',n_to_sort,&
           'values one line at a time'
!--Read in data
DO I=1,n_to_sort
  READ(UNIT=*,FMT=*) nums(I)
ENDDO
!--Sort the numbers into ascending order of magnitude
L1: DO I=1,n_to_sort-1
  L2: DO K=I+1,n_to_sort
    IF(nums(I) > nums(K)) THEN
      temp = nums(K)         ! Store in temporary location
      nums(K) = nums(I)      ! Swap the contents over
      nums(I) = temp
    ENDIF
  ENDDO L2
ENDDO L1
!--Write out the sorted list
DO I=1,n_to_sort
  WRITE(UNIT=*,FMT=*) 'RANK ',I,' VALUE IS ',nums(I)
ENDDO
ENDPROGRAM sort_any_number
```

The above program would be able to handle lists of numbers of any size.

Note that the space occupied by an allocatable array such as `nums` can be released when it is no longer needed using a `DEALLOCATE` statement. This allows the programmer to optimise the use of memory. The `DEALLOCATE` statement would take the form,

```
DEALLOCATE(nums)
```

Note, it is an error to deallocate an array that has not been allocated space previously by an `ALLOCATE` statement.

6.4 Array manipulation

Up until now all the operations on arrays have been via array elements. A significant enhancement in Fortran 90, over previous versions of Fortran, is provided by its facilities to manipulate arrays as whole compound objects. This allows arrays to be referenced, not just in terms of single elements, but also in groups of elements. In addition a large number of intrinsic procedures are provided which perform some of the common operations required for array processing. These intrinsic procedures are described in Appendix A.

6.4.1 Whole array references

References to an array name without any subscripts can appear on both sides of assignment statements and in input/output statements. For example, to set all the elements of an array `mark` to zero we could write,

```
INTEGER, DIMENSION(1:50) :: mark
mark = 0
```

The reference to `mark` on the left-hand side of the assignment statement is taken to mean 'all the elements of `mark`'. The scalar value zero is assigned to all the elements of mark by this statement.

It is also possible to assign all the elements of one array to the elements of another. For example,

```
INTEGER, DIMENSION(1:200) :: arr1,arr2
...
arr2 = arr1
```

This last statement makes the corresponding elements of `arr2` the same as those in `arr1`. Notice that `arr1` must be the same shape as `arr2` for this to be allowed. Arrays of the same shape are said to be *conformable*, and conformability is essential for one to be assigned to the other. The following example would be illegal,

```
INTEGER, DIMENSION(1:50) :: first
INTEGER, DIMENSION(1:150):: second
first = 10
second = first
```

The arrays are not conformable since `first` has shape (50) and `second` has shape (150). However,

```
INTEGER, DIMENSION(1:51) :: first
INTEGER, DIMENSION(-25:25) :: second
first = 10
second = first
```

is legal since now the two arrays have the same shape (i.e. (51)). Note that when a scalar, such as `10` above, appears in a context that requires an array, the scalar is conformable to any shape. The scalar is said to be equivalent to an array of the required shape with the same value for every element.

The right-hand side of an array assignment can be any expression which delivers an array result with the same shape as the left-hand side. Note that, given the following declarations,

```
REAL, DIMENSION(1:10,1:8) :: A
REAL, DIMENSION(1:80) :: B
```

the statement

```
A = B
```

is illegal. Although `A` and `B` have the same size, they do not have the same shape since `A` has rank 2 and `B` has rank 1.

6.4.2 Array section references

There are many problems that cannot be programmed using just whole array references since it is often necessary to access part of an array rather than the whole. Fortran 90 therefore provides the ability to use array sections as shown in the following code.

```
INTEGER, DIMENSION(1:100) :: arr1
INTEGER, DIMENSION(1:50) :: arr2
INTEGER, DIMENSION(1:100) :: arr3, arr4
arr1(1:50) = 5
arr1(51:100) = 25
arr2 = arr1(1:50)
arr3(51:100) = arr2
arr3(1:50) = arr1(51:100)
arr4(1:100:2) = arr2
```

The reference `arr1(1:50)` for instance, which means 'the elements of array from 1 to 50', is an array section. The last statement shows how an array section can be chosen in a regular pattern from the array. In the case shown the elements `arr4(1)`, `arr4(3)`, `arr4(5)`,...,`arr4(99)`, i.e. every second element, are set to the elements of arr2. Note that the array section arr4(1:100:2) is conformable with arr2 since they both have shape (50).

The general form of an array section reference is

```
array_name(<bound1>:<bound2>:<stride>)
```

where <bound1> and <bound2> are the limits of the section of the array and <stride> is the increment by which the locations are selected. They can all be integer expressions. That is to say they do not have to be constant expressions as shown in the examples above but can also be any expressions which deliver an integer result.

For example, it is perfectly legal to write,

```
X(M:N:K) = 0
```

or

```
X(M**2:N*K/3:2*K) = 0
```

where K, M and N are integers which have been calculated previously.

There is no restriction that <bound1> must be less than <bound2> or that <stride> must be positive so the following example is permissible,

```
INTEGER, DIMENSION(0:10) :: box,arr
box(8:3:-1) = arr(2:7)
```

and sets part of box to be the same as part of arr but in reverse order. Array section references can be extremely useful when dealing with multi-dimensional arrays. It is often necessary to access rectangular subsets of particular arrays. For instance, consider the following array A declared as

```
REAL, DIMENSION(1:6,1:8) :: A
```

which can be illustrated as shown in the diagram below,

X	X	X	X				
X	X	X	X			Y	
X	X	X	X			Y	
						Y	
						Y	

We could reference the top left-hand corner of `A` (marked with Xs) with the array section

```
A(1:3,1:4)
```

and the section of the 7th column marked with Ys as

```
A(2:5,7)
```

A nice short-hand is available if one of the bounds in a section is to be the bound of the whole array. In this case the bound may simply be omitted. The section `A(3:,:4)` is the same as `A(3:6,1:4)`. Similarly, `A(6,:)` refers to all the elements of the 6th row and `A(:,3)` refers to the 3rd column, and so on.

Note that the rule of conformability mentioned above for whole arrays also applies to array sections. So if we declare `B` as

```
REAL, DIMENSION(0:3,-5:5) :: B
```

we could write

```
A(2:5,1:7) = B(:,-3:3)     ! both sections have shape (4,7)
```

but

```
A(1:5,1:7) = B(:,-3:3)    ! left-hand side has shape (5,7)
                          ! right-hand side has shape (4,7)
```

would be illegal.

6.4.3 Array bound violations

The array subscript (or implied subscripts in the case of an array section) must lie within the bounds declared for the array. It is all too easy to produce array subscript values which exceed the declared bounds. Some compilers translate programs in such a way that the runnable versions can detect invalid (out of bounds) references, but there are many compilers which do not have this facility. A program which does not check for array bound violations will usually run much faster than one that does. If possible, programs should be compiled for testing with array bound checking switched on, and then, when they are working correctly, compiled again without the checks to allow them to run more efficiently.

Unchecked programs in which array subscripts do exceed their bounds can harbour some very enigmatic bugs. They may not fail with any comprehensible error message. They are more likely just to continue to run but to produce wrong results because some entirely incorrect piece of memory was accessed and misinterpreted when the array bound error occurred.

Subscript values are never allowed to exceed the bounds but section bounds can as long as the section does not actually reference elements that lie outside of the declared bounds. That is, the lower bound of a section must be greater than or equal to the declared lower bound and the upper bound of a section must be less than or equal to the declared upper bound. However, the lower bound of a section may be greater than the upper bound of a section, in which case the array referenced is said to be *zero-sized*. Zero-sized arrays are allowed since they permit a number of limiting case problems to be handled more easily.

6.4.4 Array Constructors

Values can be assigned to whole arrays using an array constructor. Thus an array with elements `10, 25, 32, 40, 54, 60` could be constructed with the following statements,

```
INTEGER :: marks(1:6)
marks = (/10,25,32,54,54,60/)
```

which assign the six values to the required elements of `marks`. The required elements are enclosed in the delimiters (/ and /), and this constructs a rank one array with six integer elements.

The general form of the array constructor is

```
(/ <list of expressions> /)
```

so it is possible to have variable expressions such as

```
(/ x, 2.0*y, SIN(t*w/3.0),...etc./)
```

Each expression must be of the same type, namely that of the array being constructed. The expressions may be simple scalar expressions in which case each contributes one element to the array. If, however, an expression is array valued, it contributes a number of elements equivalent to the size of the array in array element order to the constructed array. If all the expressions are constant expressions the constructor denotes an array constant.

Array constructors can only be used to construct rank one arrays. If higher rank arrays are required these must be produced by using the `RESHAPE` function (see Appendix A). This function in its simplest form is

```
RESHAPE( shape, source)
```

where `shape` is an array of rank 1 containing the shape of array required. The argument `source` is also an array of rank 1 which contains the values of the elements required in the new array. Thus the expression

```
RESHAPE( (/3,4/) , (/11,21,31,12,22,32,13,23,33,14,24,34/) )
```

delivers an array of shape (3,4) containing the values in the source argument. The values in `source` must be listed in the array element order of the required array. The array defined by the above expression is as shown schematically below.

```
11 12 13 14
21 22 23 24
31 32 33 34
```

6.4.5 Named array constants and initialised arrays

Whole arrays can be initialised using array constructors in declaration statements. To initialise an array B with 5 elements we could use,

```
CHARACTER, DIMENSION(1:5) :: B = (/'A','B','C','D','E'/)
```

In cases where array constructors appear as initialisation expressions, it must be possible to evaluate the list of expressions at compile time; each constructor expression must be also an initialisation expression. For example the statements

```
INTEGER,PARAMETER :: N=3,M=6,P=12
INTEGER, DIMENSION(1:3) :: arr = (/ N,(M/N),(P/N) /)
```

are permissible.

It is possible to use the RESHAPE function in initialisation expressions in declaration statements. Thus to set up the array B with shape (3,3) and bounds of 1:3 and -1:1 in its two dimensions as

```
1 5 3
9 4 4
6 7 3
```

we could write

```
INTEGER, DIMENSION(1:3,-1:1) :: B = RESHAPE( (/3,3/),&
                                  (/ 1,9,6,3,4,7,5,4,3 /))
```

In an entirely similar way named array constants can be created. Now, of course, the declaration requires the specification of the PARAMETER attribute.

```
REAL,DIMENSION(1:3),PARAMETER:: &
                          zero_vec=(/0.0,0.0,0.0/), &
                             vec_i=(/1.0,0.0,0.0/), &
                             vec_j=(/0.0,1.0,0.0/), &
                             vec_k=(/0.0,0.0,1.0/)
REAL,DIMENSION(1:3,1:3),PARAMETER:: &
        identity=RESHAPE( (/3,3/), (/vec_i,vec_j,vec_k/) )
```

The first declaration creates four vector constants, the zero vector, and the three unit vectors along the axes. The second then creates the 3x3 identity matrix.

6.4.6 Array expressions

We have seen above how an array reference can be a whole array or an array section reference. We have also seen simple examples of array expressions containing whole array or array section references. Array expressions can, in fact, take a much more general form than this. We can use all the arithmetic and logical operators and intrinsic functions in expressions involving whole arrays and array section references. The following statements illustrate this:

```
INTEGER, DIMENSION(1:50) :: A,B,C,D
REAL, DIMENSION(-10:10,-20:20) :: minutes, seconds
REAL, DIMENSION(1:10,1:20) :: lengths
REAL, DIMENSION(1:10,-100:100) :: angles
LOGICAL, DIMENSION(1:50) :: E
```

```
A = 5 * B         ! elements of A are
                  ! 5 x the corresponding elements of B
A = B + C         ! elements of A are sum of corresponding
                  ! elements of B and C
A = B/C + D
A = B ** 5
A = SIN(B) + COS(SQRT(C))
                  ! SIN(B) is the array whose elements are the
                  ! SINES of all the elements of B
A = C * EXP(B) + D
seconds = 60 * minutes
lengths = SIN( angles(1:10,0:19))
! Note that the following sets the array E to true
! where the corresponding elements of A and B are equal
! and to false elsewhere. A==B is a valid array logical
! expression
E = A==B
```

In the above, all the arrays are conformable (have the same shape). All the whole array references could equally well be array sections of appropriate shape.

All of the intrinsic operations that apply to scalar values of the intrinsic types have their meanings extended to apply to arrays of these types. The extended meanings apply element by element. The same is true of the elemental intrinsic functions (see Appendix A). In this way expressions applying to conformant arrays can be just as complex as expressions involving scalar variables of the same types. In fact they are evaluated as if they were sets of similar scalar expressions with the arrays replaced by the corresponding array elements. However, there is no order of evaluation implied as there would be if the expressions were written as loops over the array elements. This is important. Consider,

```
REAL,DIMENSION(10):: x
x(2:10)=x(1:9)
```

The assignment here moves the bottom nine elements of the array up one into the top nine. The simple element by element loop

```
DO i=1,9
 x(i+1)=x(i)
ENDDO
```

does not mean the same thing at all. The effect is to perform the sequence of assignments x(2)=x(1); x(3)=x(2); x(4)=x(3)....

which would result in all ten elements being set equal to the first.

The rule with array assignments is that all the element by element expressions on the right are evaluated, in any order the processor decides, including all at once if this is possible, and then and only then is the copy into the left hand variable performed, again in any order required.

6.4.7 Masked assignment

Circumstances often arise in practice where it is desirable to assign values to the elements of an array according to some condition based on the values that exist in it, or on the values in some other array of the same shape. For instance, suppose we wanted to set all negative values in a particular array `A` to zero. We could do this simply using the `WHERE` statement, for example,

```
REAL, DIMENSION(20,30) :: A

WHERE (A < 0.0) A = 0.0
```

The condition, `A < 0.0`, is an array-valued logical expression known as a mask expression.

The general form of the `WHERE` statement is,

```
WHERE( <mask array> ) <array assignment statement>
```

where the `<mask array>` and the array being defined in the assignment statement must be arrays of the same shape. Thus a more general statement might be

```
WHERE (A > 5.0) B = A*2.0
```

In this statement elements of a different array `B` are being given the values of twice the corresponding values in array `A` where such values are greater than `5.0`. The values of `B` where `A<=5.0` are unchanged.

If more than one assignment with the same shape needs to be performed under the control of the same mask, the compound form of the `WHERE` can be used.

```
WHERE(A>0.0)
  B=LOG(A)
  C=SQRT(A)
ENDWHERE
```

Assuming A,B, and C are all real arrays of the same shape, this group of statements causes the logarithm of elements of A to be assigned to B and the square root of the elements of A to be assigned to C for those elements which are positive and it leaves the other elements unchanged. Suppose we wanted also to make different changes to the elements for which the mask was false. Consider the following:

```
WHERE(A>0.0)
  B=LOG(A)
  C=SQRT(A)
ELSEWHERE
  B=-100.0
  C=0.0
ENDWHERE
```

This group has the same effect as before when the mask is true, but it also causes the elements of B to be set to -100.0 and C to be set to 0.0 where the mask is false.

It should be stressed that, in spite of the superficial similarity, the WHERE...ENDWHERE group of statements is not a block control construct like IF...ENDIF. It is a compound, masked assignment and it cannot be nested. Nor can anything other than conformant shape assignment statements appear in the body of the WHERE...ENDWHERE group. The other difference is that if an ELSEWHERE part is present, both it and the preceding WHERE part are always executed, whereas for an IF()THEN...ELSE...ENDIF only one or other of the contained blocks is executed.

6.5 Simple input/output of arrays

Whole array, array section, and array element references can be included in input/output statements to enable data for arrays to be both read and written. In the preceding examples for the sorting program we specified the required input and output by using array elements in statements like,

```
DO I=1,n_to_sort
   READ (UNIT=*,FMT=*) nums(I)
END DO
```

This read the data one value at a time. We could more easily have written

```
READ(UNIT=*,FMT=*) nums
```

In the first piece of code `n_to_sort` records would have to be read, since a new data record is read each time a `READ` statement is executed. This would not be too inconvenient for ten numbers but would become rather cumbersome for say 1000 numbers. The second piece of code, which means that elements to fill the whole array in array element order are to be read, would allow multiple numbers to be typed for each record.

When parts of arrays are to be read in, or written out, array sections can be used, as in the following example

```
REAL arr(1:100)
...
WRITE(UNIT=*,FMT=*) arr(1:25)
```

A useful and very common construction occurs when the number of items to be transferred is also included in the data to be read. For example we may in one run of the program want to process 25 elements, as above, but in others we may want to handle 50, 20, 75, 10, 37, etc.. This can be done as follows:

```
INTEGER :: NA
REAL, DIMENSION(1:100) :: A
READ(UNIT=*,FMT=*) NA, A(1:NA)
```

The data now starts with a record whose first value is an integer which determines how many real values follow in this set of data. This integer value is read first and its value is used determine the size of the array section. Since it is possible to use an incremental step when specifying an array section, we could write out all the odd locations of an array, say the number of people in the houses on one side of a street, with the following notation

```
WRITE(UNIT=*,FMT=*) house(1:nhouse:2)
```

where the increment has been specified as 2.

6.6 Array intrinsic functions

As mentioned previously, the Fortran 90 language includes several very useful intrinsic procedures which can save much time when programming with arrays. These functions are listed below in order to give a summary of the coverage of these functions relating to arrays. A fuller description of each function is given in Appendix A.

6.6.1 Vector and matrix multiply functions

DOT_PRODUCT(VECTOR_A,VECTOR_B)	Inner Product of two rank 1 arrays
MATMUL(MATRIX_A,MATRIX_B)	Matrix Multiplication

6.6.2 Array reduction functions

ALL(MASK,DIM)	True if all values are true
ANY(MASK,DIM)	True if any values are true
COUNT(MASK,DIM)	Number of true elements in array
MAXVAL(ARRAY,DIM,MASK)	Maximum Value in an array
MINVAL(ARRAY,DIM,MASK)	Minimum value in an array
PRODUCT(ARRAY,DIM,MASK)	Product of array elements
SUM(ARRAY,DIM,MASK)	Sum of array elements

6.6.3 Array inquiry functions

ALLOCATED(ARRAY)	Array allocation status
LBOUND(ARRAY,DIM)	Lower bounds of an array
SHAPE(SOURCE)	Shape of an array or scalar
SIZE(ARRAY,DIM)	Total number of array elements
UBOUND(ARRAY,DIM)	Upper bounds of an array

6.6.4 Array construction function

MERGE(TSOURCE,FSOURCE,MASK)	Merge two arrays under mask control
PACK(ARRAY,MASK,VECTOR)	Pack an array into a vector under a mask
SPREAD(SOURCE,DIM,NCOPIES)	Replicates an array by adding a dimension
UNPACK(VECTOR,MASK,FIELD)	Unpack a vector into an array under a mask

6.6.5 Array reshape function

RESHAPE(SOURCE,SHAPE,PAD,ORDER)	Reshape an array

6.6.6 Array manipulation functions

```
CSHIFT(ARRAY,SHIFT,DIM)                Circular shift
EOSHIFT(ARRAY,SHIFT,BOUNDARY,DIM)      End-Off shift
TRANSPOSE(MATRIX)                      Transpose of matrix
```

6.6.7 Array location functions

```
MAXLOC(ARRAY,MASK)                     Location of a maximum
                                       value in an array
MINLOC(ARRAY,MASK)                     Location of a minimum
                                       value in an array
```

6.7 An array application

As an example of how compact the code can become when using this whole array approach to programming we will look at an application for processing a set of student marks. We assume we have a class of students each of whom sits exams in nine subjects, English, French, mathematics, physics, chemistry, history, economics, technology, and geography. We want to process the class marks so as to scale the marks in each subject so that the class average is set at 50. We will need to calculate the class averages of the raw marks for each subject so as to determine the scale factor to be applied. We then want to calculate the scaled average for each student and display a report with each student's scaled marks, average marks, and scale factors used for each subject. Just to complicate the processing further we shall assume that no student is allowed to have a scaled mark in any subject that is greater than 100. (Note this could mean that class averages for the scaled marks are not exactly 50. We are not proposing to iterate the process following the clipping to an upper limit of 100 to correct for this). We are assuming that the data is to be typed as a series of records that look like,

```
35
"SMITH" 56.0 45.5 75.0 67.0 45.0 67.5 75.5 59.0 52.0
"MORGAN" 65.0 56.0 68.0 75.0 76.0 54.0 82.0 76.0 45.0
.....
```

where the first record contains the number of pupils in the class and the subsequent records contain the students name and the nine marks for that student. The following would be a program to perform this task.

```
PROGRAM exams
!-----------------------------------------------------------!
! program to read class marks, results to be scaled to      !
! produce class averages of 50 in each subject, maximum     !
! scaled mark for any student to be 100, student averages   !
! to be reported and scale factors for each subject.        !
!-----------------------------------------------------------!
INTEGER :: class_size
REAL,DIMENSION(:,:),ALLOCATABLE :: results
CHARACTER(LEN=12),DIMENSION(:), ALLOCATABLE :: name
! results array to be used to hold students marks, averages
! and scale factors
READ(UNIT=*,FMT=*) class_size
ALLOCATE(name(class_size))
ALLOCATE(results(10,class_size+1))
DO i=1,class_size
  READ(UNIT=*,FMT=*) name(i),results(1:9,i)
ENDDO
results(1:9,class_size+1) = &
  SUM(results(1:9,1:class_size),DIM=1)/class_size
! calculates the raw data class averages for each subject and
! stores this in the bottom row of the results array
results(1:9,class_size+1) = 50.0/results(1:9,class_size+1)
! converts these raw averages into scale factors needed to
! produce class averages of 50.0
DO i = 1,9
  results(i,1:class_size) = results(i,class_size+1)* &
                           results(i,1:class_size)
ENDDO
! scales each set of subject marks as required
WHERE(results(1:9,1:class_size)>100.0) &
      results(1:9,1:class_size) = 100.0
! reduces all scaled marks over 100 back to 100
results(10,1:class_size) = &
  SUM(results(1:9,1:class_size),DIM=2)/9.0
! calculates the scales average mark for each student and
! stores it in the last column of the results array
DO i=1,class_size
  WRITE(UNIT=*,FMT=*) name(i),results(:,i)
ENDDO
WRITE(UNIT=*,FMT=*) "Scaling",results(1:9,class_size+1)
ENDPROGRAM exams
```

6.8 Exercises

1. Declare an array which would be suitable for representing draughts board. Write a program to set all the black squares to unity. [A draughts board is 8x8 with alternate black and white squares]

2. Declare an array of rank 3 which might be suitable for representing a hotel with 8 floors and 16 rooms on each floor and two beds in each room. How would the second bed in the 5th room on floor 7 be referenced?

3. Give the rank, bounds, extents, and size of the arrays defined as follows:

```
REAL, DIMENSION(1:10)   :: ONE
REAL, DIMENSION(2,0:5)  :: TWO
INTEGER, DIMENSION(-1:1,3,2)  :: THREE
REAL, DIMENSION(0:1,6)  :: FOUR
```

   Which two of the arrays are conformable?

4. Write down the array element order of the arrays in question 3.

5. Write an array constructor for the rank 1 array `BOXES` containing 1, 4, 6, 12, 23.

6. Write down a declaration for the constant array of rank 2 given as,

   (2.1 5.3)
   (3.2 6.5)
   (7.4 8.9)

7. Which of the following are valid array references for the array declared as

```
REAL, DIMENSION(1:20) :: A
A(12), A(21), A(I), A(3.0), A(I*J), A( INT(SIN(Theta) )
```

8. Write a program to read in an integer matrix of any size and print out the largest element, the number of positive, negative, and zero values, and the sum of all the positive values.
   (Write your answer first using array element notation and then using whole array notation and the appropriate array intrinsic functions from Appendix A)

9. The cost, for each mile, of laying a pipeline between two towns which are 20 miles apart is given in thousands of pounds as follows:-

```
6.3 7.6 9.2 3.4 5.6 7.23 9.76 6.83 5.45 4.56
4.86 5.8 6.4 7.43 7.87 8.6 9.25 8.9 8.4 7.23
```

Write a program to calculate the most expensive 5 mile stretch.

10. A salesman travels between 5 towns A, B, C, D, E whose distances apart are given in the following table:-

	A	B	C	D	E
A	0	120	180	202	300
B		0	175	340	404
C			0	98	56
D				0	168
E					0

Write a program to calculate the shortest route he can travel, visiting all the towns once, and returning to the first town.

11. Rewrite the exams program using only array element references and DO loops, rather than the array section and SUM intrinsics used in the example.

Chapter 7

Procedures

We discussed in Chapter 2 the method of programming in which complex problems are broken down into increasingly simple problems and we showed how this relates to the use of the procedure facility in Fortran. This idea of a procedure as a piece of a program which performs a specific task, and which can be called from the main program or from any other procedure, is fundamental to efficient and effective programming. Many of the examples we have used in previous sections would in fact be very much better written so that the central tasks were performed by one or more procedures. The main program would then merely set up the necessary data required to use these procedures correctly. For example, the sorting problem would have been better programmed in terms of a main program that read in the specific data and printed out the results and a general purpose subroutine which carried out the sorting operation. This subroutine could then be reused whenever a need to sort an array of numbers occurred. In this chapter we are going to look in more detail how both subroutine and function procedures are written and how they can be employed.

7.1 Standard libraries

At this point it is worth pointing out that for many standard tasks, such as plotting curves, sorting lists of numbers, calculating various statistical quantities from a given set of observations, solving equations, evaluating integrals, and so on, it is not necessary for the average user to write new procedures. For many of these standard tasks programs have been written by professional programmers and are made available to the general user in the form of libraries. For example, a comprehensive library of procedures for solving numerical problems is provided by NAG (the Numerical Algorithms Group[1]). The software in this library has been written by experts in the relevant mathematical and computing techniques. Similarly, there are numerous proprietary libraries available which simplify many of the tasks involved in creating graphics for presentation. For the most basic

[1] The Numerical Algorithms Group resulted from a collaboration of numerical software specialists in a number of UK Universities. It is now incorporated as a non-profit making company to supply its software products more widely, and the collaboration now involves experts in a number of computing fields from at least three continents. The address is, NAG Central Office, Wilkinson House, Jordan Hill, Oxford, UK.

graphics operations an international standard called GKS exists with a Fortran binding which defines a standard library interface[2]. The reader setting out to solve a real problem is strongly advised to consult the supplier of his or her computing facilities as to the availability of such libraries of procedures. This may save months if not years of effort.

7.2 General program structure

All Fortran 90 programs must include one and only one main program. This is where the execution of the program starts. In addition the complete program may involve any number of procedures. These procedures may be *external* procedures which are defined externally to the program unit that calls them (we saw examples of these in Chapter 2), or, as we shall see later (section 7.3.2), they may be *internal* procedures. These are procedures whose definition is contained within the procedure or main program that calls them. In addition procedures may also be contained in a module subprogram. These *module-procedures* have some characteristics of both internal and external procedures and will be described in Chapter 8.

External procedures are defined separately and can be compiled independently of each other. They are appropriate for the solution of separate independent tasks. Internal procedures are contained within another *host* program unit, and cannot therefore be separately compiled. Internal procedures are useful only for purposes strictly related to the host program unit. Unlike external procedures which are visible and callable from any and every program unit in the whole executable program, internal procedures are visible and hence callable only within their host. An external procedure can contain any number of internal procedures but nesting of internal procedures is not allowed. That is, an internal procedure cannot itself contain another internal procedure.

When there are a group of inter-related procedures which perhaps call each other and which perform general actions rather than those which are specific to a particular program, we shall see later that they are more appropriately defined within a module rather than as separate external or internal procedures.

7.2.1 The main program unit

The main program starts with a `PROGRAM` statement and ends with an `ENDPROGRAM` statement. Between these delimiting statements the structure

[2] ISO 7942 and BS 6390

of a main program is always the same. The PROGRAM statement is followed by the necessary declarations and specification statements which establish the data environment of the program. These are then followed by the sequence of statements which when executed cause the program to perform the required task. If the main program is to contain any internal procedures, these will appear immediately before the ENDPROGRAM statement and they will be preceded by a CONTAINS statement. The structure is therefore

```
PROGRAM <main program name>
 ┌──────────────────────────────────┐
 │ specifications and declarations  │
 └──────────────────────────────────┘
 ┌──────────────────────────────────┐
 │ executable statements            │
 └──────────────────────────────────┘
CONTAINS
 ┌──────────────────────────────────┐
 │ internal procedure definitions   │
 └──────────────────────────────────┘
ENDPROGRAM <main program name>
```

where the CONTAINS is omitted if there are no internal procedures. The executable code of the main program will include invocations of any internal procedures and probably also of external and accessible module-procedures.

The structure of a procedure is essentially the same regardless of whether it is an external, internal or module-procedure. The major differences arise from whether the procedure is a subroutine or a function. This difference also reflects the difference in effect and method of invocation. Subroutine procedures are meant to perform some action and may or may not take input from or return results to their "calling" programs. Function procedures are intended to calculate results whose values should ideally be dependent on (be "a function of") their argument(s).

A subroutine is invoked by its appearance in a CALL statement as in,

```
CALL change_calculation(change,np,n50,n20,n10,n5,n2,n1)
```

A function is invoked by its appearance in an expression at the place where its result value is needed as in,

```
total = total + largest(I,J,K)
```

More than one function, or the same function more than once, may be invoked in the same statement. For example,

```
big = largest(I,J,K) + largest(I,M,N)
```

Fortran does not specify in such cases which function is to be evaluated first. Therefore, if a function can have some side effect which could cause the value of some other function, or some other quantity involved in the expression, to change this could result in such an expression having an unpredictable value. Functions with side effects are to be avoided if at all possible. A properly constructed function should be such that its result is uniquely determined by the values of its arguments, and the values of its arguments should be unchanged by any invocation.

The general structure of a subroutine procedure is

```
SUBROUTINE <procedure name>( <list of dummy arguments> )
 ┌──────────────────────────────────────────────────────┐
 │specifications and declarations for dummy arguments   │
 └──────────────────────────────────────────────────────┘
 ┌──────────────────────────────────────────────────────┐
 │specifications and declarations for local data        │
 └──────────────────────────────────────────────────────┘
 ┌──────────────────────────────────────────────────────┐
 │executable code                                       │
 └──────────────────────────────────────────────────────┘
CONTAINS
 ┌──────────────────────────────────────────────────────┐
 │internal procedure definitions                        │
 └──────────────────────────────────────────────────────┘
ENDSUBROUTINE <procedure name>
```

An argument list will normally be part of a subroutine, but subroutines without arguments can sometimes be useful and so the argument list (including the parentheses) is sometimes omitted. Again as with main programs, the CONTAINS and the internal procedure definitions are optional, except within a procedure that is itself an internal procedure where they are prohibited.

The structure of a function procedure is very similar.

```
FUNCTION <procedure name>( <list of dummy arguments> )
 ┌──────────────────────────────────────────────────────┐
 │specifications and declarations for dummy arguments   │
 │and the function result variable                      │
 └──────────────────────────────────────────────────────┘
```

```
specifications and declarations for local data

executable code including the definition of the
results variable
CONTAINS
internal procedure definitions
ENDFUNCTION <procedure name>
```

The key difference between a function and a subroutine, as we saw in Chapter 2, is that the result of a function is returned via a result variable which is normally declared within the function to have the same name as the function itself. The result variable must be given a defined value before the function returns. The type and the other attributes of the result variable are the same as those of the function.

7.3 The scope of data objects

The *scope* of an entity is the range of a program within which an entity is visible and accessible. Most entities have a scope which is limited to the program unit in which they are declared, but in special circumstances some entities can have a scope that is wider than this.

7.3.1 Local data

Variables and other data objects are local to the procedure in which they are declared unless they appear in the argument list for the procedure. When a procedure is compiled all local objects that are not arguments to the procedure are allocated new storage space that is local to the procedure. The names of such objects are not "visible" outside the context of the procedure in which they are declared. Consider the following program,

```
PROGRAM main
  REAL :: A,B
  B=6.0
  A=0.5*B
  CALL sub1
  WRITE(UNIT=*,FMT=*) A
END PROGRAM main
```

```
SUBROUTINE sub1
  REAL :: A
  ...
  A=2.0
  ...
END SUBROUTINE sub1
```

The variable `A` in `main` is totally unrelated to `A` in `sub1`. A compiler would allocate different memory locations to the two objects. This would mean that although the call to sub1 would cause the `A` (in `sub1`) to be assigned the value `2.0`, the value of `A` in `main` would be unaffected and the program would write out the value `3.0`.

In general, local objects are created each time a procedure is invoked and are destroyed when the procedure completes its execution and returns control to the calling program. Local variables do not retain their values between calls. However, if a local variable has the `SAVE` attribute, then it does retain its value. The `SAVE` attribute can be declared explicitly,

```
REAL,SAVE :: r,s,t
```

or it is given implicitly by a variable being initialised. Local variables may be given initial values, as we have seen in previous chapters. If they are then they automatically have the `SAVE` attribute. Note, dummy arguments cannot be given the `SAVE` attribute, nor can they be initialised.

7.3.2 Internal procedures

In the previous section `sub1` is entirely separate from `main`. Such a procedure is an external procedure. However, this separation is not so complete between the data objects declared in a host program and its internal procedures. For example in the following,

```
SUBROUTINE calculate_pay
  REAL :: pay, tax,...
  ...  statements to calculate pay
  ...
  CALL print_pay
  ...  further calculation
  ...
CONTAINS
  SUBROUTINE print_pay
    ...
    WRITE(UNIT=*,FMT=*) pay,tax...
    ...
  ENDSUBROUTINE print_pay
ENDSUBROUTINE calculate_pay
```

The `print_pay` procedure is an internal procedure of `calculate_pay`. In addition to any locally declared objects, the internal procedure has access to the data environment of its host. Therefore the names `pay` and `tax` in the subroutine refer to the same variables as defined in the host subroutine. If however a variable called `pay` was declared locally within `print_pay` this would still be a local variable. It would be different from the host variable of the same name and would make the host variable inaccessible within the internal procedure.

7.3.3 Scope of names

In the example below we show the scope, or range of program statements where various data objects are accessible.

```
SUBROUTINE sub1                                       --
  REAL :: A,B                                           |
  ...                                                   |
  CALL sub2                                             |
  ...                                                   |
CONTAINS                                                |
  SUBROUTINE sub2      --                               |
    REAL :: B            |                              |
    ...                  |- scope of sub2               |
    B = A                |                              |
    ...                  |                              |- scope of sub1
  ENDSUBROUTINE sub2   --                               |
  SUBROUTINE sub3      --                               |
    REAL :: C            |                              |
    ...                  |- scope of sub3               |
    C = B                |                              |
    ...                  |                              |
  ENDSUBROUTINE sub3   --                               |
ENDSUBROUTINE sub1                                    --
```

In this example the objects declared in `sub1`, i.e. `A` and `B`, are in scope and hence potentially accessible in `sub1` itself and in both its internal procedures. Objects declared in either of the internal procedures are in scope in their respective procedure and hence accessible only in that procedure. The name `B` declared in both `sub1` and `sub2`, refers to a variable which is local to the internal procedure `sub2` as well as to the host variable. Within sub2 this declaration of `B` creates a new name referring to new space, and this makes the host `B` inaccessible in `sub2`; even though the host `B` remains in scope, it is "masked" by the local `B`. Each procedure starting at the `SUBROUTINE` or `FUNCTION` statement and ending at the `END` of procedure statement forms a scoping unit. Except where they have the `SAVE` attribute, objects declared in a procedure are created when the execution flow enters the scope of the procedure and they disappear when the flow exits from the scope.

7.4 Procedure interfaces

The dummy arguments of a procedure, the attributes with which they are declared, and in the case of functions, the attributes of the result variable, determine the way in which a procedure must be invoked. That is, they define the procedure *interface*. In the following,

```
SUBROUTINE expsum( n, k, x, sum )
  INTEGER, INTENT(IN) :: n
  REAL, INTENT(IN)   :: k,x
  REAL, INTENT(OUT)   :: sum
  sum=0.0
  DO 50 i=1,n
    sum = sum + exp(-i*k*x)
  ENDDO
END SUBROUTINE expsum
```

which sums the series

$$e^{-kx} + e^{-2kx} + e^{-3kx} + \ldots + e^{-nkx}$$

`expsum` has an interface defined by the statements

```
SUBROUTINE expsum( n, k, x, sum )
  INTEGER, INTENT(IN) :: n
  REAL, INTENT(IN)   :: k,x
  REAL, INTENT(OUT)   :: sum
ENDSUBROUTINE expsum
```

Note that this is the definition of the procedure minus the local declarations and the executable code. Only those declarations which refer to arguments, or the function result, are part of the interface definition.

It is clear that when a procedure is invoked, in order for the compiler to check that the actual arguments are correct (in order,type, etc.) it must have access in some way to the interface of the invoked procedure. When the compiler can "see" all the details of the interface, as is the case for calls to internal procedures, the interface is said to be *explicit*.

In general, when simple external procedures are invoked, their interface has to be inferred from the properties of the actual arguments. In such situations the interface is said to be *implicit*. This was the case for the simple examples of Chapter 2. Accessing external procedures via implicit interfaces is only possible for a restricted sort of interface where the dummy arguments have a restricted set of attributes. For the majority of procedures the interface must be explicit in the calling program.

As we have noted above the interface to an internal procedure is always explicit within the scope of its host. However, an external procedure must have its interface declared in the calling program to make it explicit. This can be done by use of an interface block. Thus a program using `expsum` could be written as,

```
PROGRAM interface_example
! declare interface block for expsum
  INTERFACE
    SUBROUTINE expsum(N,K,X,sum)
      INTEGER, INTENT(IN) :: N
      REAL, INTENT(IN)   :: K,X
      REAL, INTENT(OUT)   :: sum
    ENDSUBROUTINE expsum
  ENDINTERFACE
  REAL :: sum
  ...
  ...
  CALL expsum(10,0.5,0.1,sum)
  ...
  ...
ENDPROGRAM interface_example
```

The statements from `INTERFACE,` up to and including `ENDINTERFACE,` are called an interface block. The inclusion of the interface for a procedure in an interface block declares the procedure and makes its interface explicit.

When compiling a call to a procedure with an implicit interface there is no way to check that the implied interface is correct. With explicit interfaces the correctness of actual invocations can be checked. For this reason we recommend that explicit interfaces be declared even where they are not strictly necessary. If this is done there is no need to remember the relatively complex rules about when interfaces have to be explicit and when they can be implicit. We shall see in the next chapter how to avoid much of the onerous verbosity involved when explicit interfaces are always included in the bodies of calling procedures.

7.5 Argument intent

It is possible for arguments to be used for input-only (they will not be changed by invocation of the procedure and are expected to be used only to pass information to the procedure), output-only (they may be changed by invocation of the procedure and are not expected to pass any information to the procedure) or for both input and output (they are intended to pass information both ways). The way in which a dummy argument is intended to be used is specified by the `INTENT` attribute. We have already seen examples of `INTENT(IN)` and `INTENT(OUT)` arguments. The third possibility can be specified in an obvious way by the `INTENT(INOUT)` attribute.

Fortran is quite a liberal language and does not force the programmer to specify the intent of procedure arguments. Intent can be left undeclared in which case it is inferred only from the operations performed on the dummy arguments in the body of the procedure. However, if mistakes are made in writing the body of a procedure, or in calling a procedure, they will not be detected until wrong results are obtained. It does take a little more effort to specify these attributes but it is well worth it in terms of the safety gained. With these specifications included, compilers are able to check that arguments are used correctly within a procedure. For instance a compiler could check that an argument specified with the `INTENT(IN)` attribute is not changed during the execution of a procedure. Also, if the interface of a procedure is explicit, a compiler can check that an invocation of a procedure does not violate the basic rules. For example, it can check that a constant value has not been specified as an actual argument when a dummy argument is `INTENT(OUT)` or `INTENT(INOUT)`.

When the interface is explicit and intent is specified for all dummy arguments it is possible to make the invocation much more efficient. This is another reason for always using explicit interfaces and always specifying the intent for dummy arguments.

7.6 Keyword and optional arguments

The names of the dummy arguments of a procedure define a set of keywords which can be used when invoking a procedure. This is a useful facility which optionally allows arguments to be specified in any order and helps improve the readability of the program.

Suppose we have written a subroutine (or one has been made available from a standard library) to plot an axis given the starting point, the length, the starting scale value, the ending scale value and the number of scale intervals required. Such a subroutine might have the following interface specification:

```
SUBROUTINE AXIS(X0,Y0,Length,Minimum,Maximum,Intervals)
 REAL,INTENT(IN)    :: X0,Y0,Length,Minimum,Maximum
 INTEGER, INTENT(IN) :: Intervals
ENDSUBROUTINE AXIS
```

Using positional argument invocation a call to `AXIS` might look like,

```
CALL AXIS(0.0,0.0,100.0,0.1,1.0,10)
```

where the correspondence between actual and dummy argument is determined by matching position in the argument list. Using keyword arguments this same call could be,

```
CALL AXIS(X0=0.0,Y0=0.0,Length=100.0,Minimum=0.1, &
                                  Maximum=1.0,Intervals=10)
```

which makes the argument correspondence directly visible. Each dummy argument name defines a keyword that can be used to identify which dummy argument the actual argument is to be associated with. Of course, the advantage is that the arguments can now be specified in any order. The user of the subroutine does not have to remember the order in which they have to be specified. For example the following call would be equally valid,

```
CALL AXIS(Intervals=10,Length=100.0,X0=50.0,Y0=50.0, &
                  Minimum=0.1,Maximum=1.0)
```

It is possible to specify some actual arguments with keywords and others without. The positional arguments, if any, must be those at the start of the argument list and they must be given in the correct order. Once a keyword argument is used all subsequent arguments must be specified with keywords.

Note that the interface of a procedure with keyword arguments must be explicit within the procedure in which it is invoked. Otherwise the invoking procedure would not have any way of knowing what the keywords were.

The utility of keyword arguments is further enhanced by the fact that some arguments may be optional. Developing our previous example we can observe that it is common for axes to be drawn with ten scale intervals and so it is reasonable to use this as a default in the `AXIS` routine above. If we are plotting on A4 paper then the position of the origin of coordinates can reasonably be placed at say (50.0,50.0). A reasonable default axis length could be 150 mm. Therefore we could write the `AXIS` subroutine as,

```
SUBROUTINE AXIS(X0,Y0,Length,Minimum,Maximum,Intervals)
 REAL,INTENT(IN), OPTIONAL   :: X0,Y0,Length
 INTEGER, INTENT(IN), OPTIONAL :: Intervals
 REAL, INTENT(IN)          :: Minimum, Maximum
 ! local variables
 REAL :: x,y,lnth
 INTEGER :: Intl
 ! Specify defaults
 x=50.0; y=50.0; lnth=150.0; Intl=10
 ! override if arguments present
 IF(PRESENT(X0)) x=X0
 IF(PRESENT(Y0)) y=Y0
 IF(PRESENT(Length)) lnth=Length
 IF(PRESENT(Intervals)) Intl=Intervals
 ...
   the body of the procedure would then use x,y,lnth and Intl
 ...
```

If the defaults were adequate, it would then be possible to call `AXIS` as follows,

```
CALL AXIS(Minimum=0.0, Maximum=500.0)
```

But if it was required to be more precise about the positioning of the axes or the number of scale intervals then the caller would have the option of specifying the corresponding arguments. It should be noted that once an argument has been omitted all subsequent arguments must be keyword arguments. Note again that use of keyword or optional arguments also requires the interface of the invoked procedure to be explicit.

If an optional argument is not present in any invocation of the procedure, the dummy variable must not be referenced except as the argument of the `PRESENT` function. This intrinsic function is provided to test for the presence or absence of optional arguments.
The structure shown above is very common when using optional arguments. Local variables corresponding to each optional argument are also declared and used in the body of the procedure. Such variables are assigned default values and these are replaced by actual argument values only if the argument is actually present.

7.7 Arrays in procedures

It is frequently necessary to write subroutines or functions which accept arrays as arguments, return arrays as results, and/or which manipulate arrays locally. There are a number of subtleties involved in this which we will cover in this section.

7.7.1 Explicit-shape dummy arrays

The simplest form of array argument is one where both the dummy argument and the actual argument are required to have the same explicitly declared shape. If a dummy argument is declared with explicit bounds as in,

```
SUBROUTINE clear_board(squares)
  INTEGER,DIMENSION(8,8),INTENT(INOUT) :: squares
  ...
```

then any actual argument that becomes associated with `squares` when `clear_board` is called must be exactly an 8x8 integer array. This is fine in circumstances when the size of the arrays involved is known and is fixed by the nature of the problem. This is comparatively rare and so this form is obviously overly restrictive. We need to be able to write procedures that handle arrays of various sizes.

One way of handling array arguments of variable size is to pass the bound information as well as the arrays as arguments.

```
SUBROUTINE scale_average(no_marks,marks)
  INTEGER,INTENT(IN)::no_marks
  REAL,INTENT(INOUT)::marks(1:no_marks)
  ...
```

In this case the dummy array still has an explicit shape, but now the bounds depend on the value of another dummy argument and so the size (or indeed the shape in the case of higher rank array arguments) is determined at the time of invocation.

It should be noted that in both these cases the correct correspondence of actual argument and dummy argument size and shape can only be checked if the interface is explicit.

7.7.2 Assumed-shape dummy arrays

A more flexible way of passing array arguments of variable shape is to declare the dummy array so that it assumes the shape of the actual argument. Such arrays, for obvious reasons are called *assumed-shape* arrays. Consider the following subroutine,

```
SUBROUTINE Three_Arrays(A,B,C)
  REAL,INTENT(INOUT) :: A(:)       ! an array of rank 1
  REAL,INTENT(INOUT) :: B(:,:)     ! an array of rank 2
  REAL,INTENT(INOUT) :: C(:,:,:)   ! an array of rank 3
  ...
ENDSUBROUTINE Three_Arrays
```

In this example the dimensions of `A, B,` and `C` are specified with deferred-shape array specifications. We saw a similar usage when we discussed allocatable arrays in the last chapter. In the case of allocatable arrays the declaration also included the `ALLOCATABLE` attribute to signify that the array would be allocated space later using the `ALLOCATE` statement. In this case where the array being declared is a dummy argument the deferred-shape specification indicates that the shape of the array is to be assumed from the corresponding actual argument when the subroutine is invoked. Note that dummy arguments cannot be declared as allocatable.

The above example subroutine can thus be called with array actual arguments of any size provided the ranks of the corresponding actual and dummy arguments are the same. The following program illustrates this.

```
PROGRAM Three_Array_Calls
  INTERFACE
    SUBROUTINE Three_Arrays(A,B,C)
     REAL,INTENT(INOUT) :: A(:)       ! an array of rank 1
     REAL,INTENT(INOUT) :: B(:,:)     ! an array of rank 2
     REAL,INTENT(INOUT) :: C(:,:,:)   ! an array of rank 3
    ENDSUBROUTINE Three_Arrays
  ENDINTERFACE
  REAL, DIMENSION(1:10)             :: F
  REAL, DIMENSION(1:5,1:100)        :: G1, G2
  REAL, DIMENSION(0:10,-2:2,1:12)   :: H1, H2, H3
  ...
  ...
  CALL Three_Arrays( F, G1, H )
  ...
  CALL Three_Arrays( F(2:4), G2, H2) ! pass a section of F
  ...
  CALL Three_Arrays( G1(:, 3), G2(2:4,50:100) , H3 )
  !  pass a column of G1 and a rectangular sub-section of G2
  ...
```

Note that the sections `F(2:4), G1(:,3)`, and `G2(2:4,50:100)` all have the same rank as their corresponding dummy argument. Note also that the interface block which specifies the subroutine's dummy arguments is absolutely essential when using assumed-shape arrays.

As a slightly more practical example, suppose we wished to write a subroutine to copy a two-dimensional symmetric array into a one-dimensional array containing just the set of different elements. Such a symmetric array could contain the distances between various towns, for instance. Obviously the distance from town 1 to town 2 is the same as for town 2 to town 1. The distance from town n to town n is clearly zero. It might, for some calculations, be useful to store the distance array as a full two-dimensional array. So, for example in the case where there are four towns we might have the following array,

```
| 0.0,3.0,5.0,9.0 |
| 3.0,0.0,7.0,4.0 |
| 5.0,7.0,0.0,1.0 |
| 9.0,4.0,1.0,0.0 |
```

where we store 16 elements. However, if we are short on memory it might be preferable to store only the six that are significant. This could be done by mapping the two-dimensional array onto a one-dimensional array containing only the required distances so as to produce,

```
| 3.0,5.0,7.0,9.0,4.0,1.0 |
```

That is, we would map the elements as follows,

```
2,1 to 1
3,1 to 2
3,2 to 3
4,1 to 4
4,2 to 5 etc.
```

For a small array like this such a mapping would be rather a waste of time but if we were dealing with a larger number of towns the difference could be significant. For N towns the two-dimensional array requires N*N elements, for the one-dimensional mapping we need only N*(N-1)/2. For 100 towns the difference is 10,000 elements compared to 4,450. A fairly obvious subroutine to do the copying from one form to the other is,

```
SUBROUTINE linearise_Symmetric(twod,oned)
!-----------------------------------------------------------!
! Copy symmetric zero diagonal two dimensional array into !
! a one dimensional array retaining only the significant  !
! lower triangle of elements                               !
!-----------------------------------------------------------!
  REAL, DIMENSION(:,:), INTENT(IN) :: twod
  REAL, DIMENSION(:) , INTENT(OUT) :: oned
  INTEGER :: I,J,K,L,M,N
  ! Get size of twod in its two dimensions
  N = SIZE(twod,1)
  M = SIZE(twod,2)
  L = SIZE(oned)
  IF( L >= N*(N-1)/2)THEN      ! Check that oned is big
                               ! enough to hold the lower
                               ! triangle
   IF(M == N)THEN
   ! The following code copies the lower triangular portion
```

```
    ! of twod into oned
     K=1
     DO I=2,N
      DO J=1,I-1
       oned(K) = twod(I,J)
       K = K + 1
      ENDDO
     ENDDO
    ELSE
     WRITE(UNIT=*,FMT=*) 'Array is not square'
    ENDIF
   ELSE
    WRITE(UNIT=*,FMT=*)'Insufficient space in output array'
   ENDIF
END
```

Note the use of the SIZE intrinsic function to determine the size of twod and oned. SIZE takes two parameters, the first being the name of the array and the second, which is optional, being the dimension for which the size is required.

7.7.3 Automatic arrays

For many algorithms which are programmed using arrays it is often necessary to use workspace for temporary storage. In such cases the workspace usually takes the form of one or more local arrays whose size depends on the size of the actual arrays which are being used, or on some other dummy argument. The following example shows this,

```
SUBROUTINE image_process( pixel_map )
 INTEGER, DIMENSION(:,:) :: pixel_map
 INTEGER, DIMENSION(SIZE(pixel_map,1),SIZE(pixel_map,2))::work
 ...
```

In this case work is defined to be the same size as pixel_map using the SIZE intrinsic function we saw earlier. The caller of the subroutine does not need to know anything about the array work since it is automatically created when the procedure is invoked and destroyed when it returns. Such arrays are called *automatic* arrays.

It is also possible to use the value of an argument to define the size of an automatic array. Thus

```
SUBROUTINE process_part( sparse, M, N)
  REAL, DIMENSION(:,:) :: sparse
  REAL, DIMENSION(M,N) :: work
  ...
END
```

This subroutine might process some sparse subsection of the array `sparse` in which case a much smaller work array may be sufficient to hold temporary values during the calculation. In this example the calling subprogram provides the necessary sizes in each dimension.

Note that since automatic arrays may have different sizes and shapes each time the procedure is invoked, they may not have the `SAVE` attribute nor may they be initialised.

7.7.4 Array-valued functions

As well as the dummy arguments being arrays, it also possible for the result of a function procedure to be an array. Consider the common image processing operation of "smoothing". To understand this it is necessary to be aware that an image can be represented as a two-dimensional array of integers. Each integer represents the intensity or colour of an image at each pixel or picture element position. It is not uncommon for an image to be distorted by "noise"; the snow seen on a badly tuned TV is a familiar example. The effect of such noise can often be reduced by smoothing the image.

One method of smoothing is to replace the value at each pixel by an average of all the pixels surrounding it. Since pixels lie on a square grid each pixel has 8 neighbours in its nearest vicinity and 24 neighbours if the region of interest is extended to the nearest 2 pixels etc. For obvious reasons then, when the distance is chosen as 1, the smoothing is known as 9-point averaging and when the distance is 2 it is known as 25-point averaging. Since noise involves random errors this averaging process will tend to cancel the noise and to enhance the image quality.

A function for the averaging is included in the following program. The program illustrates the power of the Fortran 90 array language when combined with the facilities for writing procedures.

```
PROGRAM Averaging
 INTERFACE
   FUNCTION image_average(image,width)
   INTEGER,INTENT(IN) :: image(:,:)
   INTEGER,INTENT(IN) :: width
   INTEGER :: &
       image_average(SIZE(image,DIM=1),SIZE(image,DIM=2))
!(The SIZE intrinsic function is defined in Appendix A)
   ENDFUNCTION image_average
 ENDINTERFACE
 INTEGER,PARAMETER :: M=6
 INTEGER,DIMENSION(M,M) :: IM2, &
                 IM1 = RESHAPE( (/1, 4, 3, 5, 3, 6, &
```

```
                                       7, 4, 6, 5, 2, 7, &
                                       7, 3, 7, 6, 5, 1, &
                                       1, 9, 4, 8, 5, 2, &
                                       4, 2, 9, 5, 6, 3, &
                                       1, 5, 6, 3, 8, 3/), &
                                       SHAPE=(/M,M/) ),&
 ! The above statement defines a 6 x 6 array
 ! which is used for testing purposes

 ! Smooth the image in array IM1 and store in IM2
 IM2 = image_average(IM1,1)
 ! Write out the two images for checking
 ! Note that the FMT= parameter specifies a
 ! format that is discussed in Chapter 11.
 DO I=1,M
   WRITE(UNIT=*,FMT='(6I3,''  '',6I3)') IM1(I,1:M),IM2(I,1:M)
 ENDDO
ENDPROGRAM averaging

FUNCTION image_average(image,width)
INTEGER,INTENT(IN) :: image(:,:)
INTEGER,INTENT(IN) :: width
INTEGER::image_average(SIZE(image,DIM=1),SIZE(image,DIM=2))
 N = SIZE(image,DIM=2)
 M = SIZE(image,DIM=1)
 image_average = 0 ! Set average to be zero everywhere
 IF(width>=1)THEN
   ! We assume that the image is large enough to
   ! justify ignoring the edge pixels
   DO I=width+1,N-width
     DO J=width+1,M-width
       image_average(I,J) = &
           SUM(image(I-width:I+width,J-width:J+width)) &
               /(width+2)**2
     ENDDO
   ENDDO
 ENDIF
ENDFUNCTION image_average
```

The function has an assumed shape dummy argument and the shape of the result is declared to be the same by using the `SIZE` intrinsic function to determine the bounds that are required when the procedure is invoked. The width dummy argument determines whether 9-point, 25-point etc. averaging will be done.

7.8 Character dummy arguments and functions

In an analogous way to that for arrays, character dummy arguments may be declared either to be of explicit length or to assume the length of their associated actual arguments by specifying their length as an asterisk.

```
SUBROUTINE char_example(fix_string)
  CHARACTER(LEN=10),INTENT(INOUT) :: fix_string
  ...
```

would declare `fix_string` to be an explicit length dummy argument. Such an argument should be matched by an actual argument of the same fixed length when the subroutine is invoked.

As an example of assumed length dummy arguments the following is a logical valued function, `palindrome`, which returns the value true or false depending on whether its character argument reads the same from left to right as it does from right to left.

```
FUNCTION palindrome(word)
  LOGICAL :: palindrome
  CHARACTER(LEN=*), INTENT(IN) :: word
  INTEGER :: word_length,I,J
  word_length = LEN(word)
  J=word_length
  !   Compare characters from each end of word until either
  !   there is a mis-match or we run out of characters.
  comp: DO I = 1,word_length/2
    IF( word(I:I) /= word(J:J) )THEN ! mismatch
      palindrome = .FALSE.
      RETURN
    ENDIF
    J=J-1
  ENDDO comp
  ! If we reach here all characters match
  palindrome = .TRUE.
END FUNCTION palindrome
```

In the above note the declaration of `word` specifies a length of `LEN=*`. This means that `palindrome` will assume the length of `word` from the associated actual argument. The function `palindrome` could be used in statements such as

```
IF( palindrome( typed_word ) THEN
  WRITE(UNIT=*,FMT=*) 'This word is a palindrome'
ENDIF
```

The following statement

```
logical_value = palindrome('minim')
```

would assign true,

```
logical_value = palindrome('unsymmetric')
```

would assign the value false.

7.8.1 Character-valued functions

It is also possible to write character-valued functions. Fixed length functions can be defined by declaring the result length explicitly. But it is more useful to have variable length character results. Suppose we wished to write a function which returns the contents of its argument in reverse order. The function should return a character string of the same length as its argument. This can be achieved as follows:

```
FUNCTION reverse(word)
 CHARACTER(LEN=*) :: word
 CHARACTER(LEN=LEN(word)) :: reverse
 INTEGER::lw
 lw=LEN(word)
 ! copy characters from right to left order into reverse
 DO I=1:lw
    reverse(lw-I+1:lw-I+1) = word(I:I)
 ENDDO
ENDFUNCTION reverse
```

The length of the function result is determined automatically to be the same as that assumed by the argument word. As with arrays we can also have local character variables whose length is determined automatically in similar ways.

7.9 Passing procedures as arguments

It is often necessary to have an argument which is not a data object but is a function or subroutine. For example, suppose we wish to write a general purpose subroutine to calculate the area under a given curve, i.e. to evaluate the definite integral of some function. The problem is one of taking an arbitrary curve represented by the function, f(x) say, and finding an approximate value for the area bounded by, y=0, x=A, x=B, and y=f(x). This is the area shown shaded in Figure 7.1.

One way of approximating the area is to divide the interval from A to B into a number of small sections. If we then assume that these are small enough that f(x) does not change much from one part of the section to another we can approximate the area of the section as if it were a rectangle; one side being f(x) at the start and the other being the thickness of the rectangle. We can then get an approximate area for the whole region by adding up all the small rectangles. If we take, say, N sections then the thickness of one section, H, is obviously given by,

```
H = (B - A)/N
```

and the points at the start of each rectangle will be

```
A, A+H, A+2H, A+3H, ....,
                 A+(N-1)H
```

The required approximate area will therefore be the sum of,

```
H*f(A) + H*f(A+H) +
  H*f(A+2H) + ... +
    H*f(A+(N-1)H)
```

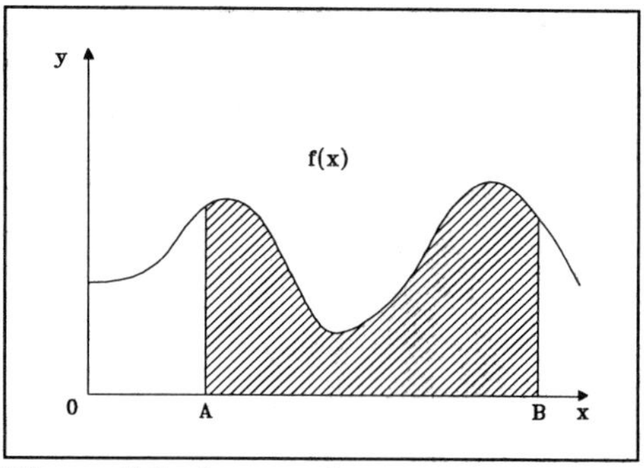

Figure 7.1: Area under a curve

N.B. It should be noted that this algorithm for approximating the area is the simplest possible. It has been chosen to illustrate the programming point, not for its quality as a method. In fact it is a poor method and very much better techniques exist for this problem. Even the simple refinement of taking not the value of the function at the start of the interval but the average of the functions value at the two end points makes a dramatic improvement, but it complicates the program somewhat. In fact this type of problem is a very general one and a great deal of work has been done to develop very high quality, efficient, and accurate methods for its solution. Subroutines implementing some of these methods can be found in system libraries such as the NAG Library mentioned earlier.

It would be useful to have a subroutine that could calculate this sum for any function, any values for `A` and `B`, and with any number of subsections `N`. One way of doing this would be,

```
SUBROUTINE farea(n,a,b,area)
!---------------------------------------------------!
! Calculates the area under a curve defined by the   !
! function f(x) between x=a and x=b                  !
! Divides the range into n subintervals in which the !
! function is assumed to be approximately constant.  !
! The area is approximated as the sum of these small !
! rectangles                                         !
! --------------------------------------------------!
  ! Subroutine arguments
  INTEGER, INTENT(IN)  :: n
  REAL,    INTENT(IN)  :: a,b
  REAL,    INTENT(OUT) :: area
  ! Local variables
  INTEGER :: i
  REAL :: h
```

```
  ! Interface for integrand
  INTERFACE
    FUNCTION F(x)
    REAL,INTENT(IN)::x
    REAL::F
    ENDFUNCTION F
  ENDINTERFACE
  ! Calculate subinterval width h and initialise area to zero
  area = 0.0
  h=(b - a)/n
  ! Loop from zero to n-1, sum function values into area
  DO i=0,n-1
    area = area + F(a+i*h)
  END DO
  ! Calculate area
  area = area*h
END
```

This is a reasonably simple and general subroutine. However it can only calculate the area for one function, the function called `F`. In any program the subroutine could only be used to calculate the area under this one function. This is not very convenient or useful since we often want to call the function by some name that is meaningful. We may already have the function defined with some other name, and perhaps most importantly we may want to calculate the area for a number of different functions in the same program. We do not want to have to write a different area subroutine for each function. The way out of this problem is to pass the function to be used by the subroutine as an argument. That is, we can modify the above subroutine including `F` as a dummy argument. For example,

```
SUBROUTINE FAREA(N,A,B,F,AREA)
```

By making `F` into a dummy argument the interface declaration no longer declares the interface of an external procedure but a dummy procedure. Now in any calling program an actual argument must be provided to match `F` when the subroutine is called. This must be the name of a function subprogram that can be referenced in the same way as `F`. That is, it must have an interface that can match that declared for `F`, except that the names of the actual procedure interface may be different from the dummy ones. In the particular case it must be a the name of a function which returns a real result and takes a single real argument. This actual function must have been declared explicitly in the calling program. (Note, although explicit by definition internal procedures cannot be passed as actual procedure arguments).

The actual function becomes associated with the dummy function when the subroutine is called. When the subroutine is executing and it encounters a reference to the dummy function `F` this causes the associated actual function to be invoked. For example,

```
  PROGRAM FUNARG
  REAL ST,FN,AREA1,AREA2,POLY,FUN
  INTERFACE
    FUNCTION POLY(T)
      REAL :: POLY,T
      INTENT(IN) :: T
    ENDFUNCTION POLY
    FUNCTION FUN(X)
      REAL :: FUN,X
      INTENT(IN) :: X
    ENDFUNCTION FUN
  ENDINTERFACE
  ...
  CALL FAREA(100,-1.0,1.0,POLY,AREA1)
  ...
  CALL FAREA(250,ST,FN,FUN,AREA2)
  ...
ENDPROGRAM FUNARG
```

where the functions `POLY` and `FUN` might be defined as

```
FUNCTION POLY(T)
REAL :: T,POLY
INTENT(IN) :: T
POLY = ((0.001*T + 0.01)*T + 0.1)*T + 1.0
ENDFUNCTION POLY

FUNCTION FUN(X)
REAL :: X,FUN
IF ( X .LT. 0.0 ) THEN
 FUN = 0.0
ELSE
 FUN = SIN(X)*EXP(-X)
ENDIF
ENDFUNCTION FUN
```

7.10 Recursive subprograms

In general procedures are not allowed to call themselves. However, there are situations where this can be a very convenient thing to do. This is known as *recursion* and is a very powerful facility for expressing a wide class of problems. A simple example of an algorithm that incorporates all the essential features of recursion is that of calculating the factorial of a number. The factorial of a positive integer number, say, 5, usually written as 5!, is obtained by multiplying together the integer number itself and all the positive integer numbers less than it. Thus

```
5! = 5 * 4 * 3 * 2 * 1
```

This can be generalised for any integer N so that

```
N! = N * (N-1) * (N-2) * ... * 1
```

from which it can be seen that

```
N! = N * (N-1)!
```

A function to calculate the factorial of a number `N` (assuming the usual convention that 0!=1) can therefore be written as

```
RECURSIVE FUNCTION FACTORIAL(N) RESULT(N_Factorial)
 INTEGER, INTENT(IN)   :: N
 INTEGER               :: N_Factorial
 IF(N > 0)THEN
   N_Factorial = N * FACTORIAL(N-1)
 ELSE
   N_Factorial = 1
 ENDIF
ENDFUNCTION FACTORIAL
```

Notice that the function statement begins with the keyword `RECURSIVE` and also contains a `RESULT` keyword followed by the name of the result variable. For recursive functions it is necessary for the result name to be distinct from the name of the function itself and it is therefore specified separately using the `RESULT` keyword.

In a program, the function could be invoked just as for any other function. For example,

```
Combinations = FACTORIAL(N)/(FACTORIAL(N-R)*FACTORIAL(R))
```

gives the number of ways of choosing `N` things `R` at a time.

It should be pointed out that recursion can be quite an expensive way of programming a particular problem and, in fact, most recursive solutions can be expressed in terms of repeated loops if resources are scarce. However the benefit of recursive solutions is in their expressive power and problems do exist which would be very difficult to program any other way.

7.11 Exercises

1. Which variables in the following piece of code are **local**?

```
SUBROUTINE Example(V1,V2)
   REAL :: V1,V2
   INTEGER :: V3,V4
   ...
 END
```

2. What are internal procedures and why are they useful/convenient?

3. What is wrong with the following piece of code?

```
SUBROUTINE Mistaken(A,B)
 REAL, INTENT(IN) :: A
 REAL, INTENT(OUT), OPTIONAL :: B
 A = 2*B
 IF( PRESENT(B) ) B = 2*A
END
```

4. Write a subroutine which draws circles. The routine takes two arguments, the first defines the radius of the circle and the second is optional and defines the colour by which the circle is shaded. The default colour for the circle shading should be green. Assume you have two library subroutines available, one called Circle which takes one real argument, the radius, and one called Shade_Circle which takes one character argument which defines the colour as a character string, e.g. "RED" or "GREEN".

5. Write an interface block for the subroutine in 4.

6. In the following subroutine, which are the **automatic** and which are the **assumed shape** arrays?

```
SUBROUTINE Array_Types(A,B,C,D)
 INTEGER, INTENT(IN) :: D
REAL, DIMENSION(:,:) :: A,C
REAL, DIMENSION(:)   :: B
REAL, DIMENSION(SIZE(A)) :: E
INTEGER, DIMENSION(1:D,1:D) :: F
...
```

7. Write a function which returns the standard deviation from the mean of an array of real values. Note that if the mean of a sequence of

values (xi, i=1,n) is denoted by m then the standard deviation, s, is defined as:

$$s = \sqrt{\frac{\sum_{i=0}^{n} (x_i m)^2}{n}}$$

8. Write a function which simulates a throw of two dice and returns the total score. Use the intrinsic subroutine `RANDOM` to obtain pseudo-random numbers to simulate the throw of the dice.

9. Write a function which returns the position of a particular number in an array of integers sorted into ascending order using the so-called "binary cut" method. This method proceeds by determining in which half the number is and then concentrating on that half. It is easily implemented using two indices to point at the low and high positions of the current area of interest. It is assumed that if there is more than one occurrence of the number then the one with the higher index will be chosen. This method is very efficient for very large arrays.

10. Write a function `day` which, given the day of the week as an integer, returns a three character string denoting the day. For example `day(1)` and `day(2)` should return `'Sun'` and `'Mon'` respectively.

11. The following code sets the number of days in February (N_Feb):

```
IF( leap(year) )N_Feb=29
```

where `year` is an integer of the form 19XX. Write the function `leap`.

Chapter 8

Modules and Facility Packaging

In this chapter we shall consider an additional variety of program unit called a *module*. Modules, and the facilities they provide, are perhaps the most important feature of Fortran 90. They provide the "glue" which binds together many of the other features of the language. A module is a program unit in which a number of different data objects and procedures may be declared and defined and these entities can then be made available for use in other programs and program units. Modules can be used to provide *global data* access by making the same set of data objects accessible from a number of different program units. They can also provide a convenient way of making the interface declarations of a number of external procedures explicit in a number of different program units. Modules can be used for much more elaborate applications where whole sets of facilities are packaged together in such a way as to effectively extend the expressive capabilities of the language. Programmers can extend the types of data supported by the language by defining new data types and the operations that may be performed on them and encapsulating them in a module.

8.1 Simple modules

We shall begin by describing two relatively simple uses of modules, first their use for defining global data, and then their use for making procedure interfaces explicit in a convenient way.

8.1.1 Global data access

Information is normally passed between subprograms via arguments. This process operates by establishing a temporary association between the actual argument and the corresponding dummy argument. For many situations this is the most appropriate way of passing information from procedure to procedure in a program. However, in some applications and for some sorts of information it is necessary for a number of different procedures to have direct access to the same data in much the same way as internal procedures all have access to their host's data environment. That is, we need a mechanism to allow a number of external procedures to access the same data without each having to pass the data via argument lists.

It would become rather cumbersome and confusing if in cases where a number of procedures all needed access to the same large set of data objects, all these had to be passed via long argument lists. It would be useful if such data could be defined once in some area that could be made accessible to all the subprograms needing access to that data. In fact this can be achieved by declaring the required objects in a module subprogram and then attaching the module (with a `USE` statement) to each program unit that needs to have access to the module data. The module data is then said to be global to all the procedures that access it.

As an example, consider a program simulating the behaviour of a region of the atmosphere. A number of subroutines might need access to arrays holding the state variables temperature, pressure, humidity, and fluid velocity etc., as shown in the following program.

```
MODULE state_variables
 INTEGER ,PARAMETER :: NX=100, NY=100, NZ=10
 REAL, DIMENSION(NX,NY,NZ) :: temp, pres, humid, &
                              vx, vy, vz
ENDMODULE stat_variables

PROGRAM atmosP
 USE state_variables
 DO IZ = 1,NZ
  DO IY = 1,NY
   DO IX = 1,NX
    ...
    CALL update_temp(IX,IY,IZ)
    CALL update_pres(IX,IY,IZ)
    CALL update_humi(IX,IY,IZ)
    ...
   ENDDO
  ENDDO
 ENDDO
 ...
ENDPROGRAM atmosP

SUBROUTINE update_temp(I,J,K)
 USE state_variables
 INTEGER, INTENT(IN) :: I,J,K
  ...
 temp(I,J,K) = { updated value of temperature }
  ...
ENDSUBROUTINE update_temp

SUBROUTINE update_pres(I,J,K)
 USE state_variables
 INTEGER I,J,K
  ...
 pres(I,J,K) = { updated value for pressure }
  ...
ENDSUBROUTINE update_pres
```

```
SUBROUTINE update_humi(I,J,K)
 USE state_variables
 INTEGER I,J,K
  ...
 humid(I,J,K) = { updated value for humidity }
ENDSUBROUTINE update_humi
```

In this sort of application the updating process for one physical quantity such as the pressure in a given cell will usually depend on the temperature, humidity, flow velocities, etc., that currently apply in the adjacent cells. So each update procedure needs to access not just the array element it is updating but a large number of array elements from many of the arrays involved in the problem. It is not difficult to see how inconvenient it would be to handle this situation via argument lists.

The constants and variables required are declared in the module `state_variables`. The inclusion of a `USE` statement naming this module in the main program and each of the subroutines makes the objects declared in the module accessible via the names specified in the module. This is the simplest of the ways in which the `MODULE/USE` facility can be employed. It is worth noting that the parameters which control the size of the problem, the contants `NX`, `NY` and `NZ`, are defined in one place and one place only, i.e. in the module. This makes modification and adaptation of the program, say, to different sizes of problem, a simple safe process. Changes to the specifications of global data items only have to be made in one place. This can be compared to the situation in the past, using Fortran 77, where such parameters were necessarily declared and defined separately, using `COMMON` statements (see Chapter 13), in every program unit that required them.

8.1.2 Making interfaces explicit

One of the problems of adopting a policy of explicitly declaring the interfaces for all external procedures in any program unit that invokes them, is the amount of code that has to be written for each interface. This is not a great problem when only one fairly simple procedure is called from a single program unit. However, it is common for a single executable program to be made up of a large number of procedures each of which might themselves call several other procedures. This could result in a large amount of duplicated source code used in just declaring the interfaces to procedures. This problem can be made much more tractable by use of modules. As with data objects, interface declarations can be incorporated in a module and these can be accessed in any other program unit by naming the module in a `USE` statement as shown in the following example.

```
MODULE my_interfaces
INTERFACE
  SUBROUTINE sub1(A,B,C)
    REAL,INTENT(IN) :: A(:)
    INTEGER,INTENT(IN) :: B
    CHARACTER(LEN=*),INTENT(IN) :: C
  ENDSUBROUTINE sub1
  SUBROUTINE sub2(time, dist)
    REAL,INTENT(INOUT) :: time, dist
  ENDSUBROUTINE sub2
  SUBROUTINE sub3(arr)
    REAL,INTENT(INOUT),DIMENSION(:) :: arr
  ENDSUBROUTINE sub3
ENDINTERFACE
ENDMODULE my_interfaces

PROGRAM use_of_module
USE my_interfaces
REAL :: a(-10:10),t,d
 ...
CALL sub1( (/1.0,3.141,0.57112/), 2, 'Hello')
 ...
CALL sub2(t,d)
 ...
CALL sub3(a(2:9))
ENDPROGRAM use_of_module

SUBROUTINE sub1(A,B,C)
  REAL,INTENT(IN) :: A(:)
  INTEGER,INTENT(IN) :: B
  CHARACTER(LEN=*),INTENT(IN) :: C
  ...
ENDSUBROUTINE sub1
SUBROUTINE sub2(time, dist)
  REAL,INTENT(INOUT) :: time, dist
  ...
ENDSUBROUTINE sub2
SUBROUTINE sub3(arr)
  REAL,INTENT(INOUT),DIMENSION(:) :: arr
  ...
ENDSUBROUTINE sub3
```

The interfaces for the subroutines `sub1`, `sub2`, and `sub3` have been gathered together in a `MODULE` called `my_interfaces`. The main program can then make the interfaces for all three procedures explicit by including the statement

```
USE my_interfaces
```

as its first specification statement.

8.1.3 Module procedures

The above simple organisation for the inclusion of a collection of interfaces in a module is adequate for a situation where a set of independent external procedures are to be called from other program units. This is not appropriate for the very common situation where the procedures are interrelated and hence call each other. In this situation we need to make the interfaces of the procedures explicit in each other as well as in any program that uses them. It is not permissible for each of the procedures to include a `USE` statement for a single module containing all their interface declarations. This would result in a procedure having access to two definitions of its own interface, one being its own definition and the other coming from the module declaration.

The solution to this dilemma is to place not just the interface declarations, but the whole definition of the procedures that form the interrelated set, in the module. To illustrate this we modify the previous example as follows:

```
MODULE related_procedures
CONTAINS
  SUBROUTINE sub1(A,B,C)
    REAL,INTENT(IN) :: A(:)
    INTEGER,INTENT(IN) :: B
    CHARACTER(LEN=*),INTENT(IN) :: C
    ...
  ENDSUBROUTINE sub1
  SUBROUTINE sub2(time, dist)
    REAL,INTENT(INOUT) :: time,dist...
    REAL :: arr_1(100)
    CALL sub1( (/5.0,27.67/), 6,'Bye-bye')
    ...
    CALL sub3(arr_1(25:45:3))
    ...
  ENDSUBROUTINE sub2
  SUBROUTINE sub3(arr)
  REAL,INTENT(INOUT),DIMENSION(:) :: arr
  ...
  ENDSUBROUTINE sub2
ENDMODULE related_procedures
```

When procedures are contained in a module in this way they are called *module procedures* and they must be separated from the rest of the module (which is empty in the above example) by a `CONTAINS` statement. Notice that in this example `sub2` calls `sub1` and `sub3` and it is essential that `sub1`'s and `sub3`'s interfaces are explicit in `sub2`. By including the procedures within the module (making them essentially internal to the module) their interfaces are automatically made explicit to each other. The inclusion of a `USE` statement for this module will again make these procedures and their interfaces explicitly accessible in any other program unit. Thus the main program above could be written in the same way as before.

8.1.4 Type and procedure packaging

In Chapter 4 we described user-defined types and structured data objects. In that chapter we described little more than the definition of such objects. There are no intrinsic operations defined for them as there are for the intrinsic types and with this limitation there is not much they can be used for. However, since procedure arguments can be of a derived type and since functions can return results of derived type, it is possible, using modules, to define procedures which specify operations that can be used to manipulate objects of these types.

It is important to note that two objects are of the same derived type if and only if they are declared using a reference to the same unique type definition. An actual argument and a dummy argument cannot therefore be made to match in type by just including identical type definitions in both the calling and called program unit. As with variables, types declared in different program units are entirely independent, even if they happen to have the same structure and the same names. Thus, in the following example,

```
PROGRAM main
 TYPE WHEEL
  INTEGER :: spokes(30)
  REAL    :: rim_size
 ENDTYPE
 type(WHEEL) :: W1
 CALL sub(W1)
 ...
END PROGRAM main
SUBROUTINE sub(W)
 TYPE wheel
  INTEGER :: spokes(30)
  REAL    :: rim_size
 ENDTYPE
type(WHEEL) :: W
 ...
END SUBROUTINE
```

the call to sub would be illegal since the dummy argument w does not correspond in type with the actual argument w1. This is because the two definitions of the type WHEEL occur in different program units and are therefore considered to be entirely distinct even though the actual definitions are identical.

It follows from the above that both the actual argument and the dummy argument must be declared by reference to a type definition which must be accessible globally to both the procedure and the calling program. This can only be achieved by putting the type-definition in a module which is accessed by a USE statement in both program units. For example, if we wanted to write a procedure to read some data and return an object of, say, type HOUSE and then employ this in a program creating a list of houses to model a city, we could write,

```
MODULE HOUSE_DEFS
  TYPE HOUSE
    CHARACTER(LEN=16) :: owner          ! name of owner
    INTEGER           :: residents      ! number of residents
    REAL              :: value          ! value of property
  ENDTYPE HOUSE
ENDMODULE HOUSE_DEFS

PROGRAM CENSUS
  USE HOUSE_DEFS
  type(HOUSE),DIMENSION(100,50) :: city
  INTEGER                       :: ioerr
  ...
  city:DO j=1,50
    street:DO i=1,100
      CALL GET_HOUSE(city(i,j),ioerr)
      IF(ioerr == 0)THEN ! normal processing
        ...
      ELSEIF(ioerr == -1)THEN; EXIT city ! all data processed
      ELSEIF(ioerr == -2)THEN; EXIT street ! street complete
      ELSE ! fatal error in input
        WRITE(UNIT=*,FMT=*) &
             "Fatal Error reading city data",ioerr
      ENDIF
    ENDDO street
  ENDDO city
  ...
ENDPROGRAM CENSUS

SUBROUTINE GET_HOUSE(place,ioerr)
  USE HOUSE_DEFS
  type(HOUSE),INTENT(OUT) :: place
  CHARACTER(LEN=16),PARAMETER :: no_more="                "
  INTEGER,INTENT(OUT)      :: ioerr
  READ(UNIT=*,FMT=*,IOSTAT=ioerr) place%owner
```

```
  IF(ioerr > 0)THEN ! fatal error
    RETURN
  ELSEIF(ioerr < 0)THEN ! end of data
    ioerr = -1; RETURN
  ELSEIF(place%owner == no_more)THEN ! no more residents
                                     ! in street
    ioerr = -2; RETURN
  ELSE
    READ(UNIT=*,FMT=*) place%residents,place%value
  ENDIF
ENDSUBROUTINE GET_HOUSE
```

The module is now employed to make the type definition available to both the main program and the subprogram thus allowing an object of `type(HOUSE)` to be passed as an argument.

Another way of writing the above example that is even more useful is to include the procedure definition within the module. This has the advantage that it ensures that the procedure defining a fundamental manipulation of an object of `type(HOUSE)` and the type definition are packaged together. In the fashionable jargon of *object-oriented* programming this ability to package together type definitions, and procedures for the manipulation of objects of the type, is called *encapsulation*. In Fortran 90, encapsulation is achieved by including the requisite information in a module. In the example we are considering, the module would look like,

```
MODULE HOUSE_DEFS
  TYPE HOUSE
    CHARACTER(LEN=16) :: owner
    INTEGER           :: residents
    REAL              :: value
  ENDTYPE HOUSE
CONTAINS
  SUBROUTINE GET_HOUSE(place,ioerr)
    type(HOUSE),INTENT(OUT) :: place
    CHARACTER(LEN=16),PARAMETER :: no_more="   "
    INTEGER,INTENT(OUT)     :: ioerr
    READ(UNIT=*,FMT=*,IOSTAT=ioerr) place%owner
    IF(ioerr > 0)THEN ! fatal error
      RETURN
    ELSEIF(ioerr < 0)THEN ! end of data
      ioerr = -1; RETURN
    ELSEIF(place%owner == no_more)THEN ! no more residents
                                       ! in street
      ioerr = -2; RETURN
    ELSE
      READ(UNIT=*,FMT=*) place%residents,place%value
    ENDIF
```

```
  ENDSUBROUTINE GET_HOUSE
ENDMODULE HOUSE_DEFS
```

Notice in the above example that the procedure is now internal to the module and hence automatically has access to the entities declared or defined in its host module. It does not need a USE statement specifying its host module; in fact such a statement would be illegal.

8.2 General form of a module

In general a module starts with a MODULE statement and finishes with an ENDMODULE statement, both of which specify the name of the module. Between these two delimiting statements a module is very like a main program but without an executable part.

```
MODULE <module name>
 declarations and specifications statements
CONTAINS
 definitions of module procedures
ENDMODULE <module name>
```

The specification part of a module may start with USE statements that make the entities of other existing modules accessible in this module. Note, entities that are made accessible by a USE statement are said to be accessed by *use-association*. The possibility of one module accessing the definitions of another module by use-association permits a chain of dependent definitions to be established. However, for obvious reasons circular definition is not permitted.

Within the specification part, any data object that could be included in a main program can be declared. Named constants and initialised or uninitialised variables of any accessible type, including derived types, may be specified. However, only fixed size explicit-shape and allocatable arrays are allowed. The bounds of an explicit shape array may depend on the values of named constants, including those accessed by USE association from other modules.

A module may include the type definition for a derived type. In fact, most derived type definitions will be placed in a module since this is the only convenient way of making such a definition accessible to more than one external program unit.

Finally, as we saw above, a module may include interface blocks in its specification part. These can declare the interfaces for external procedures, and as we shall see later in this chapter such interface blocks have a very important additional function of permitting the construction of *generic* procedure sets.

The definitions of module procedures, if such are included, must follow a `CONTAINS` statement. Module procedures are like internal procedures in that they have access to the data environment of their host, i.e. the module in which they are defined. Similarly, module procedures have explicit interfaces that are visible to all other module procedures defined in that module. They also have explicit interfaces in any program unit in which they are made accessible by use-association.

Module procedures are also rather like external procedures in that they are themselves permitted to contain internal procedures with all the normal internal procedure properties. They are also like external procedures in that they are accessible, albeit in a controlled way, to other external program units.

Note that the above discussion points to a way of writing general programs which differs radically from the traditional Fortran 77 style in which there is a main program followed by several subprograms. With the availability of modules and the great benefits obtainable by the use of explicit interfaces it is usually more convenient to write programs in terms of a module which encapsulates the global data environment of the program along with the bulk of the related subprograms. The program will then consist of a main program and a small number of external procedures which `USE` this or other modules.

8.3 Generic procedures and operators

Most of the intrinsic procedures are *generic*. This means that the type of their result is determined by the type of their argument(s). For example, the intrinsic procedure `ABS(X)`, which calculates the absolute value of its argument, returns an integer value if the argument `X` is an integer and a real value if the argument has type real, and so on. This is implemented by having the processor compile an invocation of a different *specific* procedure depending on the type of the argument. An integer argument causes the generic name `ABS` to be replaced by the specific name `IABS` which is the name of the specific intrinsic procedure for returning the absolute value of an integer argument. For a real argument the specific name happens also to be `ABS`.

8.3.1 User-defined generic procedures

The user can also define a set of different specific procedures to be associated with a common generic name. This is done by using a generic interface block. Suppose we wanted to create a set of procedures which clear arbitrary rank one arrays to zero. It would be useful to be able to call any such procedure CLEAR regardless of the type of its argument. This could be done by use of an interface block

```
INTERFACE CLEAR
  SUBROUTINE clear_int(a)
    INTEGER,DIMENSION(:),INTENT(INOUT) :: a
  ENDSUBROUTINE clear_int
  SUBROUTINE clear_real(a)
    REAL,DIMENSION(:),INTENT(INOUT) :: a
  ENDSUBROUTINE clear_real
ENDINTERFACE
```

This associates the generic name CLEAR with the two specific names `clear_int` and `clear_real`. If such an interface declaration was included in a program where the following declarations were in force,

```
REAL:: prices(100)
INTEGER :: counts(50)
```

we could include the calls

```
CALL CLEAR(prices)
CALL CLEAR(counts)
```

The first of these where the argument is real matches the interface for the specific routine `clear_real` and hence this is the procedure which would be invoked. The second would resolve the generic call by matching the interface for `clear_int` and this specific procedure would be invoked.

The set of procedures associated with a given generic name must form an unambiguous *overload* set. That is, by matching actual and dummy arguments, it must be possible to determine that any invocation is a reference to one an only one specific procedure in the set. This basically means that the procedures in such a set must differ from each other in the type and/or ranks of their non-optional arguments.

Generic procedures may be functions as well as subroutines but the type and rank of a function result does not resolve the ambiguity of an overload. This must still be done by the arguments.

8.3.2 User-defined operators

Functions with one or two arguments can be defined as part of *generic operator* overloads. Instead of a generic name on the INTERFACE statement a generic operator symbol is specified. For example, suppose we had defined a data type for rational arithmetic to have two components, a numerator and a denominator. We could extend the meaning of the operator, *, to apply to rational numbers by the following.

```
MODULE RATIONAL_ARITHMETIC
  TYPE RATNUM
    INTEGER :: num,den
  ENDTYPE RATNUM
  ...

  INTERFACE OPERATOR(*)
    MODULE PROCEDURE rat_mult_rat, int_mult_rat, rat_mult_int
    ! the above three procedures will cater for
    ! the three possible types of multiplication
    ! expression i.e. r*r, i*r, r*i, where r and i
    ! are a rational number and an integer respectively
  ENDINTERFACE
  ...
CONTAINS
  FUNCTION rat_mult_rat(l,r)
    type(RATNUM),INTENT(IN) :: l,r
    type(RATNUM) :: rat_mult_rat
    rat_mult_rat%num = l%num * r%num
    rat_mult_rat%den = l%den * r%den
  ENDFUNCTION rat_mult_rat
  FUNCTION int_mult_rat(l,r)
    INTEGER,INTENT(IN) :: l
    type(RATNUM),INTENT(IN) :: r
    type(RATNUM) :: int_mult_rat
    int_mult_rat%num = l * r%num
    int_mult_rat%den = r%den
  ENDFUNCTION int_mult_rat
  ...
ENDMODULE RATIONAL_ARITHMETIC
```

In this case the operator symbol being overloaded is the intrinsic *. The three procedures defined above which are to be added to the multiply overload set can be invoked as operations in a normal arithmetic expression by the normal operator. Which function is actually executed to perform the operation is determined by the types of the operands. The left operand matches the first argument (here named l), and the right operand matches the second argument (r). If, in a program that accessed the above module, we had the following declaration,

```
type(RATNUM) :: ra,rb,rc
```

the following two statements would be valid and would have exactly the same effect.

```
rc = 2*ra*rb
rc = rat_mult_rat(int_mult_rat(2,ra),rb)
```

The expression is evaluated according to the precedence rules for the operators. In this case both operators are `*` and so they are evaluated from left to right. This means the operator `*` is to be applied between the integer `2` and the `RATNUM` `ra`, and then `*` is to be applied between the result and `rb`. Because of the generic operator interface definition made accessible from the module, the first operation resolves to an invocation of `int_mult_rat` and the second to `rat_mult_rat`. Even in this simple example the advantage in clarity of expression of the operator form is obvious.

Another point to note from this example is that where a module procedure is to be added to a generic overload set, the full interface is not specified as for an external procedure but its specific name is declared on a `MODULE PROCEDURE` statement. This merely establishes the connection between the module procedure and the overload set identified by the generic interface statement; the actual specific interface is already explicit and declared by the procedure's definition.

The whole set of intrinsic operator symbols can be overloaded in this manner and new operators can be defined. Any new operators have operator symbols which follow the form for the logical operators like `.AND.`. User-defined operator symbols thus have the form,

```
.<letters>.
```

We can define *monadic* prefix operators which are overloads of functions of one argument, and *dyadic* operators which are overloads of functions with two arguments. If the overloads are for existing intrinsic operator symbols the relative precedence is the same as for the the intrinsic symbol. If the operators define new, `.<letters>.`, symbols the monadic operators bind more tightly that any intrinsic operator and the dyadic operators bind less strongly that any intrinsic operator.

8.3.3 User-defined assignment

There is a yet further form of generic identifier. This allows the assignment operation to be extended to new types. If we consider the rational number type defined above, the default assignment defines assignment for variables of type RATNUM to variables of type RATNUM, but it would clearly be useful to be able to assign integers to RATNUMs and possibly RATNUMs to reals, and so on. This can be done by defining the extended meanings by appropriate subroutines which have two arguments. The first argument must be a variable to receive the assigned value and the second is an expression whose value is converted as necessary to enable the assignment. For example, the interface declaration would be,

```
INTERFACE ASSIGNMENT(=)
  MODULE PROCEDURE rat_ass_int, real_ass_rat
ENDINTERFACE
```

The actual procedures could be,

```
SUBROUTINE rat_ass_int(var,exp)
  type(RATNUM),INTENT(OUT) :: var
  INTEGER,INTENT(IN) :: exp
  var%num = exp
  var%den = 1
ENDSUBROUTINE rat_ass_int
SUBROUTINE real_ass_rat(var,exp)
  REAL,INTENT(OUT) :: var
  type(RATNUM),INTENT(IN) :: exp
  var = exp%num/exp%den
ENDSUBROUTINE real_ass_rat
```

If these definitions were also included in the above module we would be able to write statements such as,

```
ra = 50
x = rb*rc
```

where we have assumed that x is declared to be real.

As with all overloads the arguments are matched with the left and right sides of the operator (assignment in this case) and the specific procedure that is appropriate used to determine the meaning of assignment between objects of the specified types. However, assignment overloading differs from all other in one significant feature. Assignment overload sets do not have to produce an unambiguous set of overloaded procedures as do all other overloads. Later assignment overloads override earlier ones if there is an ambiguity. This means that it is possible for the user to redefine the meaning for intrinsic assignment in those cases where simple component by component copy is not appropriate.

Finally, it is perfectly legal for there to be more than one accessible generic interface block with the same generic identifier. In such a situation the effective generic set is the sum of the individual sets. Except for assignment the combined sets must remain unambiguous.

8.4 Semantic extension modules

The real power of the `MODULE/USE` facility is in its ability, when coupled with derived types and operator and procedure overloading, to provide a *semantic extension* of the language. Semantic extension allows the user to express a problem in terms of the natural objects and operations relating to that problem. A semantic extension module requires several crucial features,

1. There must be a mechanism for deriving new types.
2. There must be a method of defining operations on those types.
3. There must be a way of overloading the operations (i.e. allowing the same operator to be used to operate on objects of different type) so that the user of the new types can use them in a natural way.
4. There must be a way of encapsulating all these features in such a way that the user can access these facilities as a combined set.
5. It is desirable that the details of the underlying data representation and the implementation of the associated operations be kept hidden. This is often called *data hiding* and it allows the user to manipulate the new type only through the facilities provided by the semantic extension.

The module facility described so far has all these capabilities with the exception of the fifth. This is provided by the ability for the module to contain declarations for objects that are private to the module and hence invisible to any using program. By default all entities declared or otherwise made accessible in a module are also made accessible by a `USE` statement that names the module. This can be changed for individual entities by including the `PRIVATE` attribute in their declaration. We might want to define a private work array that could be employed by a number of module procedures but which we did not want any other program to access. This could be done,

```
MODULE working-procs
...
! declarations of public data
REAL,DIMENSION(1000,1000),PRIVATE :: work
...
! more declarations of public data
CONTAINS
...
! definitions of public procedures which access
! the private work array
...
ENDMODULE working_procs
```

When this module was accessed in another program the array work would not be visible. It would exist and be employed by the module procedures but it would not be accessible within the `USE`ing program.

There is also a `PRIVATE` statement form. This allows the entities to be declared as normal, without the `PRIVATE` attribute, and then to be made private by the inclusion of their name in a `PRIVATE` statement.

```
PRIVATE :: work,auxil
```

The names that can be declared on a `PRIVATE` statement may be of any type and rank, they may be the names of procedures, the names of derived types, and operators. In this last case they have to appear in the form

```
OPERATOR(<symbol>)
```

The default accessibility of entities in a module can be changed from public to private by the inclusion of a `PRIVATE` ststement with an empty list. If this is done then only those entities explicitly declared to be public are made visible outside the module. Objects are declared to be public by use of a `PUBLIC` attribute in their declaration or by their inclusion in a `PUBLIC` statement.

A particularly important feature of this visibility control facility is that it is possible to declare the internal structure of a derived type to be private while leaving the type itself publicly visible. We could have declared the internal structure of the rational number type to be private,

```
TYPE RATNUM
  PRIVATE
  INTEGER :: num,den
ENDTYPE RATNUM
```

The user of the module could then still declare objects to be of type `RATNUM` but they could only manipulate them via the procedures also declared in the module. The user cannot access the component names `num` and `den`. They are rendered invisible by the structure of the type being made private. A full semantic extension module for rational arithmetic would have to define meanings for all the arithmetic operations and comparisons. It would also have to define conversions from and to other numeric types and probably also ways of converting to and from values represented as character strings of digits for input/output. In this way a set of facilities mirroring those for the intrinsic numeric types, but now for a very different number representation, could be built up.

The major benefit of making the internal structure of the type private is that the module can be changed to use an alternative, perhaps better representation for the data object. Provided all the internal code for the operations etc. are changed as needed for the new representation, user programs would not need to be changed. This allows quite major corrections and improvements to supporting modules to be made without effecting the programs that depend on them. Improvements might even include replacing the Fortran bodies of some operations by procedures in other languages that are more efficient at exploiting particular features of the target computer architecture.

The use of semantic extension modules is not restricted to types which are analogous to the intrinsic types such other forms of numbers. The technique can be used to build extensions in a vast range of areas. The following example illustrates this. It defines a module that provides facilities for handling straight line segments as single objects. Lines are assumed to be defined by the x and y coordinates of their endpoints. For simplicity only two functions are defined i.e. a function to create a line given its endpoints, and a logical binary operator which can be used to check whether two lines intersect. The latter is implemented as a function with two arguments of type `LINE` returning a logical result. However, it would be possible to build up a complete module defining a wide variety of facilities for manipulating lines.

```
MODULE Lines
  !-- Definition of derived type for lines ---------------!
  TYPE LINE
    PRIVATE
    REAL :: X1,Y1,X2,Y2
    ! (X1,Y1) and (X2,Y2) are the endpoints of the line
  ENDTYPE LINE
```

```
  !-- Interface Definitions for Generic names-------------!
  INTERFACE Create_Line
    !-- This Procedure creates a line between two points.
    !-- The arguments of the function will be (X1,Y1,X2,Y2)
    !-- and they can be either all REAL or all INTEGER.
    MODULE PROCEDURE Real_Line_Constructor, &
                     Integer_Line_Constructor
  ENDINTERFACE
  INTERFACE OPERATOR(.CROSSES.)
    !-- This operator tests if two lines intersect.
    MODULE PROCEDURE Line_Line_Crosses
  ENDINTERFACE
CONTAINS
  !-- Definitions of specific procedure bodies -----------!
  FUNCTION Integer_Line_Constructor(X1,Y1,X2,Y2)
    INTEGER     :: X1,Y1,X2,Y2
    type(LINE) :: Integer_Line_Constructor
    Integer_Line_Constructor%X1 = X1
    Integer_Line_Constructor%Y1 = Y1
    Integer_Line_Constructor%X2 = X2
    Integer_Line_Constructor%Y2 = Y2
  ENDFUNCTION Integer_Line_Constructor
  FUNCTION Real_Line_Constructor(X1,Y1,X2,Y2)
    REAL        :: X1,Y1,X2,Y2
    type(LINE) :: Real_Line_Constructor
    Real_Line_Constructor%X1 = X1
    Real_Line_Constructor%Y1 = Y1
    Real_Line_Constructor%X2 = X2
    Real_Line_Constructor%Y2 = Y2
  ENDFUNCTION Real_Line_Constructor
  FUNCTION Line_Line_Crosses(L1,L2)
    type(LINE) :: L1,L2
    LOGICAL     :: Line_Line_Crosses
    REAL :: X1L1,X2L1,X1L2,Y1L2,X2L2,Y2L2,m,c
    REAL :: Cth,Sth
    REAL, PARAMETER :: tol = 1.0E-03   ! a small number
    ! angle L1 makes with x-axis
    IF((L1%X1 - L1%X2) < tol)THEN
      th = pi/2
    ELSE
      th = ATAN ((L1%Y2-L1%Y1)/(L1%X2-L%X1))
    ENDIF
    Cth = COS(th)
    Sth = SIN(th)
    ! Find x coordinates of L1 in new axis system
    X1L1 = L1%X1*Cth - L1%Y1*Sth
    X2L1 = L1%X2*Sth - L1%Y2*Cth
    ! Find coordinates of endpoints of L2 in new axis system
    X1L2 = L2%X1*Cth - L2%Y1*Sth
    Y1L2 = L2%X1*Sth + L2%Y1*Cth
    X2L2 = L2%X2*Cth - L2%Y2*Sth
    Y2L2 = L2%X2*Sth + L2%Y2*Cth
```

```
    ! find m and c for equation of new line
    Line_Line_Crosses = .FALSE.
    IF( (X2L2-X1L2) > tol) THEN   ! lines not parallel
       m = (Y2L2-Y1L2)/(X2L2-X1L2)
       c =  Y2L2 - m* X2L2
       xcross = -c/m
       ! Test to see if crossing point is inside line segment
       IF( X1L1 <= xcross . AND. X2L1 >= xcross) THEN
         Line_Line_Crosses = .TRUE.
       ENDIF
     ENDIF
   ENDFUNCTION Line_Line_Crosses
ENDMODULE Lines
```

The body of the `line_line_crosses` procedure is included for completeness. The less mathematically-minded reader can safely ignore the details since they are not essential to the points being considered. The approach adopted is to rotate the axes so that the x-axis is aligned along `L1`. This simplifies things since, in the new axes system the equation of `L1` is y=0 therefore if `L2`'s equation is y=mx+c then `L2` crosses `L1` at xcross = -c/m and y=0. If `xcross` lies between the x coordinates of the endpoints of `L1` in the new coordinate system then the lines cross.

The following is a complete program using the `Lines` module,

```
PROGRAM Using_Lines
  ! Make the definitions of the module accessible
  USE Lines
  type(LINE) :: L1,L2  !-- Declare two objects of type Line
  ! Create two lines, one using the INTEGER interface and one
  ! using the REAL interface
  L1 = Create_Line(50,50,100,100)
  L2 = Create_Line(20.4,12.56,150.0,265.75)
  IF ( L1.CROSSES.L2 ) THEN
    WRITE(UNIT=*,FMT=*) 'line 1 crosses line 2'
  ELSE
    WRITE(UNIT=*,FMT=*) 'line 1 does not cross line 2'
  ENDIF
END PROGRAM
```

The above example illustrates all the points mentioned earlier as being crucial to providing semantic extension capabilities.

It is desirable to hide the internal representation of a type because a module that uses the type can then use a different internal representation for that type without affecting programs that use the module. For example, instead of representing a line by its two end-points we might find it more convenient to use one end-point, the slope, and the line length since it might allow us to implement a number of operations on lines more efficiently. In fact this might have helped us in writing the `Line_Line_Crosses` routine above. We might then rewrite the module thus,

```
MODULE Lines
  !-- Definition of derived type for lines----------------!
  TYPE LINE
    PRIVATE
    REAL :: X1,Y1,SLOPE,LENGTH
    ! (X1,Y1) is the start of the line
  ENDTYPE LINE
  !-- Interface Definitions for Generic names-------------!
  INTERFACE Create_Line
    !-- This Procedure creates a line between two points.
    !-- The arguments of the function will be (X1,Y1,X2,Y2)
    !-- and they can be either all REAL or all INTEGER.
    MODULE PROCEDURE Real_Line_Constructor, &
                     Integer_Line_Constructor
  ENDINTERFACE
  INTERFACE OPERATOR(.CROSSES.)
    !-- This operator tests if two lines intersect.
    MODULE PROCEDURE Line_Line_Crosses
  ENDINTERFACE
CONTAINS
  !-- Definitions of specific procedure bodies -----------!
  FUNCTION Integer_Line_Constructor(X1,Y1,X2,Y2)
    INTEGER      :: X1,Y1,X2,Y2
    type(LINE) :: Line_Constructor
    Line_Constructor%X1 = X1
    Line_Constructor%Y1 = Y1
    Line_Constructor%slope = REAL(Y2-Y1)/(X2-X1)
    Line_Constructor%length = &
            SQRT(REAL((Y2-Y1)**2+(X2-X1)**2))
  ENDFUNCTION Integer_Line_Constructor
  FUNCTION Real_Line_Constructor(X1,Y1,X2,Y2)
    REAL         :: X1,Y1,X2,Y2
    type(LINE) :: Line_Constructor
    Line_Constructor%X1 = X1
    Line_Constructor%Y1 = Y1
    Line_Constructor%slope = (Y2-Y1)/(X2-X1)
    Line_Constructor%length = SQRT((Y2-Y1)**2+(X2-X1)**2)
  ENDFUNCTION Real_Line_Constructor
  ...{rewrite of the whole module to use the new structure}
ENDMODULE Lines
```

The dependent main program using the module would not need to be changed because it could only access the visible public parts of the module which are unchanged. This capability is extremely important as an aid to the production of much more maintainable programs.

The interface for `Create_Line` has been overloaded to allow the user to specify either `INTEGER` or `REAL` arguments but the internal structure of the type stores the co-ordinates as reals. Note that a mixture of real and integer arguments is not allowed by the interface supplied. To provide for a mixture of argument types in any combination would require the definition of 16 specific versions of `Create_Line` since there are 16 possible combinations of arguments if reals and integers are to be allowed in any position in the argument list. The above module could be extended to allow circles to be handled as well as lines. The data type for circles could be

```
TYPE CIRCLE
  REAL :: Centre_X, Centre_Y, Radius
END TYPE CIRCLE
```

To allow for checking whether circles and lines intersect we could overload the `.CROSSES.` operator with three new specific function definitions called

```
Circle_Line_Crosses
Line_Circle_Crosses
Circle_Circle_Crosses
```

which could take arguments of type `Circle` and `Line`, `Line` and `Circle`, and `Circle` and `Circle` respectively. Given the following object declarations

```
type(LINE)   :: L1,L2
type(CIRCLE) :: C1,C2
```

we could then write statements like

```
IF( L1.CROSSES.C1 )THEN...
IF( C2.CROSSES.L2 )THEN...
IF( C1.CROSSES.C2 )THEN...
```

As another example we might consider providing the functionality of variable length strings[1]. Fortran 90 does not have an intrinsically defined variable length character string facility. Character strings are treated as

[1] In fact such a module is being defined as a auxiliary standard by the International Standards Organisation. One of the present authors (JLS) is the international project editor for this work and has produced a fully tested implementation in Fortran 90.

fixed length objects. A module to provide such functionality must define a suitable data type with an internal structure capable of storing a value that is a character string of any length. It must define overloads for the character string manipulation operations of assignment, concatenation, and comparison. It must extend the generic intrinsic functions that apply for fixed length strings to have the correct meanings for variable length strings, and it must define procedures for the essential substring manipulations. Finally the module must define procedures to perform basic input/output operations on arbitrary length strings. A module of this size is too large (over 5000 lines) and too detailed to include in a book of this kind but the fact that such a module is possible is a good illustration of the power which the semantic extension facilities provide.

8.5 The USE statement

The USE statement in its simplest form simply names the MODULE whose public definitions are to be made accessible. It can, however, also be used to control the entities that are made visible and the names by which these should be known locally. The simple USE statement has the form,

```
USE module-name
```

This makes all of the public entities defined in the named module accessible. It is illegal for any local entity to exist with a name the same as one of these module entities. If for some reason a local entity with one of these names is essential, the USE statement can be modified to give the module entity a different name for use locally. For example, suppose we wished to use the module HOUSE_DEFS in a program that already had a procedure called GET_HOUSE. We could rename the module procedure GET_HOUSE as GET_HOME using the statement,

```
USE HOUSE_DEFS, GET_HOME => GET_HOUSE
```

The local name GET_HOME points to, or references, the module procedure GET_HOUSE. Any local use of the name GET_HOUSE will refer to a local entity of that name.

The general form of a USE statement with renamed procedures is,

```
USE module-name, local-name=>use-name,...
```

where the `local-name=>use-name` combinations can be repeated for as many times as required, separated by commas. The `use-name` in each case is the name of one of the public entities from the module.

Another way of handling possible name clashes is to restrict the entities that are accessed from the module to only those that are essential. Again if in the above example we did not want to use the procedure `GET_HOUSE` but we merely wanted to gain access to the type definition, we could employ the statement,

```
USE HOUSE_DEFS, ONLY:HOUSE
```

In this case only the type `HOUSE` is made accessible. All the other public entities remain hidden and inaccessible.

The general form may have a list of the entities to be made accessible following the `ONLY:` again separated by commas. In fact these entities can be further controlled by renaming in the `ONLY` list. We could have therefore a statement like,

```
USE lines, ONLY: LINE, make_line=>create_line
```

which would allow access only to the type and the `create_line` set of procedures from the module `Lines`, and would also cause the local name for the `create_line` procedure to be `make_line`.

The `USE` statement with its renaming and restrictive access facilities gives great control over the naming of entities accessed from modules. It would be quite possible for two modules containing entities of the same names to be accessed within the same program with only the minor inconvenience of having to rename some of the entities. This is in contrast to the insoluble problem for two libraries of external functions with a name clash in Fortran 77.

8.6 Exercises

1. What is meant by global data, and how can a global data area be set up in Fortran?

2. Why is it often preferable to put subprograms in a module?

3. Explain what is meant by data hiding. What facilities in Fortran 90 allow its implementation?

4. Explain what is meant by operator overloading.

5. Write a module defining a generic subroutine `gsort` which will sort elements of an integer or real array into ascending numerical order. Write a program to test the subroutine.

6. Write a generic function which will sort the elements of one-, two- and three-dimensional integer arrays into ascending numerical order. Assume that the subroutine `SORT(A)` which does this for one-dimensional arrays is available.

7. Write a complete module which allows a user to declare objects of type `CIRCLE`, create constants of this type, read in and write out data of type `CIRCLE`, and determine whether circles cross or not. Write a program to test your module on the following data where each line specifies the x and y coordinates of the centre of a circle followed by its radius.

   10 10 30
   10 10 40
   15 10 40
   16 10 15
   14.5 15.5 34
   5 5 23
   4 4 32
   3 3 45
   5 5 78
   10 3 23

Chapter 9

Pointers and Targets

To date, the data objects we have discussed have been constants or variables. Constants are either literal (such as 3.45 or 'some text') or symbolic (as defined in type statements with the `PARAMETER` attribute). A symbolic constant is a name for a fixed value of the appropriate type. In a sense a symbolic constant has a name which refers to some space containing a value and the relationship between the name the space and the value are all fixed. The variables we have used so far (scalars and arrays) have all had names which referenced some fixed storage space in which variable values could be stored. These normal variables allow the value referenced to change but the space associated with the name remains fixed. For a number of applications it is useful to have variables where the space referenced by the variable name can be changed in addition to the value contained in the space. Such variables are called *pointers*. The different sorts of data objects can therefore be tabulated as,

data object	**refers to**	**contents of location**
constant	fixed location	fixed
variable	fixed location	variable
pointer	different locations	variable

The space to which a pointer points is called its *target* and when a pointer has a particular target it is said to be *associated* with the target and a reference to the pointer will, in general, be a reference to the target. A pointer can be made to point at various different targets during the course of a program, or can be made to have no target. In this latter case the pointer is said to be *disassociated.* Pointers are invaluable for producing efficient programs where large objects are manipulated. Judicious use of pointers may avoid a good deal of copying of variables. Additionally, pointers are essential if arbitrary-sized lists of objects are to be handled. In fact, in all cases where the size and organisation of data objects is dynamically determined, the use and manipulation of pointers is virtually essential.

9.1 Pointer and target declaration

A pointer is a variable declared with the `POINTER` attribute. It has a static type and static rank that is determined by the declaration, e.g.

```
REAL,POINTER :: ptor
REAL,DIMENSION(:,:),POINTER :: ptra
```

The first declaration specifies that the name `ptor` is a pointer to a scalar real target, the second that `ptra` is a pointer to a two-dimensional array of reals. It should be noted that the declaration determines the type and rank of any possible target the pointer may have. Therefore `ptor` may not have a target of any other type than real and `ptra` may only be associated with targets that are rank 2 real arrays. Note also pointers to arrays are always declared with deferred-shape array specifications that determine the rank only and not the shape. The shape is always determined from the target.

If ordinary variables are to become targets of a pointer they must be declared as such with the `TARGET` attribute.

```
REAL,TARGET :: x,y,z
REAL,DIMENSION(100,150),TARGET :: a,b,c
```

With these declarations each of the variables `x,y,z` might at some stage in the program become associated with the pointer `ptor`, and any of `a`, `b`, or `c`, or any two-dimensional section of these, could become associated with `ptra`.

9.2 Pointer manipulation

There are a number of special statements which are used to manipulate pointers. These are used to change or to test the association of a pointer with a target. The simplest of these is *pointer assignment* which associates a given target with a pointer as shown in the following statements:

```
ptor => y
ptra => b
```

The first of these statements associates the target `y` with the pointer `ptor`. The second associates `b` with `ptra`.

The pointer assignment symbol is different from the ordinary value assignment because the action is different. The statements

```
x = 3.14159
ptor => y
ptor = x
```

are all valid. The first assignment sets the value of the `x` variable. The second makes `ptor` refer to the same space as `y`, and the last assigns the value of x to the space referred to by `ptor`. If we now executed the statement,

```
x = 10.0
```

the value of `x` is changed but not that of `ptor` or `y`. However if we executed,

```
ptor = 5.0
```

we would find that the values of both `y` and `ptor` were now 5.0. The pointer assignment makes the pointer and the variable refer to the same space, whereas an ordinary assignment causes the value contained in the space to be set.

A pointer to an array may be associated with the whole of a target variable or if required it may be associated with a section of a target variable as long as the section has the correct rank. For example,

```
ptra => a(35:70,26:49:3)
```

associates the pointer with a rather strange section of the target. A subsequent reference to, say, `ptra(1,1)`, would be equivalent to a reference to `a(35,26)`, `ptra(2,2)` to `a(36,29)`, and so on.

Targets for pointers can also be created dynamically by *allocation*. As well as allocating space for allocatable arrays, the `ALLOCATE` statement can allocate space to be the target of a pointer.

```
ALLOCATE(ptor)
ALLOCATE(ptra(n*n,2*k-1))
```

These statements allocate new space, the first a single real and the second a rank 2 real array, and makes these objects the targets of the pointers `ptor` and `ptra`, respectively. When arrays are being allocated the bounds may be determined by any expression that has an integer result.

The allocation of a pointer creates a target for the pointer, and this target may then be referenced and defined through the pointer. Since such a target implicitly has the `TARGET` attribute, other pointers can be associated with this space by pointer assignment,

```
ptor => ptra(i,j)
```

would associate the `(i,j)` element of the target of `ptra` with `ptor`. This could have considerable advantages in both convenience of expression and efficiency. For example, if the particular element was being used frequently inside a nested loop the calculation of the particular element need only be done once. Subsequent references to the element can then be made through the scalar pointer. This saves having to write the subscript information every time and it also saves the processor from having to calculate which element is involved every time.

Note that when a new association for a pointer is established either by allocation or by pointer assignment, any previous association with a target is broken. This means that if the previous target was created by allocation via the pointer, the space will become inaccessible, unless of course some other pointer is still associated with the previous target and this can be used to access the space.

Pointers can be disassociated with their targets by nullification or by deallocation. The latter also deallocates the space. The statement,

```
NULLIFY(ptor)
```

simply breaks the connection of its pointer argument with its target, if any, and leaves the pointer in a disassociated state. The statement,

```
DEALLOCATE(ptra)
```

breaks the connection between the pointer and its target and it also deallocates the target. Nullification does nothing to the target and may be applied to any pointer at any time. Deallocation may only be applied to a pointer that was previously associated with its target by allocation.

Both the `ALLOCATE` and `DEALLOCATE` statements have in addition to the pointer argument an optional error indicator variable specifier,

```
ISTAT=<integer variable>
```

such a variable can be used to check that an allocation or deallocation action has been completed successfully by the processor. In the statement,

```
ALLOCATE(ptra(n,m), ISTAT=ierr)
```

if the allocation is successful the variable `ierr` will be set to zero. If an error occurs during the attempt at the allocation `ierr` will be set to a positive value. The most likely cause of error is that the system has too little free memory space available for the required allocation. If the `ISTAT` indicator is not included any error causes the program to stop.

It should be noted that the association status of a pointer is undefined when it is declared. Before a pointer can be used in any other way it must be given a defined status by pointer assignment, nullification or allocation. An undefined pointer must not be deallocated. This list of statements are the only contexts in which a pointer's association status can be changed. When a pointer appears in a normal expression it is the current target that is referenced.

The status of a pointer may be tested by the intrinsic function, `ASSOCIATED`. Thus,

```
ASSOCIATED(pointer1)
```

will return true if `pointer1` is currently associated with some target and false otherwise.

```
ASSOCIATED(pointer1,object1)
```

would return true if `pointer1` was currently associated with the specific target `object1`, and false otherwise. As we shall see later, the `ASSOCIATED` function is useful in list processing problems where the end of a list can be detected by the presence of a null (not associated) pointer.

9.3 Use of pointers in iterative problems

Iteration is a method used to solve many problems in numerical computing. The method starts by making a guess at the required solution and then uses this guess or approximation as the input to some calculation that produces a better approximation. The new approximation is then used as the input to calculate yet another hopefully better approximation. The process is repeated, or iterated, until the required degree of accuracy is obtained. A simple example of such an algorithm is the well known iterative approximation method for finding the square root of a number. This is that successive approximations, X_n, to the `sqrt(Y)` are given by

$$X_n = (X_{n-1} + Y/X_{n-1})/2$$

This is such a stable and rapidly convergent algorithm that even though much better initial approximations are possible, starting with the value one would still produce an acceptable value for the square root in a fairly small number of iterations. A program fragment implementing such an algorithm could be,

```
...
REAL :: Y,tolerance=1.0E-4
REAL :: prev_approx,next_approx
! set initial approximation
prev_approx =1.0
ITERATE: DO
  ! calculate next approximation using the previous as input
  next_approx = (prev_approx + Y/prev_approx)/2.0
  ! check if error in next approximation is less than
required
  ! tolerance
  IF( ABS((next_approx - prev_approx)/next_approx) &
           < tolerance ) EXIT ITERATE
  ! copy next_approx to prev_approx and repeat iteration
  prev_approx = next_approx
ENDDO ITERATE
! next_approx now contains the required result
...
```

This structure is typical of many such iterative processes, but more often than not the objects involved are not simple real variables and the update process is not just a simple arithmetic expression and assignment. It is frequently the case that the objects which hold the approximations are large arrays and the cost of the copy operation, moving the result of one iteration to become the input to the next, is a significant proportion of the total cost of an iteration. In such cases it is much more efficient to use pointers to avoid having to do the copying operations. The following illustrates this,

```
REAL,DIMENSION(1000,1000),TARGET :: approx1,approx2
REAL,DIMENSION(:,:),POINTER :: prev_approx,next_approx,swap
prev_approx => approx1
next_approx => approx2
prev_approx = initial_approximation(.....)
DO
  next_approx = iteration_function_of(prev_approx)
  IF( ABS(MAXVAL(next_approx - prev_approx)) < 0.0001 ) EXIT
  swap => prev_approx
  prev_approx => next_approx
  next_approx => swap
ENDDO
```

The two object arrays `approx1` and `approx2` which will hold successive solutions are declared with the `TARGET` attribute. The variables `prev_approx`, `next_approx` and `swap` are declared with the `POINTER` attribute. We associate the pointers, `prev_approx` and `next_approx`, with target objects by pointer assignment.

```
prev_approx => approx1
next_approx => approx2
```

We have assumed that the functions `initial_approximation` and `iteration_function_of` do the work of setting up the initial guess and of performing the iteration calculation, and that the latter has an interface,

```
INTERFACE
 FUNCTION iteration_function_of(in)
  REAL,DIMENSION(:,:) :: in
  REAL,DIMENSION(SIZE(in,1),SIZE(in,2)) :: &
                             iteration_function_of
 ENDFUNCTION
ENDINTERFACE
```

In the invocation of the function the pointer actual argument, `prev_approx`, is dereferenced to pass the array that is the current target, and the result which is required to be of the same shape as the argument is copied into the current target array associated with `next_approx`. (If the pointer is to be manipulated as a pointer in the procedure then the dummy argument must be declared as a pointer. In such cases the dereferencing does not occur when the procedure is invoked. The pointer itself is passed rather than the target.)

Similarly in the expression, `(next_approx-prev_approx)`, the pointers are dereferenced and the subtraction applied to the target arrays. It is only in the three pointer assignments at the end of the loop that the pointers themselves are manipulated. In these, `swap` is made to point at the same target as `prev_approx`. Then `prev_approx` is made to point at the `next_approx` target, and finally `next_approx` is made to point at the same space as `swap`. The net effect is that `prev_approx` and `next_approx` pointers have been swapped over. The cost, which is quite small, is three pointer assignments. This is much more efficient than swapping the actual objects which would require `1000*1000 = 1000000` real assignments on most processors.

9.4 Pointers and derived types

The components of a derived type may be declared to be pointers. This allows for dynamically sized structures to be created and manipulated. For example, we could define a type such as,

```
TYPE STRING
 CHARACTER,DIMENSION(:),POINTER :: chars
ENDTYPE STRING
```

which has a component that is a pointer to a one-dimensional array of characters. By use of such a type we could build facilities for manipulating fully dynamically varying length strings[1].

Since it is possible to create arrays of objects of such types, it is possible to create, what are in effect, arrays of pointers (as distinct from a pointer to an array). For example, suppose we declared,

```
type(STRING),DIMENSION(100) :: lines
```

In this case the component selection

```
lines%chars
```

is illegal. There is no context where arrays of pointers such as this can be used. In expression contexts, where pointers are dereferenced and so refer to their targets, this would produce an array of arrays, possibly of variable lengths, and hence is not allowed. The basic rule is that dereferencing can only be applied to a scalar pointer and only scalar pointers can have their association changed. (A pointer to an array is a scalar pointer even though the target is an array). The expression,

```
lines(5)%chars
```

is perfectly valid, either in a pointer context (where the pointer association can be changed) or in an expression context where it will be dereferenced to produce the current array of characters that is the target of this pointer.

9.4.1 Pointers and processing lists

The use of pointers with derived types also provides support for structures such as linked lists. This is achieved by allowing a derived type to contain a pointer to an object of the same type as itself. For example, such a recursive type could be defined as

---

[1] In fact just such a type has been used in a Fortran 90 module written by one of the authors(JLS) implementing facilities that conform with the proposed ISO standard for "Varying Length Strings in Fortran". This is an auxiliary standard to that for the Fortran 90 language defining the functionality for varying length strings via the module interface.

```
TYPE CELL
  INTEGER :: val                   ! list item
  type(CELL),POINTER:: next_cell ! pointer to next list item
ENDTYPE CELL
```

The pointer `next_cell` is defined to point at an object of type `CELL`. We can use such a type to write code to create a linked list. For instance,

```
type(CELL),TARGET :: head
type(CELL),POINTER :: current,temp
INTEGER :: ieom,k
head%val = 0                  ! sets head of list to default
NULLIFY(head%next_cell)       ! starting values
current => head              ! current points to head of list
DO
  READ(UNIT=*,FMT=*,IOSTAT=ieom) k
                              ! read next value, if any
  IF( ieom /= 0 ) EXIT
  ALLOCATE(temp)              ! create new cell
  temp%val = k                ! assign new value to new cell
  NULLIFY(temp%next_cell)     ! set disassociated status for
                              ! new cell pointer
  current%next_cell => temp ! attach new cell to current
                              ! end of list
  current => temp             ! make current point to new
                              ! end of list
ENDDO
```

This program fragment would create a linked list of cells starting at `head` and terminating with a cell in which the `next_cell` pointer is disassociated. A "walk through" such a list, say, printing its contents could be written as,

```
current => head
DO
  WRITE(UNIT=*,FMT=*) current%val
  IF( .NOT.ASSOCIATED( current%next_cell )) EXIT
  current => current%next_cell
ENDDO
```

All sorts of multiply-linked lists can be created and manipulated in analogous ways. This simple example should be sufficient to show the basic principles involved.

A point to note regarding structures containing pointer components is that the meaning of intrinsic assignment between such structures is subtly different. Whereas, all normal components are assigned by copying the value, the pointer components are pointer assigned. Pointer components are assigned by copying the descriptor values not by copying the target values. Thus the statements

```
type(CELL) :: A,B
A=B
```

where `CELL` is as defined above, are equivalent to

```
A%val = B%val
A%next_cell => B%next_cell
```

unless of course the meaning of assignment for objects of type `CELL` is deliberately redefined by the program.

9.5 Pointer input/output

Pointers which appear in input/output lists are always dereferenced and values are either read into, or written out from, current targets. It should be obvious therefore that a disassociated pointer may not appear in an input/output list since it cannot be dereferenced to any target. The following example should emphasise these points.

```
REAL, DIMENSION(3), TARGET :: arr=(/1.,2.,3./)
REAL, DIMENSION(:), POINTER :: p
p => arr
WRITE(UNIT=*,FMT=*) p
```

These statements would write out the values `1.`, `2.`, `3.` since `p` in the `WRITE` statement is dereferenced to its target `arr`. If the statement `p => arr` was not present then the `WRITE` statement would be illegal since `p` would not be associated with any defined target. An undefined pointer like an undefined variable is not permitted in any context that requires its value. This goes even further for a pointer. A disassociated pointer may not appear in an input/output list either since it has no target into which values could be read or from which values could be written.

It should be noted that structured objects with pointer components may not appear in input/output lists. The normal component by component expansion followed by the dereferencing rules cannot be applied, since it would not, in general, be possible for this process to terminate. A little thought, given the above list structure, will show that if we were to place `head` in an output list, say, and then apply the above process, we would scan down the list but eventually we would end up on a disassociated pointer. If this was the only difficulty it might have been possible for this to be used in general to terminate the process and so give us an easy way of outputting lists. However, consider what would happen if we included a statement such as

```
current%next_cell => head
```

after the input loop above. We now have a list that is linked in a closed loop. The process of expanding structures by component and dereferencing pointers never ends. Structures with pointer components are therefore not allowed in input/output lists. The values involved in such objects must be specifically selected and handled explicitly as far as input or output is concerned.

9.6 Exercises

1. Define a type that might be used to hold a list of integers but with links both to the previous list item and the following list item. (Such a structure is called a *doubly-linked* list)

2. Write a procedure (assumed to be internal to the program containing the above type definition) to insert a new item into a doubly-linked list of the above objects at an arbitrary position indicated by a given pointer.

Chapter 10

Input and Output

All the programs we have seen so far in this book have been written to be run interactively at a terminal. The input/output statements we have used have all taken the form

```
READ(UNIT=*,FMT=*) <input list>
```

or

```
WRITE(UNIT=*,FMT=*) <output list>
```

These statements transfer data to and from the system default input/output unit, which is usually set as the keyboard and display. The fact that the default input/output unit is to be used is indicated by the asterisk(*) following the `UNIT=` specifier inside the parentheses in each statement. The asterisk following the `FMT=` specifier denotes that the external data is in the form of a sequence of records, each of which is a string of characters. On input it is assumed that there are enough values to fill the variables included in the input list. The layout of the values is essentially unrestricted. It can be considered as one long stream of items with each item separated from the next by spaces, commas or end-of-record markers. For output the values in the list are converted to character string representations and transferred to the output unit using whatever system-defined default layout conventions are provided. We will discuss these layout conventions in more detail in Chapter 11.

Default input/output, as described above, is called *list-directed. It* is particularly useful for constructing quick "one-off" programs, where the terminal is the only device with which communication is needed and where layout and presentation of results is not particularly important. For programs which need to perform input/output to devices other than keyboard/display terminals, and where a greater degree of control over the layout and presentation of results is important, Fortran provides quite extensive facilities. In this chapter we shall consider how Fortran handles input/ouput to files, and also some of the different ways in which the information and its transfer to and from a Fortran program can be managed. The layout and presentation of results will be dealt with in Chapter 11.

Most modern computer systems incorporate a filestore which is stored on magnetic disc of some sort. The filestore is managed by the computer's operating system and so, to access files, Fortran must provide an interface between its own input/output system and the file system provided by the operating system. The nature of this interface and how information is transferred across it, between Fortran programs and operating system files, is the main subject of this chapter.

10.1 Files and units

Computer operating systems normally organise their permanent storage into named blocks of information called files. The user of such systems need not be concerned with how or where a particular file is stored on the magnetic medium used for the permanent storage. All the user needs to know is the name of the file. The operating system then uses this name to access the file and the information stored in it. In this book we have assumed a scheme where file names are of the form *filename.ext* where *filename* is a name of up to eight characters and *ext* is a three character extension that is usually used to indicate the type of information contained in the file. For example: a Fortran program source code file could be called `MAINPROG.FOR`; a file containing data on which such a program might work could be called `EXAMRES.DAT`; the results produced by the program could be called `EXAMREP.RES`.

Fortran organises its input/output in terms of numbered *units*. Each program has available to it a number of potential input/output units which are essentially channels along which data can flow. Data is transferred by `READ` or `WRITE` statements which identify the source or destination of the data by specifying a particular unit. For example,

```
READ(UNIT=3,...
WRITE(UNIT=8,...
```

The unit is identified by a positive integer or by an asterisk as we have seen previously. If an asterisk is used then the unit is assumed to be connected to the system default input/output device. Data which is transferred via a particular unit may be input from, or output to, a particular file by connecting the unit to that file. If a unit is not connected to a file no data can be transferred via that unit.

The interface between Fortran and the operating system can be illustrated diagrammatically in Figure 10.1. The area above the dashed line represents the operating system with its group of named files and a terminal from which the program is initiated. The Fortran system and program is represented below the dashed line. The Fortran system provides the

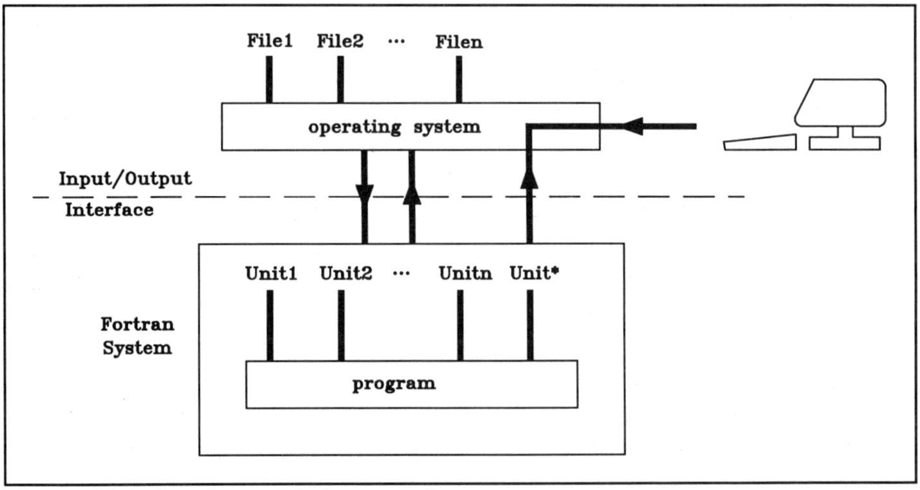

Figure 10.1: Interface with the operating system

program with a set of units which are numbered from 1 to n, where n is some processor dependent positive integer. The additional unit, denoted by an *, is connected by default to the terminal via the operating system. Any of the numbered units may be connected to any one of the operating system files. Such connections are specified by means of an `OPEN` statement. For instance,

```
OPEN(UNIT=7,FILE='RESULTS.DAT')
```

connects the unit numbered 7 to the file known to the operating system as `RESULTS.DAT`. From then on the programmer need only refer to the unit number 7 in an input/output statement in order to read from or write to that file. For example,

```
READ(UNIT=7,FMT=*) a,b,c,d
```

would read the values `a, b, c`, and `d` from the file `RESULTS.DAT`. Similarily,

```
WRITE(UNIT=7,FMT=*) a,b,c,d
```

would write the values in the output list to the file `RESULTS.DAT`.

There is also a statement which allows the programmer to close a file when it is no longer required. For example,

```
CLOSE(UNIT=7)
```

closes the file connected to unit 7 and breaks the connection between the Fortran unit and the file. No more input/output to the unit will be allowed until it is reconnected to the same or a different file.

As a more complete example suppose we wish to write a program to create a personal telephone directory. The program must read in a list of names and telephone numbers and store them permanently in a disc file so that they can be recalled later or printed out for reference. The program could consist of the following steps:

1. set up necessary variables
2. open disc file for output
3. start loop to read names and numbers from terminal and store in a file
   3.1 prompt for name
   3.2 read name
   3.3 if name is a special end-of-input indicator exit from loop
   3.4 prompt for telephone number
   3.6 write name and number to file
   end of loop
4. close file
5. end of program

In Fortran this becomes:

```
PROGRAM TELDIR
!-----------------------------------------------------------!
! Program to create a personal telephone directory file    !
! uses UNIT 1 for disc output to FILE 'TELEPH.DIR'          !
! NAME is expected as surname followed by initials,         !
! e.g. Smith J.    PHONE is expected in the form            !
!  (STD AREA CODE)LOCAL NUMBER                              !
!-----------------------------------------------------------!
CHARACTER(LEN=16) name,phone
OPEN(UNIT=1,FILE='TELEPH.DIR')
  DO
    WRITE(UNIT=*,FMT=*) ' Input NAME?'
    READ(UNIT=*,FMT=*) name
    IF(name == 'END-INPUT') EXIT loop
    WRITE(UNIT=*,FMT=*) ' Input PHONE number?'
    READ(UNIT=*,FMT=*) phone
    WRITE(UNIT=1,FMT=*) name,phone
  ENDDO
CLOSE(UNIT=1)
ENDPROGRAM TELDIR
```

The three main input/output statements illustrated in this simple program are shown in boldface type.

The `OPEN` statement establishes a connection between the unit number, `1`, and a file on disc called `TELEPH.DIR`. By default this file is assumed to be formatted, i.e. the records of the file must be strings of characters, and any `WRITE` (or `READ`) statements must have an associated format specification. This format controls how the information is to be converted between the external representation and the internal representation. In the above example default formatting has been specified with the `FMT=*` specifier. In addition, and again by default, the file is connected for sequential access. The records of the file must be written (or read) in order starting at record one.

The simple form of the `OPEN` statement used above makes no assumption about the status of the file before making the connection. If the file does not exist it is simply created. If it does exist then it is connected to the unit. In the present example because we are writing to the file the existing contents of `TELEPH.DIR` could be destroyed in which case a new file would be created with the same name[1].

The `WRITE` statement specifies that output of information is to go to unit `1`, that is to the file connected to unit `1`. The format to be used is simply the default which is indicated by the `*`. This specifies that each record of the file is to have two fields (since there are only two items in the list) that are character strings of length 16 each. The first of these will contain the name and the second the telephone number.

The final `CLOSE` statement is an instruction to complete the transfer of all the information to the file and to perform any operating system functions necessary to break the connection between unit and the file. Strictly speaking the `CLOSE` statement is not necessary in this program. In this simple example the execution of the final `END` statement of the program would cause any currently open file-unit connections to be closed properly.

A program could be written to read the file `TELEPH.DIR` and display the directory of telephone numbers twenty lines at a time. For example,

---

[1]Exactly what happens depends on how the operating system positions a file. In most cases an existing file is opened and data-transfer operations start at the first record in the file. With some systems, particularly if the file had been used previously in the same program, the file might be left at some later position so some of the old file might not be over-written.

```
PROGRAM TDIRRD
!----------------------------------------------------------!
! Program to read and display a personal telephone         !
! directory. Uses UNIT 1 for input from FILE 'TELEPH.DIR'  !
! NAME is expected to be surname followed by initials,     !
! e.g. Smith J.                                            !
! PHONE is expected to be of the form                      !
!    (STD AREA CODE)LOCAL NUMBER                           !
*----------------------------------------------------------!
CHARACTER(LEN=16) :: name,phone
CHARACTER :: yorn
INTEGER :: i
OPEN(UNIT=1,FILE='TELEPH.DIR')
  DO
    DO 20 i=1,20
      READ(UNIT=1,FMT='(A16,A16)') name,phone
      WRITE(*,*) name,phone
    ENDDO
    WRITE(*,*) ' Display some more (Y/N)?'
    READ(*,FMT='(A1)') yorn
    IF(yorn /= 'Y') EXIT loop
  ENDDO
CLOSE(UNIT=1)
ENDPROGRAM TDIRRD
```

This program again opens the file connecting it to unit `1`, but this time it reads the information recorded in the file by the previous program. It reads 20 records from the file and prints them one per line on the terminal display. It then asks if more are to be displayed. If the response is '`Y`' the next 20 are displayed and so on. Any other response will cause the program to terminate and the file to be closed.

It should be noted that this time we have used explicit format specifications in the two `READ` statements. In the first,

```
READ(UNIT=1,FMT='(A16,A16)') name,phone
```

the second item in the parentheses, following the `FMT=`, is a character constant and not an asterisk as in all previous examples. This character constant is called a format specification. The items in the format list are matched with the variables in the input list. They indicate where on the input record the input list value is to be found and how it is to be converted. In this case both input list items are character variables of length 16. The format specification `(A16,A16)` indicates that the first 16 characters are to be read as the data for the first list item and the next 16 for the second. Since the file was previously written with each record containing two 16 character strings, the data will be read back in exactly the same form as it was written.

We have also used an explicit format, `A1`, in the statement

```
READ(*,FMT='(A1)') yorn
```

so that the first character typed as the response to the question is read and stored in the variable `yorn`.

We have used explicit formats in the above examples since the default (*) format for input assumes that character values in data are represented in the form of character constants, ie. with delimiting quote(' or ") characters included. The default format for output, however, is such that character constants are output without the quote marks. The explicit, `A16`, format simply takes the next 16 characters from the record, whatever they are and so no delimiting quotes are required.

A program can have more than one unit open at a time and can therefore transfer information to, or from, several files during the same program run. A program could be written, for example, to update the telephone directory file of the above example. This could read the existing file on unit `1` and write a new version on unit `2`, say. The number of simultaneously open, connected files allowed is system dependent. On some small systems it may be as few as four or five whereas on some large mainframe machines it may be possible for hundreds of files to be open at the same time.

10.2 The OPEN and CLOSE Statements

A connection between an external file and a Fortran unit is established by the execution of an `OPEN` statement and is broken by a `CLOSE` statement. The general form of the open statement is:

```
OPEN(<open-specifier>,<open-specifier>,...)
```

where each `<open-specifier>` takes one of the `keyword=value` combinations shown below:

```
UNIT= integer expression       -   specifies the unit
                                   number to be connected

FILE= character expression     -   specifies the name of
                                   the file to be connected
```

STATUS= character expression	-	specifies the required status for the file, whether it is required to currently exist or not, or if the connection is for temporary working storage.
ACCESS= character expression	-	specifies the way in which the file may be accessed sequentially or randomly.
RECL= integer expression	-	specifies the length of record for a random access file.
FORM= character expression	-	specifies the nature of the file externally, whether it is formatted as strings of characters or is in some system dependent "binary" form
BLANK= character expression	-	specifies whether blank characters in numeric data are to be treated as zeros or are to be ignored.
POSITION= character expression	-	specifies the position of the file when it is opened.
ACTION= character expression	-	specifies the direction of allowed data-transfer for the file connection, input,output or both.
PAD= character expression	-	specifies whether short records are to be logically padded with blanks or not.
IOSTAT= integer variable	-	provides a failure monitor flag, is set to zero if operation is sucessful, nonzero otherwise.

The UNIT= specifier must appear but all the other specifiers are optional. The UNIT= keyword may be omitted, in which case the integer expression determining the unit must be the first specifier in the list. Thus the statement

```
OPEN(UNIT=4,...)
```

is equivalent to

```
OPEN(4,...)
```

Each individual specifier may occur at most once in any open statement. It is permissible for an open statement to appear without a FILE= specifier, but apart from when a connection is being established for a temporary scratch working space file, when the FILE= must not be present, most OPEN statements include both unit and file specifiers.

More than one OPEN statement for the same unit may occur in a program. If the file involved in the second open is the same as the currently connected file, or the FILE= specifier is omitted then the only other specifier which may have a different value from that which applies for the existing connection is the BLANK= specifier. If the FILE= specifier is present on the second OPEN statement and is different from that of the existing connection then the OPEN statement has the effect of closing the existing file and establishing a new connection for this unit.

A connection can be closed explicitly without creating any new connection for the unit by a CLOSE statement. The general form of the CLOSE statement is:

```
CLOSE(<unit-specifier>,<status-specifier>,
                              <iostat-specifier>)
```

The specifiers have the same form as above for the OPEN. Again the unit specifier is always required but the other specifiers are optional. The execution of a CLOSE statement breaks the connection of a file to a unit if one existed and does nothing if the unit was already disconnected. The status specifier now indicates the required disposition of the file, whether to keep it or delete it.

It is worth noting here that the values of the parameters (apart from IOSTAT) are all general expressions yielding integer or character values. It is possible therefore for the expression following a FILE= to be calculated; in particular it is a common technique to read in the name of a file from data typed in by the user at the time the program is run. This allows the same program to access many different files without change. The following program fragment illustrates this.

```
CHARACTER(LEN=12) fn
WRITE(*,*) 'Type in the name of the file to be processed'
READ(*,FMT='(A12)') fn
OPEN(UNIT=5,FILE=fn)
!--Statements to process the file follow
    ...
    ...
    ...
CLOSE(UNIT=5)
    ...
```

The user of such a program would be prompted for the name of the file to be processed, whereupon the program would open the file and continue to read from or write to it. If these statements were included in a loop the user could type in a different file name each time around the loop.

10.2.1 FILE= and STATUS= specifiers

For many programs the simple open statements already shown are quite adequate, but for more complex programs it becomes desirable to employ some of the further options that exist with the OPEN statement. For instance, the simple forms of OPEN used in the example programs are a little unsafe. In the first example if the file already exists it will be overwritten, which may not be what is required at all. In the second program if the file does not exist the program will fail, but not until the first attempt to read from it. In a complex large program this first attempt to read the file may well be a long way into the program and so quite a lot of computer time may be wasted before this error is detected.

The above deficiencies can be overcome by using the STATUS= qualifier in the OPEN statement when the file is opened. The character expression in the STATUS= specifier of an OPEN statement must have one of the values:

'NEW'	-	the file must not already exist
'OLD'	-	the file must exist already
'UNKNOWN'	-	the existence or otherwise of the file is unknown (This is the default if the specifier is omitted)

'SCRATCH' - this file is to be used for temporary space for the duration of the connection

'REPLACE' - a new file is to be created replacing the existing file, if any.

The STATUS='NEW' qualifier causes the file specified in the FILE= qualifier to be created. The file must not already exist. If it does the OPEN statement will fail and no file will be created.

A file opened with STATUS='OLD' must already exist. If no file of the name specified in the FILE= qualifier exists the OPEN statement will fail.

An 'UNKNOWN' file is one where it does not matter whether the file exists or not. This is the default. The status of a file connected by an OPEN statement without a STATUS= qualifier is 'UNKNOWN'. The file is created if it does not exist and is connected if it does. The two example programs given previously use this default case[2]. The STATUS='REPLACE' option is used when the creation of a new file is required regardless of whether a file exists or not. This option is more tightly specified by the standard and is probably safer than the default for that reason.

A 'SCRATCH' file is used when a temporary file is needed by the program. The temporary file is created by the OPEN statement. Information may be written to it which may then be read back in the same program. When the close statement on the relevant unit is executed the file is automatically deleted. A 'SCRATCH' file must not be named. That is the FILE= qualifier must not be used in an OPEN statement which opens a scratch file.

It can now be seen that the OPEN statements in the two example programs would have been safer if they had been written as:

```
OPEN(UNIT=1,FILE='TELEPH.DIR',STATUS='NEW')
```

in the program to create the telephone directory file, and

```
OPEN(UNIT=1,FILE='TELEPH.DIR',STATUS='OLD')
```

in the program to display the directory. By using statements of this form it is possible to protect information from accidental loss.

---

[2]It should be noted that STATUS='UNKNOWN' is said in the Fortran 90 standard to be system dependent, and therefore the above interpretation is not necessarily valid on all systems. However it is one that has been found useful and it has been implemented on several well-known systems.

The STATUS= specifier can also be used with the CLOSE statement. The allowed values for the character expression now are:

```
'DELETE'    -    the file is to be deleted and not retained in
                 the permanent filestore.

'KEEP'      -    the file is to be disconnected but kept in
                 the filestore.
```

The defaults are DELETE for scratch files and KEEP for all other files. These defaults are usually exactly what is required and so the STATUS= qualifier is rarely used in practice on CLOSE statements.

10.2.2 Access methods (use of ACCESS= and RECL=)

A file in Fortran is considered to be a set of records numbered from one upwards. Files are classified as sequential-access or direct-access according to whether input/output operations on the file are performed strictly in order (i.e. from the first to the last) or whether they may be performed in arbitrary order. Since for a direct access file the tenth record, say, could be read, or written, before the first, all records in such files must have the same length (since the system must know how much room to leave in the file for previous records). Sequential files however, which must be processed record by record in strict order, may contain records of different lengths.

The OPEN statement has two qualifiers relevant to files which are to be accessed in different ways. These are the ACCESS= and RECL= qualifiers. The character expression following the ACCESS= keyword must have one of the values:

```
'SEQUENTIAL'    -    the file is connected for sequential
                     access and records must be written or
                     read in order (the default is
                     sequential)

'DIRECT'        -    the file is connected for direct access
                     and records may be written or read in
                     any order
```

For direct access files the

```
RECL = integer expression
```

is mandatory. The integer expression delivers a value which is the record length for a file connected for direct access. This qualifier must be specified for a file that is accessed by the direct method. In this case it specifies the fixed length of each record. It may be specified for a sequential file, in which case it specifies the maximum length of record to be found in the file.

For a formatted file the record length is measured in characters. For an unformatted file the record length is measured in units which are processor dependent. An explanation of the terms formatted and unformatted is given in the next sub-section. On many processors the record length will be in units of words, where a word is the space needed to store a single integer or real number value, but on others it may be in "bytes", where a byte is the storage unit for a character. On such processors a real or integer number typically requires four bytes of storage.

10.2.3 Formatted and unformatted files

Files may also be classified as *formatted* or *unformatted.* A formatted file contains data which is stored as strings of characters whereas an unformatted file is one that has been written by the current or some previous program. The representation of the data in an unformatted file is system dependent. Essentially the information is transferred between program and file in whatever way the system prefers with each `READ` or `WRITE` statement processing one record. Unformatted files are usually written by one Fortran program to be read by another. They are often implemented by tranferring to or from disc a direct copy of the internal pattern of bits used to represent the values of the various items of data involved in the read or write operation. For this reason they are sometimes referred to as *binary files.* The normal operating system commands for displaying or printing, applied to formatted files, give a perfectly meaningful display of the contents of the file. The same commands applied to unformatted files does not.

In transferring information between formatted files and a program the information must be converted from the external character representation to the internal forms appropriate to the particular types of data. How the character strings representing the values are positioned in the records of the file must also be controlled by the program. This control of conversion and external data layout is called *formatting* and will be covered in the next chapter.

Direct-access files are usually used for internal program needs such as temporary storage areas or for holding data that is to be accessed by other programs. Such files are usually unformatted for efficiency reasons since this avoids the overheads associated with converting from external format to internal form. Sequential-access files on the other hand are often used for holding data that is to be read by the programmer and so these files are usually formatted. On occasions however, unformatted sequential files are required and perhaps less frequently formatted direct access files are useful, so Fortran does allow both possibilities.

The qualifiers that can be used with the `OPEN` statement which relate to the nature of the file representation are `FORM=` and `BLANK=`. The character expression following the `FORM=` keyword must evaluate to:

'FORMATTED'	-	the file is a formatted file and must be read or written with an associated format (the default is FORMATTED for sequential access)
'UNFORMATTED'	-	the file is unformatted and data will be transfered to and from the program without conversion (the default is UNFORMATTED for direct access)

The `BLANK=` specifier only applies to formatted files and only to read operations. The character expression following the keyword may have the values:

'NULL'	-	meaning that in reading numeric fields in a formatted file all blank characters are ignored for the purposes of determining the value except if the whole field is blank then the value is taken to be zero (NULL is the default)
'ZERO'	-	meaning that blanks in a numeric field are treated as zeros

That is if we had the field containing the characters

```
bb123bbb
```

(`b` represents blank) and this was read as an integer, with `BLANK='NULL'` the value would be interpreted as 123, but if `BLANK='ZERO'` was used the value would be 123000.

The meaning of blanks may be changed as often as required during the lifetime of a given connection. This is the only characteristic of a connection that may be changed.

The `PAD=` specifier is permitted only for sequential formatted files, and effects only input from such files. If `PAD='YES'` is specified and an attempt to read a record that is longer than that actually present in the file, the record is read as if it had been padded on the right with as many blanks as required. If `PAD='NO'` is specified an attempt to read past the end of record must not be made. The number of characters read from each record must be less than the number actually stored in the file. If this specifier is omitted `'YES'` is the default.

10.2.4 File positioning and action control

When a sequential file is opened the position at which the first data transfer will occur is controlled by the `POSITION=` specifier. The allowed values for this are:

`'REWIND'` - the file is positioned at the start of the file, just before the first record of the file.

`'APPEND'` - the file is positioned at the end of the file, just after the last record of the file and before the end-of-file record if the file has one.

`'ASIS'` - the file is left positioned where it was left by the system. If the file has not been previously connected this position may be system dependent. This is the default specification.

On most systems a newly opened file is by default at its `REWIND` position, that is at its start. It is a minority of machines that will even allow an `ASIS` file to be set at some position other than at the start, but the fact that there are some such machines means that it is desirable for the file to be opened explicitly either at the start, using `POSITION='REWIND'`, or at the end, `POSITION='APPEND'`.

10.2.5 The direction of transfer

A file can be opened for reading, writing, or both through use of the `ACTION=character expression` specifier. The character expression values are,

`'READ'` - the file is connected for input only, WRITE and ENDFILE statements must not refer to this connection

`'WRITE'` - the file is connected for output only, READ statements must not refer to this connection

```
'READWRITE'      -    the file is connected for both input and
                      output
```

These actions must be possible for the file. For example, an error would result if a `READ` or `READWRITE` specifier were included for connection where the file was in fact a printer. In general, the default for this specifier is system and file dependent. This specifier should be used where it is important to control the use of the connection. It can protect the programmer from accidentally writing to a file and possibly corrupting valuable data. Examples are,

```
OPEN(UNIT=5, ACTION= 'READ',...)
OPEN(UNIT=9, ACTION= 'READWRITE',...)
```

10.2.6 Error detection

Both the `OPEN` and the `CLOSE` statements may optionally have the `IOSTAT=` specifier included. This, if present, is used to report errors which may occur in the connection or the disconnection operation. It has the form

```
IOSTAT = integer variable
```

where `integer variable` is set to zero if the operation is completed successfully and to a positive value if an error occurred in trying to make the connection or disconnection.

For example, if in the telephone directory creation program above, we had used the statement

```
OPEN(UNIT=1,FILE='TELEPH.DIR',STATUS='NEW',IOSTAT=ioerr)
```

and a file called `TELEPH.DIR` already existed on the disc, the program would not terminate with a failure message, as it should if the `IOSTAT` qualifier was omitted. Instead the variable `ioerr` would be set to some positive value and the program would continue. This allows the program to detect such failures and to modify what it does, or to print its own message before stopping. The value of the `IOSTAT=` variable can be tested following the `OPEN` or `CLOSE` and the appropriate action taken depending on its value.

10.3 Data transfer statements

As we have seen in many of the previous example programs the way in which the computer is instructed to transfer information to and from a program is by use of `READ` and `WRITE` statements. The `READ` statement causes information to be read from the file currently connected to the unit specified, into a list of variables which forms part of the statement. The `WRITE` statement performs the reverse operation. It causes the transfer of values listed as part of the statement from the program to the file currently connected to the specified unit.

In this section we shall consider some additional aspects of the `READ` and `WRITE` statements which apply when using files, other than the default.

The general form of a data transfer statement is:

```
READ(control_list) input_list
```

or

```
WRITE(control_list) output_list
```

where `control_list` can contain the following qualifiers:

```
UNIT=integer expression     -    specifies the unit number to
                                 be used for the data
                                 transfer

FMT=character expression, asterisk, or label
                            -    defines the format to be
                                 used to control the
                                 transfer, indicates the use
                                 of the default format, or
                                 identifies the statement
                                 that contains the format to
                                 be used.

REC=integer expression      -    specifies the record number
                                 in a direct access file to
                                 be used for the data
                                 transfer

IOSTAT=integer variable     -    provides a failure monitor
                                 flag

ADVANCE='YES' or 'NO'       -    specifies whether file
                                 positioning is by record or
                                 character
```

10.3.1 `UNIT=` specifier

The `control_list` must specify a unit from which the information is to be read, or to which it is to be written. This can be in the form `UNIT=integer expression`, in which case it may appear anywhere in the list, or it may simply be an integer expression which yields the number of the unit. In this latter case it must be the first item in the `control_list`. Other items that may appear in the `control_list` depend on the nature of the file and the connection that is currently in effect for the unit.

10.3.2 `FMT=` specifier

If the file is formatted then the `control_list` must contain a format specifier. This may be specified using the `FMT=` keyword, in which case it can appear anywhere in the list, or the first two items in the list can be the unit-number integer and the format expression or label. If the file connected is unformatted then no format specifier may be present. For an unformatted transfer each `READ` or `WRITE` transfers a record to or from the file. For formatted files the data transfer starts at the next available record or character depending on whether `ADVANCE='NO'` is present. If it is then the next available character in the file is used, if it is not then each new statement starts a new record. However, the number of records read or written is determined by the interaction of the list of items to be transferred and the relevent format specification (see next chapter). Similarly following an `ADVANCE='NO'` transfer the file is in general positioned just after the last character transferred but still within the last record. Otherwise following a transfer the file is positioned between the previous record and the next.

10.3.3 `REC=` specifier

If the file is connected for direct access then the `control_list` must include a record number for the record to be read or written. This record number can be any integer value between one and the number of records in the file. When a direct access file is being written for the first time it can in principle be written in any order, but on some systems this can cause problems. The `OPEN` statement that establishes the connection does not have any way of specifying how many records the file is to contain. This is not a problem for sequential files since they simply keep on adding data to the end of what is there. The space on disc is extended smoothly and this is an operation that all operating systems can perform. However when a direct access file is created the possibility that record 100 say might be written before record 1 causes some systems considerable difficulty. The space for record 100 and all the previous 99 records has to be reserved just to write one record and this may actually require all the earlier 99 records in fact to be written with dummy values. When creating direct access files for the first time it is a good idea to write them sequentially i.e. write with `REC=1`, then with `REC=2` and so on.

Since direct access records must all be the same length it is usually possible to write and read the same file on the same unit, provided only that an attempt to read a record that has not yet been written is not made. The record may have been written previously in the same program or in a previous program. All that matters is that the record has been written to the file before it is read. However since records in sequential files may be of variable length it is not usually possible for a sequentially accessed file to be both written and read at the same time. It is usually necessary for sequential files to be opened and then written completely, and if the same file must be read in the same program it must be closed and reopened before it can be read. Some systems may have a particular method of organising their file storage which allows sequential files to be read and written simultaneously but this is relatively rare, so any program which depends on doing this is likely to be non-portable. The `REC=` item must not be included on a read or write statement for a unit connected for sequential access since in this case each statement starts its transfer from the next available character of the file.

10.3.4 `IOSTAT=` specifier

`READ` or `WRITE` statements may contain an `IOSTAT=` specifier. This causes the operation of the input/output operations to be monitored. For each operation a return code is placed in the variable specified by the `IOSTAT=` specifier. A zero value signifies that the operation was a success whereas a positive value signifies some system-dependent error has occurred. For `READ` statements on sequential files a negative value signifies that an attempt has been made to read past the end of the file. Therefore files with an unknown number of records can be read by testing the `IOSTAT` variable each time around a loop and exiting the loop when a negative value is found. In such a case a `READ` statement without an `IOSTAT` specifier would cause the program to terminate with an error message when the end of file was reached.

10.3.5 `Additional ADVANCE=` specifiers

There are two other special specifiers that are only allowed when `ADVANCE='NO'` reading is being done. These are:

`SIZE=integer variable`

`EOR=label`

If when reading a record with a `READ` statement that is specified to be `ADVANCE='NO'` on a file with `PAD='YES'` and an attempt to read past the end of record is made, then control is passed to the statement indicated by the `label` in the `EOR=label`. The iostat-variable, if present would also be set to a negative value different from the end-of-file value. The `SIZE=integer variable` would also be set to the number of characters transferred from the file via data-item edit-descriptors to list-variables. Characters added by the padding to satisfy the last item read are not counted. For example,

```
INTEGER :: num_chars
CHARACTER(LEN=80) :: line
OPEN(UNIT=1,FILE='myfile.txt',PAD='YES')
...
record_loop: DO ! until end of record
  READ(1,FMT='(A)',ADVANCE='NO',EOR=999,SIZE=num_chars) line
  ...
  ! process 80 characters read into line
  ...
  CYCLE record_loop
999 CONTINUE
  ...
  ! process num_chars characters read into line and
  ! the end of record special factors
  ...
  EXIT record_loop
ENDDO record_loop
...
```

This fragment of program would enable records of any length to be read and processed in chunks of 80 characters. When an attempt to read more characters than were left in the record the `EOR` branch to statement `999` would be taken. The number of characters actually read from the record into `line` on this last read, which must be less than 80 because an attempt to read past the end of record has occurred, is now contained in the variable `num_chars`. The processing of these characters and any special end-of-record processing can be done and the loop terminated. This is a fairly simple method of using these facilities to enable arbitrary length records to be processed.

10.3.6 The input and output lists

These two lists specify the data objects which are to be involved in the transfer. The `input_list` is the list of variables into which values taken from the file are to be placed by the read statement. The `output_list` is a list of expressions determining the values which will be written to the file by the `WRITE` statement. Both lists are made up of items separated by commas.

An input item may be a variable of any type. If it is an array it stands for all the elements of the array in the array element order. If it is a structured object of a derived type it stands for all the components of the structure in the order that they are defined in the type-definition. An input item may also be an implied-do which contains an `input_list`.

An output item may be an expression, or an implied-do containing an `output_list`. If an array name appears in an output list the values stored in the array are transferred element by element in array element order.

The following are examples of valid `READ` and `WRITE` statements.

```
REAL :: x,y,z,arr(1:10),mat(1:3,1:3)
INTEGER :: i,j,k,ioerr
CHARACTER(LEN=4) :: code
   ...
READ(1,*,IOSTAT=ioerr) code,k,x,y,z,arr(1:k),mat
   ...
WRITE(2,*,IOSTAT=ioerr) code,k,x,y,z,2.0*arr(1:k),mat
   ...
```

10.4 Internal files

It is sometimes desirable to store data in files in such a way that the format of a record, or of a number of records is dependent on the value of one of the items of data in the record. To read such a record correctly requires that it be read first in some universal format that is independent of the the data values. The value of the key item must be checked and the record re-read using the appropriate format for converting the values. This is not possible for a normal external sequential file which allows records to be read once only for any connection. It could be done with a direct access file, but it would require the information to be transferred from the file to the program twice. Since file transfers are in general very much slower than operations in program memory this is undesirable. Fortran 90 therefore includes a facility for reading, and writing, formatted information using an internal file rather than an external unit and file.

An internal file is a character variable, substring, or a character array. It is an area of memory used to simulate a file. A `READ` or `WRITE` statement can be made to operate on an internal file by replacing the unit number in the statement with the name of a character variable or array. If the internal file is a single variable, or substring, then the input/output operation treats the characters in the internal file as a single record with a length that is the length of the character string. If the internal file is a character array then each element in the array is considered to be a record in a formatted sequential file. In this case the file is considered to be positioned at the beginning of the first element at the start of data transfer.

Suppose we had data that had been recorded from a number of different experiments. This data might have been kindly collected together and sent to us as a file on a floppy disc. Suppose that in some experiments the data had been recorded as real numbers in a formatted record, 10 characters to a value and the fixed-point format has been used. In some others it has been recorded 20 characters to a value and in floating-point format. The problem is that the number of records in each experiment is also variable, so we can't know before reading a record whether it contains 8 values in F format or 4 values in E format. To process this file we must read each record from the file into a character variable, check to see which type of record it is and then read the record according to the appropriate conversion format from the internal file, the character variable. The following program reads such a file and reorganises it so that it has every record the same, viz. 8 values each in an unformatted file.

```
PROGRAM reorg
!-----------------------------------------------------------!
! Program to reorganise data file                            !
! Records with a space character at position 11 are          !
! recorded as 8F10.0                                         !
! Records with a non-space character at position 11 are      !
! recorded as 4E20.0 and are always in pairs                 !
!-----------------------------------------------------------!
CHARACTER(LEN=80) :: infile
INTEGER :: ioerr
REAL :: data(8)
OPEN( UNIT=1,FILE='EXPT.RES',STATUS='OLD' )
OPEN( UNIT=2,FILE='EXPT.DAT',STATUS='NEW',&
                     FORM='UNFORMATTED' )
read_loop: DO
  READ(UNIT=1,FMT='(A80)',IOSTAT=ioerr) infile
  IF( ioerr /= 0 ) EXIT read_loop
  !-- test record for form
  IF( infile(11:11) == ' ' )THEN  !-- F FORMAT RECORD
    READ(UNIT=infile,FMT='(8F10.0)') data
    WRITE(UNIT=2) data
  ELSE  !-- E FORMAT RECORD
    READ(UNIT=infile,FMT='(4E20.0)') (data(i),i=1,4)
    READ(UNIT=1,FMT='(A80)') infile
```

```
    READ(UNIT=infile,FMT='(4E20.0)') (data(i),i=5,8)
    WRITE(UNIT=2) data
  ENDIF
ENDDO read_loop
!-- END OF FILE OR READ ERROR PROCESSING
IF( ioerr > 0 ) WRITE(6,*) " READ ERROR -- IOSTAT=",ioerr
CLOSE(UNIT=1)
CLOSE(UNIT=2)
END
```

Data can be transferred from normal variables to a character variable or array by `WRITE` statements with the character variable or array being used as the internal file in an analogous way.

10.5 Inquire

It will often be necessary in a program to find out if a file exists, whether it is connected, or what type it is, before some other input/output statements are executed. An `INQUIRE` statement is provided which allows this to be done. The form of the `INQUIRE` statement is:

```
INQUIRE(inquiry_list)
```

There are two basic types of inquiry, inquiry by file and inquiry by unit. An inquiry by file requests the status of a named file and the `inquiry_list` must contain an item of the form:

```
FILE=fname
```

where `fname` is a character expression whose value is the name of a file. The file of this name may or may not exist. It may or may not be currently connected to a unit.

In an inquiry by unit `inquiry_list` must contain a unit specifier of the form:

```
UNIT=unum
```

where `unum` is a positive integer expression for the unit number. The inquiry is in this case is about the unit and any file that might be connected to the unit at the time the statement is executed.

When the `INQUIRE` statement is executed it will cause values to be assigned to the variables included in the `inquiry_list` to indicate the current status of the file named. The additional items that may be included in an `inquiry_list` are:

`EXIST=lex` - where `lex` is a logical variable that is assigned the value true if a file with the name, `fname`, exists. If the file does not exist `lex` is assigned the value false. Similarly if the inquiry is by unit `lex` is assigned the value true or false according to the existence or otherwise of the unit, `unum`.

`OPENED=lod` - where `lod` is a logical variable that is assigned the value true if the specified file, or unit, is currently connected. It is assigned the value false otherwise.

`NUMBER=num` - where `num` is an integer variable that is assigned the value of the unit number that is currently connected to the file. It becomes undefined if the file is not currently connected to a unit. This inquiry item is useful only for inquire by file statements.

`NAME=fnm` - where `fnm` is a character variable that is assigned the name of the file. If the inquiry is by unit it is the name of the file currently connected or is undefined if no file is connected. Note that, if the inquiry is by file the value of `fnm` need not be identical to that specified by the `FILE=` item. It may contain other information which allows the name to identify the file more exactly, e.g., the user identification of the user who owns the file might be added, or a disc volume name, etc. This extra information may not have been necessary for the identification of the file in the `FILE=`, being provided by system defaults. However the value `fnm` must be useable in any subsequent `OPEN` statement to identify the same file.

`ACCESS=acc` - where `acc` is a character variable that is assigned the value `'SEQUENTIAL'` or `'DIRECT'` depending on the access method which applies for the current file connection. If there is no connection then the result is undefined.

`SEQUENTIAL=seq` - where `seq` is a character variable that is assigned the value `'YES'` or `'NO'` depending on whether the file can be accessed sequentially or not. If the processor cannot determine whether sequential access is possible or not it returns the result, `'UNKNOWN'`.

`DIRECT=dir` - where `dir` is a character variable that is assigned the value `'YES'` or `'NO'` depending on whether the file can be accessed directly or not. If the processor cannot determine whether direct access is possible or not it returns the result, `'UNKNOWN'`.

`FORMATTED=fmt` - where `fmt` is a character variable that is assigned the value `'YES'` or `'NO'` depending on whether the file can be connected for formatted input/output. If the processor cannot determine whether formatted input/output is possible the result returned is `'UNKNOWN'`.

`UNFORMATTED=unfmt` - where `unfmt` is a character variable that is assigned the value `'YES'` or `'NO'` depending on whether the file can be connected for unformatted input/output. If the processor cannot determine whether unformatted input/output is possible the result returned is `'UNKNOWN'`.

`FORM=frm` - where `frm` is a character variable that is assigned the value `'FORMATTED'` or

'UNFORMATTED' depending on whether the file is connected for formatted or unformatted input/output. If the file is not currently connected the result is undefined.

NEXTREC=recn - where recn is an integer variable that is assigned the value n+1 when the last record written to or read from the file connected was record number n. If the file is connected but no input/output has yet been done on the file the result is 1. This inquiry applies only to files connected for direct access. If the file is not so connected the result becomes undefined.

RECL=recl - where recl is an integer variable that is assigned the value of the record length for the file currently connected. This inquiry applies only for files connected for direct access. If the file is not so connected then the result is undefined. Note that, to be strictly consistent with the Fortran 90 standard the record length must always be specified when opening a file for direct access and if the file being opened already exists the specified record length and the existing record length must be the same, unless a new file is being created with the same name. This makes this inquiry one of rather limited utility. However many implementations have allowed an existing file to be opened for direct access without the inclusion of the RECL= specifier, the value being taken from the existing file. In this case the inquiry is very useful for finding what the actual value is.

A typical use of the INQUIRE statement would be to find out if a file exists before processing some data. For example, one might want to modify the telephone directory creation program so that it could either update an existing file or create a new directory. Such a program would need to test to see if a file already existed and if so new records could be written to the same file, otherwise the file would need to be created. We will assume that we are going to use an unformatted direct access file to hold the directory.

```
   ...
LOGICAL :: oldfil
   ...
INQUIRE(FILE='PHONE.DIR',EXIST=oldfil)
IF(oldfil)THEN  !-- FILE EXISTS
  OPEN(UNIT=1,FILE='PHONE.DIR',ACCESS='DIRECT',RECL=32, &
        FORM='UNFORMATTED',STATUS='OLD')
ELSE  !-- FILE DOES NOT EXIST
  OPEN(UNIT=1,FILE='PHONE.DIR',ACCESS='DIRECT',RECL=32, &
         FORM='UNFORMATTED',STATUS='NEW')
ENDIF
   ...
```

10.6 Exercises

1. Write a program to open a new sequential file on unit 4 called MARKS.DAT. The program should then read a student's name followed by his/her marks for four exams from the keyboard (the default unit) and write these to the file. Repeat the read/write process until a student with the name "END" is entered. Close the output file.

2. Write a program to read the file produced above and to print a list of students and their average marks.

3. Amend the program in Exercise 1 to allow the optional appending of records to MARKS.DAT.

4. Explain the difference between a sequential file and a direct access file. When would the latter be used in preference to the former.

5. Write a program to create a sequential file of 10 records containing the names and addresses of a group of people. Assume that 32 characters each is enough to hold the names and addresses. Having written the file, read back the records in reverse order and print them out. (Hint: after creating the file, re-open it as a direct access file.)

6. Write a program which opens a file for reading specified by typing its name at a terminal. Check that the file has been opened correctly and,

if it hasn't, allow the user to specify an alternative or stop the program.

7. Modify the program of Exercise 6 to check that the file exists before trying to open it.

Chapter 11

External Data Layout, Formats

In the previous chapter we described how external files could be connected to a Fortran program for formatted or unformatted input/output. Unformatted files are represented as a series of records, one record for each `READ` or `WRITE` statement. They are recorded in a file in whatever manner the Fortran processor chooses. Unformatted files are usually stored as a direct copy of computer memory and as such cannot be read easily by computer users. They are not meant to be edited, displayed, or printed by standard operating system commands. Formatted files are also represented as a series of records but each `READ` or `WRITE` statement from or to a formatted file can correspond to more than one input or output record. Formatted files consist of records which contain strings of characters which are human readable. They can be edited, created or manipulated by means other than Fortran.

Formatted files are represented in a form that is understandable to the external world, therefore when they are read or written, data must be converted to and from the internal (binary) representation used for storing data inside the computer. On input this means that the computer must be programmed to "understand" what an input record means; it must be told where on each record a data value is situated. The program can then convert the data to an appropriate internal form corresponding to the item being read. On output the machine must be told where on an output record a particular data item is to be positioned and also how it is to appear. The specification of this input/output information is called formatting.

When considering input/output there are three main input/output devices that we are concerned with. These are disc files, displays, and printers. In the following we shall consider input/output to files. When we talk of records we mean records in a file. For the purposes of formatting, a display can also be thought of as a file. Each input record is a line typed on the keyboard, each output record is a line displayed on the screen. Printers are slightly different and so we shall talk about these separately.

There are two ways in which format information can be specified in Fortran:

List-directed formatting: This is the form we have used almost exclusively up until now. It is chosen by specifying an asterisk for the `FMT=` qualifier of a `READ` or `WRITE` statement. Thus for list-directed formatting to the default unit we would have, for input `READ(UNIT=*,FMT=*)` and for output `WRITE(UNIT=*,FMT=*)`. These can be shortened to `READ(*,*)` and `WRITE(*,*) where the first asterisk specifies the unit and the second specifies the format.` On input, data must be presented in a form which is defined by the Fortran 90 standard and which is described below. On output, data will appear in a form which is strictly processor dependent although the general appearance will be similar on different machines.

Explicit formatting: With this method the user defines precisely the form that external data should take. This means that for input and output the user determines both the position and the appearance of data in a particular record. Use of explicit formatting ensures that the behaviour of input/output is consistent across different machines.

11.1 List-directed formatting

Although in most cases a file written by list-directed formatting is suitable for reading by this method of formatting, there are cases where this may not be totally true. There are a number of subtle differences between input and output using list-directed formatting so these will be treated separately.

11.1.1 List-directed input formatting

For list-directed input the data values must be represented in a file as character strings of the form used for constants of the relevant type. For reals the data values can take the form of fixed point constants or floating point constants. The file must be broken into records and the data must be organised in these records in such a way as to take account of the fact that each new read statement starts a new record. Otherwise the data are represented as a sequence of values of the appropriate types separated by one of the following value separators:

- one or more contiguous blanks
- a comma surrounded by any number of contiguous blanks, including none
- a slash surrounded by any number of contiguous blanks, including none
- end of record preceded or followed by any number of blanks

Note that for logical data a value may be `.TRUE.` or `.FALSE.` but could also be any character string beginning with `T` or `F`.

It should also be noted that if the list item is of type character the data constant should normally be delimited by apostrophes, or quotes, in which case the value may contain blanks, commas, and slash characters, which in this context are not treated as separators. The data character string may, if necessary, be continued from one record to the next. In this case the end of record is ignored. It does not result in any characters being transferred into the list variable. The delimiter apostrophes, or quotes, may be omitted when the variable in the input list is of type character but in this case the value may not contain blanks, commas or slash characters. If this is done the value read is the string from the first non-blank character until the first value separator.

The following example which reads variables of different types using two READ statements illustrates the above points.

```
REAL                :: R1,R2,R3
INTEGER             :: I1,I2
CHARACTER(LEN=10)   :: C1,C2
LOGICAL             :: L1,L2
READ(UNIT=*,FMT=*) I1,R1,C1,L1
READ(UNIT=*,FMT=*) I2,R2,C2,L2,R3
```

Data records for this program fragment could be (using spaces as delimiters):

```
5    6.3    'TEST' TRUE
312  1.0E-05 'TEST2' F   .3245
```

or using commas as delimiters and omitting the apostrophes,

```
5,6.3,TEST,TRUE
312,1.0E-05,TEST2,F,.3245
```

or with a slight rearrangement and using the fact that the end-of-record can be a delimiter,

```
5   6.3 'TEST'
TRUE
312 1.0E-05
'TEST2' F .3245
```

The following arrangement however would not have the desired effect,

```
5   6.3 'TEST' TRUE 312
 1.0E-05 'TEST2' F .3245
```

With this arrangement the first four values would be read correctly into the variables `i1,r1,ch1,l1` but the fifth value would be ignored. The variables `i2,r2,ch2,l2` would be read off the next record (since each `READ` statement starts a new record) and then the program would attempt to read the value for `r3` off the next record.

11.1.1.1 Repeated data items: If the same value is to be read into a number of consecutive input-list variables the constant representing the value can be preceeded by an appropriate repeat factor. For example, if we had wanted to read the value zero into a whole array of size 100, say, we could write,

```
REAL,DIMENSION(100) :: a
   ...
READ(*,*) a
   ...
```

and we could type the data as,

```
100*0.0
```

In general the form

```
      r*c
```

is permissible where `c` is any valid constant and `r` is a positive integer constant. This is equivalent to having the data

```
      c,c,c, ...
```

with `c` repeated `r` times in the file. The corresponding `READ` statement must therefore have `r` consecutive variables of the same type as `c` in the input-list. Note, the repeated data form may not be used for character strings where the delimiters are omitted.

11.1.1.2 Null values: List-directed input works as if the external constant was assigned by an assignment statement to the corresponding list variable, except in the case when the external constant represents a null value. This can happen if:

- the first non-blank character in the first record read by a READ statement is a separator (comma, slash, end of record). This means that the first value for the first variable in the list is null.
- two separators appear with no intervening non-blank characters. This is interpreted as a null value for the corresponding list variable.
- the input contains a string of the form `r*` with no constant following the `*`. This is taken to mean read `r` consecutive null values.
- a slash separator is encountered in the input. This means that if there are any variables remaining in the input-list they are taken as having null values assigned to them to complete the execution of the READ statement.

The effect of assigning a null value to a variable via a list-directed READ statement is to leave the value of that variable unchanged. This particular facility can be useful for handling the situation when a program is controlled by a number of parameters which are given default values, say by initialisation in a declaration statement, but where one or two of them may need changing. However, some care needs to be exercised when using this facility since counting commas can be a hazardous pastime. Programs that require the changing of, say, the 7th and the 13th variable in a `READ(*,*)` list are apt to go wrong, since use of the null/default facility in these circumstances would require the user to type,

```
,,,,,,15,,,,,,3.141
```

The risks of mis-counting are all too obvious.

11.1.2 List-directed output formatting

For list-directed output the values will be written out in the form of constants separated by one or more blanks or a comma surrounded by any number of blanks. The processor can end a record and start a new record anywhere it needs to, except it may not end a record in the middle of a value other than a character constant. This means that the programmer does not have precise control over where a data item will appear within a record.

Integer values are output as ordinary integer constants, employing enough characters to represent the largest representable integer value (including a sign) with one or more spaces in front of the value. Real numbers are also represented with a few spaces preceding the actual constant, which will be in fixed-point form for values of a reasonable magnitude and floating-point form for more extreme values. The exact values at which the form changes are processor-dependent. The number of characters used to represent the value will also be processor-dependent and will normally be sufficient to represent the effective number of decimal figures that can be stored correctly by the processor.

Logical data is output as a `T` or an `F`. The forms used for numeric or logical data output are suitable for input using list-directed formatting. However this is not necessarily the case for character data. Character values are normally transferred as character strings without the delimiting apostrophes that may be required for an input character constant. Nor does the processor insert any value separator before or after the output of a character value. It can however insert an end of record if required. In this case the first character of the new record is an added blank for use as printer carriage control if the file is printed. Character data written by list-directed formatting may well not be readable by list-directed formatting. It is possible to ensure that such output is readable by causing the delimiters to be used. This is achieved by adding the

```
DELIM='QUOTE'
```
or
```
DELIM='APOSTROPHE'
```

to the `OPEN` statement for the file connection.

11.2 Explicit formatting

The `FMT=` specifier on a `READ` or `WRITE` statement may be given as a character value which contains the format list or as a statement label of a `FORMAT` statement which includes the format list. The format list is a list of edit descriptors which specify how data is to be transferred between the items in the input/output list and the records of the external file. We therefore have the following possibilities for formatted `READ` and `WRITE` statements:

```
READ                                     <char value>
or     (UNIT= <unit number>, FMT=          or          ) i/o-list
WRITE                                    <label>
```

where the `<char value>` must be of the form of a format list and the `<label>` refers to a labelled statement of the form,

```
<label> FORMAT format-list
```

A format list is enclosed in parentheses and like most lists in Fortran is a sequence of items separated by commas. Each item is either a data value edit descriptor, a layout control descriptor, or an embedded format list enclosed in parentheses.

For example, we may need to read three integers from a formatted file that has been connected to unit 1. The record containing these values holds the first integer in the first five character positions, the second in the next three and the third in the following two. Figure 11.1 below, with the character positions shown by the "scale", shows the layout of the values. In the examples below, where it is necessary to be precise, we shall indicate a blank or space character by a lower case 'b'. The record can be thought of as being split up into fields containing different numbers of characters. The type of data and the number of characters in each field is defined by a *data value edit descriptor*, often just called an *edit descriptor*.

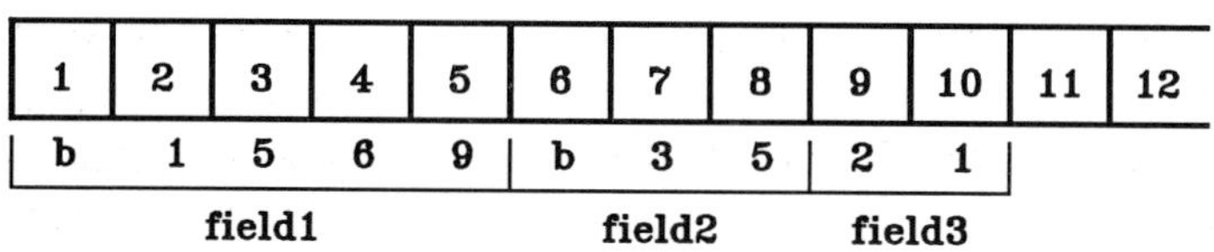

Figure 11.1: A formatted record

The required `READ` statement for the above record could be either

```
READ(UNIT=1,FMT='(I5,I3,I2)') int1,int2,int3
```

or the combination

```
      READ(UNIT=1,FMT=1000) int1,int2,int3
 1000 FORMAT(I5,I3,I2)
```

The items `I5,I3,I2` are the edit descriptors for the three integer values. The effect of the `READ` statement coupled with the format information is that the program starts to scan the input list, the format list and the input record all in parallel. The first input variable in the input list is matched with the first edit descriptor in the format list. This results in the variable `int1` being matched with the edit descriptor `I5`. The `I5` indicates that the representation of the value to be converted to the internal form for the integer data type is located in the first five characters of the input record. The characters,

```
blank 1 5 6 9
```

are therefore converted to the internal form for the value 1569 and assigned to the variable `int1`. The second input variable is then processed by matching it with the second data value edit descriptor in the format list. The correspondence is now between `int2` and `I3`. This again indicates that the conversion is to be for an internal form for an integer but that this time the external value is to be found in the next three characters of the record. The characters are,

```
blank 3 5
```

and the result will be the value 35 assigned to `int2`. The input list still has the third item to be processed, `int3`, this is matched with the next data value descriptor, `I2`, which causes the next two characters from the input record to be converted to an integer value, 21, and this is assigned.

All formatted input/output operates in this way with parallel scanning of the input/output list, the format list and the input/output record. The format list is always scanned so that an edit descriptor is made to correspond with an item in the input/output list.

It is possible for a format specification to contain layout edit descriptors as well as data value edit descriptors. For example in the format `'(I3,T5,I5)'` the `T5` causes five character positions to be skipped before the characters specified by `I5` are read. Layout descriptors may even cause a change of record to occur. When a format list is scanned in order to match an input/output list item with a valid format descriptor, any layout descriptors are processed as they are encountered. This allows new records to be taken, captions to be added, or position in the record to be changed before the next data item is processed. Thus in the statement:

```
READ(*,'(I5,T10,I4/I5)') I,J,K
```

`I` will be read from the first five character positions of the record, `J` will be read from character positions 16 to 19 and `K` will be read from the next record since / indicates a change of record.

The main[1] data value edit descriptors are:

```
Iw       -   for integer data

Fw.d }
Ew.d }   -   for real data
Gw.d }

Aw       -   for character data

Lw       -   for logical data
```

These edit descriptors must match with an input/output list item of the corresponding type. They control how the characters of the external record are related to the internal data value.

The most important layout edit descriptors are:

```
nX                 -   skip n characters
Tc                 -   tab to character position c
TLn                -   tab left n characters
TRn                -   tab right n characters
/                  -   end current record
'<any string>'     -   insert <any string> in the record
                       (output only)
```

The same edit descriptors, (except for an embedded string), may appear in a format controlling a READ statement as well as in one controlling a WRITE statement, but their meaning in the two cases is subtly different. We shall therefore explain the meaning of the edit descriptors for input and output separately.

11.2.1 Input data value edit descriptors

The effect of the data value edit descriptors for each of the basic Fortran data types is described in what follows. The main function of each of these edit descriptors is to specify the number of characters (representing a value)

---

[1] We are only covering the most commonly used of the format descriptors in this chapter. There are a large number of specialist descriptors defined in the language. For example descriptors to use a non-decimal radix for the representation of integers or represent real values in engineering notation where the exponent is divisible by 3. These specialist descriptors differ only in detail from those covered and the details are probably best found from the documentation for the particular system actually being used.

which are to be taken from the current input record and assigned to the corresponding variable in the input list.

11.2.1.1 Integers: The integer edit descriptor is the letter `I` followed by an integer constant,

```
Iw
```

where `w` is the width of the input field. When `Iw` is encountered in a format list it must be associated with an input list variable that is of type integer. The constant, `w`, indicates that the next w characters in the input record are to be interpreted as containing an integer value. The following are some typical examples of the use and effect of `I` format:

```
Record         READ statement                  Values assigned

b31            READ(1,'(I3)') k                k=31
b31b21         READ(1,'(I3,I3)') k,m           k=31 m=21
b31b21         READ(1,'(I4,I2)') k,m           k=31 m=21
                                               (if BLANK='NULL')
                                               k=310 m=21
                                               (if BLANK='ZERO')
b31b21         READ(1,'(I1,I5)') k,m           k=0 m=3121
                                               (if BLANK='NULL')
                                               k=0 m=31021
                                               (if BLANK='ZERO')
bb-12345       READ(1,'(2I4)') k,m             k=-1 m=2345
```

These examples should be fairly self-explanatory. It should be noted that if there are a number of adjacent integers that are to be read each with the same format descriptor then the effective format can be repeated by putting the number in front. For example, we used a format `'(I3,I3)'` above, which could have been written more compactly as `'(2I3)'`. The compact form was used above in the last example.

In the above examples there is one format descriptor corresponding to each item of the input list of variables. Each descriptor indicates which characters of the record are to be used to determine the value. The third and fourth examples also show how the different interpretations of blank characters can affect the value. That is, they show the potential effects of the `BLANK=` specifier of the `OPEN` statement. If `BLANK='ZERO'` is in force then it is particularly important for the integer value to be "right-justified" in the input field since any trailing blanks will be interpreted as zeros and will have the effect of multiplying the value assigned to the input variable by ten. This of course could produce unintended results.

11.2.1.2 Reals: The possible descriptors are `Fw.d`, `Ew.d`, or `Gw.d`, and the corresponding input variable for any of these must be of type real. These descriptors, as we shall see later, differ in their effects on output but, on input they are all essentially equivalent. The `w.d` must be a string of characters in the form of a fixed-point constant. For example, `F10.6`, `E12.5`, `G3.1`. The `w` part determines the number of characters from the input which will contain the value; that is `w` determines the width of the input field for the value. The `d` indicates how many of the characters in the input field are to be considered to be to the right of the decimal point unless the input field contains an explicit decimal point, in which case this determines the number of decimal places involved regardless of the value of `d`.

If the external numbers are all represented with decimal points included explicitly, then for input the only two things that matter about the format descriptor are that:

a) it be one of the real descriptors, and

b) that the width of field is correct.

That is, any of the `F`, `E`, or `G` format descriptors would be acceptable and the value of `d` would be irrelevent. The following would be a suitable statement to read three real numbers,

```
READ(1,'(F12.3,F12.3,F12.3)') a,b,c
```

or since the three formats are the same this would usually be written using a repeat factor as,

```
READ(1,'(3F12.3)') a,b,c
```

Valid input records that could be read by such a statement and which would read the same values into `a,b,c` could be:

```
bbbbb3.14159bbbbbb2.1789bbbb-156.123
```

where all the values are recorded in fixed-point form with explicit decimal points,

```
b0.314159E+1bb0.21789E+1b-1.56123E+2
```

where all values are recorded in floating-point form with explicit decimal point and explicit exponent character, `E`, or

```
bbbb314159-2bbbbb21789-1bbbbb-156123
```

where no explicit decimal point is used but the `d` part of the format descriptor is used along with exponents (without the explicit `E` exponent character) where necessary. The last example is interpreted by assuming an exponent is present if a sign is encountered in the middle of digits within the field. The sign and the digits to the right of it are taken as the decimal exponent (-2 in the first number). The decimal point is then assumed to be d (in this case 3) digits to the left of this exponent, or d digits to the left of the end of the field if there is no exponent. The value of `a` above is therefore interpreted as

314.159×10^{-2}

The above input forms can be mixed at will but the data is very much easier to read if explicit decimal points and explicit exponents are used. The form illustrated in the last example where implicit decimal point and implicit exponents are used is useful when the amount of data is large since it can significantly reduce the number of key strokes required to enter the data into the machine.

11.2.1.3 Characters: The character format descriptor is, `Aw`, is used for controlled input of character strings. As for other formats the `w` in the `Aw` format determines how many characters are to be used to determine the value to be assigned to the corresponding character variable in the input list. For example,

```
READ(UNIT=5,FMT='(2A10)')  surnam,fornam
```

This statement would accept any record with at least 20 characters. It is the user's responsibility to ensure that these 20 characters are correctly made up of two fields of ten, each containing the required information. For example, the following records would all be read without problem by the above statement:

```
(scale line to show position in record)
12345678901234567890

     JONES      JOHN
      TELL   WILLIAM
  EINSTEIN    ALBERT
    FORMBY    GEORGE
  NICKLAUS      JACK
SCHONFELDER   LAWRIE
```

All of these records would be read with the desired effect except the last. In this case `surnam` would end up containing the value `'SCHONFELDE'` and `fornam` would contain `'R   LAWRIE'`. Some care is obviously needed with character input/output to ensure that such cases (e.g. people with perversely long names!) are allowed for, otherwise data can easily be inadvertently mis-read.

With character edit descriptors and input it is necessary to consider what happens when the field-width, `w`, is equal to, less than, or greater than the length of the corresponding character variable. In the following examples the character variable `NAME` is assumed to be declared as

```
CHARACTER(LEN=12) :: NAME
```

Consider the statement

```
READ(UNIT=5,FMT='(A12)') NAME
```

which is similar in structure to the previous example in that the length of the character variable is exactly the same as the width of the input field. In this case the effect is obvious and the first twelve characters of the record are assigned to `NAME`. In this special case where the field width is equal to the length of the corresponding character variable, the field width may be omitted. Thus the above statement could be written as,

```
READ(UNIT=5,FMT='(A)') NAME
```

This form has the advantage that if the length of any character variable is altered there is no need to modify associated formats since these will, in effect, adjust automatically to the change.

The effect of the statement

```
READ(UNIT=5,FMT='(A7)') NAME
```

where the field width is less than the length of the corresponding character variable, is that the first seven characters are read in, padded out on the right by blanks up to the length of `NAME` and assigned to the variable `NAME`. If the input record was

```
WILLIAMSONbbbbbbb...
```

then `NAME` would contain `WILLIAMbbbbb`. In general, if `w` is less than the length of the variable, w characters are read from the input record and are assigned to the left-hand end of the variable and the right is padded with blanks to fill the variable.

If the field width specified in character edit descriptors is greater than the length of the corresponding character variable then the rightmost characters of the field are assigned to the input variable. For example the statement,

```
READ(UNIT=5,FMT='(A15)') NAME
```

where `NAME` is a character variable of length 12 were used to read the record

```
BUCKINGHAMSHIRE
```

then `NAME` would contain `'KINGHAMSHIRE'`, not `'BUCKINGHAMSH'` as might have been expected from the rules of assignment.

11.2.1.4 Logicals: The format edit descriptor for logical data is `Lw`. Again `w` determines the width of the field in the input record in which the value will be found. The field may have any number of leading blank characters followed by,

`T` or `.T`

meaning a value of true, or

`F` or `.F`

meaning false.

The remaining characters in the field, if any, are ignored. The following would be a valid `READ` statement with a number of suitable input records,

```
READ(UNIT=8,FMT='(3L7)') MALE,ON,ERROR

(scale line to show field positions)
123456712345671234567

bbbbbbTbbbbbbFbbbbbbT
TANYG89FCHARS6TAT ALL
b.TRUE..FALSE.b.TRUE.
```

All three records would produce the same result with MALE set to true, ON to false and ERROR to true. The last record indicates that the form for logical constants is also a valid logical input form.

11.2.2 Input layout edit descriptors

The layout descriptors are used on input to skip over characters in the record and to force new records to be read at appropriate places. Normally, when a READ statement is executed a new record of the file is started. The input record is processed from the first character of the indicated record if the file is being read as direct access (i.e. FORM='DIRECT') or from the first effective character of the file if it is being processed sequentially. This will be the first character of the next record if either the previous READ or this one is of the ADVANCE='YES' type, even if the previous READ and FORMAT did not read all the characters of the previous record. If this READ is of the non-advancing type the first character is the next available character in the file. If the previous READ was also non-advancing then the first character may be in those remaining unread from the previous record.

Having determined the first character to be processed in the input stream it is necessary to locate the characters to be used as the input field containing the required value. To do this it may be necessary to skip some characters. It may also be necessary to start a new record or skip some characters in the middle of processing a single READ statement. These actions are caused by including the appropriate layout descriptors in the format list.

Layout descriptors are not associated with any input list items. When the parallel scan of input list and format list encounters a layout descriptor it is processed before the next value is input. If the last variable in the input list is read and the format has not reached the end of the format list any layout descriptors that are in the format before the next data value descriptor, or the end the format whichever is first will be acted upon before the execution of the READ statement is completed.

11.2.2.1 Positioning within a record: Most of the layout descriptors control the positioning within a record. The nX and TRn descriptors cause a skip right. When the scanning process encounters either of these descriptors the current processing position in the input record is moved to the right by n characters. The parameter n must be an integer constant. For example if the statement,

```
READ(UNIT=1,FMT='(I3,TR3,I3)') J,K
```

was used when reading a record such as

```
b10123999
```

the values 10 and 999 would be assigned to `J` and `K`, respectively. The characters `123` in the middle would be skipped because of the `TR3` layout edit descriptor. The use of `3X` instead of `TR3` would have had exactly the same effect.

The `TLn` descriptor causes the record processing position to be moved to the left `n` characters. This allows the same portion of a record to be read more than once in possibly different ways. The statements

```
INTEGER :: DAY,MONTH,YEAR,CENT
   ...
READ(UNIT=2,FMT='(I2,TR1,I2,TR1,I4,TL4,I2)') &
DAY,MONTH,YEAR,CENT
```

would read a record with the date recorded as

```
b3-b9-1939
```

and produce the results `DAY=3,MONTH=9,YEAR=1939,CENT=19`.

The `X` and `TR` descriptors are basically "tab-right-relative" instructions. The `TL` descriptor is a "tab-left-relative" instruction. The descriptor `Tc`, where `c` is again an integer constant, is a "tab absolute" instruction. The effect is to move the current processing position to the `c`th character position in the record. The `T` edit descriptor is useful in allowing a record to be read and then re-read in another way. A `T1` will cause scanning to start again at the start of the record. The record can then be re-read using different edit descriptors. Note, the absolute tab or the tab-left-relative descriptors are not permitted to cause the current character position to move back past the start of the current record or the first character position of this read.

11.2.2.2 Forcing new records: The slash `/` edit descriptor causes processing of the current record to be terminated. Any subsequent processing will occur from the next record. Any characters remaining in the current record when a `slash` is encountered in the format list are ignored. The slash may be used as an edit descriptor, separated from other descriptors in the list by commas, or it can be used as an alternative separator to a comma. Two consecutive slashes cause a record to be skipped, n consecutive slashes causes n-1 records to be skipped.

11.2.3 Output edit descriptors

The same edit descriptors are used to control the conversion and positioning of values to be output as are used for input, but the effects are subtly different, particularly for the real edit descriptors.

11.2.3.1 Integer formats: The descriptor is, as for input, `Iw`, and a repeat factor may be used if the same descriptor is to be used a number of times. The number of characters written to the output record, the width of the output field, is again given by `w`. The value of the corresponding output list item, which must be an expression of type integer, is converted into a string of characters of length `w`. The rightmost characters are the numeric characters necessary to represent the absolute value of the integer as a decimal number. These are preceded by a sign if the number is negative and the string padded on the left with blanks to the required length. The output value is said to be right-justified in its field. For example, if we have a set of integer variables with values defined by:

```
I = 3
J = 1001
K = 12
L = -5
```

the statements

```
WRITE(UNIT=6,FMT='(I4)') I
WRITE(UNIT=6,FMT='(4I5)') I,J,K,L
```

would produce output records containing,

```
bbb3
bbbb3b1001bbb12bbb-5
```

If the value of the integer is too large to fit into the width of field allowed, including the space for any sign if one is needed, the whole field is filled with asterisk, `*`, characters.

11.2.3.2 Real formats: As for input there are `F`, `E`, and `G` format edit descriptors. However, for output formatting there are quite significant differences between the three formats. The `F` format causes the value to be converted into a character string in fixed-point form, the `E` format converts to floating-point form, and the `G` format uses fixed or floating-point form depending on the magnitude of the value being output.

11.2.3.2.1 F format - This format is used when numbers are required to be output in fixed-point form. The descriptor has the form, `Fw.d`, where `w` is the field width and `d` is the number of digits which are required after the decimal point. The value of the corresponding expression in the output list is converted to a character string of length `w` which is transferred to the output record. The value will be converted to a normal decimal number with `d` digits after the decimal point. There will then be one or more digits to the left of the point depending on the value, and a sign if necessary. The value will be right-justified in the field and padded on the left with the required number of blank characters. If the value requires more than `d` decimal places to represent it correctly, it is rounded to `d` places during the conversion process. If the magnitude of the number is too great for it to fit into the allowed field width, the field is filled with asterisk characters.

The following is a table showing the effect of different values and different F formats.

Value	Format	Output field
4.63	F8.3	bbb4.630
4.63	F5.2	b4.63
-4.63	F5.2	-4.63
4.63	F5.1	bb4.6
4.69	F5.1	bb4.7
101.5	F5.1	101.5
-101.5	F5.1	*****

N.B. with F format the range of values that can be represented is limited. For example, with a format of `F5.1` the most negative value that can be represented is -99.9 and the largest positive value is 999.9 or +99.9 depending on whether the sign is included or not.

11.2.3.2.2 E format - This descriptor is used for the output of numbers in floating-point form. The form of the descriptor is, `Ew.d`, where `w` is the field width and `d` is the number of digits of precision required in the output representation. The value of the corresponding expression in the output list is rounded to `d` significant decimal digits and the output field is constructed as a character string of length `w`. The value is represented in the form,

$\texttt{b...bs0.}D_1D_2\texttt{...}D_d\texttt{Eexp}$

where `s` is the sign of the value, $D_1 \ldots D_d$ are the digits of the value and `exp` is the signed decimal exponent. The field is padded on the left with blanks as required. The exponent may be represented as a two-digit or three-digit signed integer depending on the range of values available on the particular processor. This means that `w` must be greater than `d+6`, or `d+7`, for the value to fit into the field. This is to allow space for the four or five characters needed for the exponent and the E, the decimal point, the zero before the point and the sign as well as the significant digits. However provided this is the case E format can be used to output any representable real value regardless of magnitude.

The following shows the effect of E format.

Value	Format	Output field
4.63	E10.3	b0.463E+01
4.63	E10.2	bb0.46E+01
4.63	E10.1	bbb0.5E+01
-4.63	E10.3	-0.463E+01
101.5	E11.4	b0.1015E+03
0.1015	E11.4	b0.1015E+00
0.001015	E11.4	b0.1015E-02

E formats are normally used if the magnitudes of the output values are known to be very large or very small so that F format would have to be of unreasonable width for them to be represented. It is also common to use E format when the magnitudes are unknown before the program runs since E format guarantees output of the values, not a field full of asterisks.

11.2.3.2.3 G format - With this descriptor, which again has the form `Gw.d`, the output field always represents `d` significant digits, but floating-point form is used only if the value being output is less than `0.1` or is greater than `10**d`. For other values a fixed-point representation is used. That is the effect of `Gw.d` can be expressed as equivalent E or F formats depending on the value of the corresponding output list item. If `x` is the magnitude of the value of the output item then the various ranges of values of `x` and the equivalent effective formats are shown below, where `'bbbb'` indicates an extra four blanks added to the right of the field to pad it out to the required width of `w`.

Value Range	Effective Format
0.0 < X < 0.1	Ew.d
0.1 < X < 1.0	F(w-4).(d),'bbbb'
1.0 < X < 10.0	F(w-4).(d-1),'bbbb'
10.0 < X < 100.0	F(w-4).(d-2),'bbbb'
....	....
10**(d-2) < X < 10**(d-1)	F(w-4).1,'bbbb'
10**(d-1) < X < 10**d	F(w-4).0,'bbbb'
10**d < X	Ew.d

G format is useful when the range of output values is large or unknown but where the extra readability of fixed-point is considered desirable whenever this is possible.

11.2.3.3 Character editing: As for input the A format descriptor is used to output character information. The form is `Aw` where `w` is the field width. As with input `w` may be omitted, in which case the width of field is taken to be the length of the corresponding character item in the output list. Where the length of the character item and the output field are the same the character item is simply transferred whole to the output record. If `w` is greater than the length of the character value, the character value is right-justified in the field and the field is padded on the left with blanks. If the character value is longer than the field width then the `w` leftmost characters of the value are transfered to the output. For example,

Value	Format	Output Field
'LIVERPOOL'	A	LIVERPOOL
'LIVERPOOL'	A9	LIVERPOOL
'LIVERPOOL'	A15	bbbbbbLIVERPOOL
'LIVERPOOL'	A5	LIVER

11.2.3.4 Logical editing: The logical edit descriptor for output is again the same form as for input; that is `Lw`, where `w` is the width of output field. In this case the effect is to fill the output field with `w-1` blanks followed by a `T` or an `F` depending on whether the corresponding output list item has the value true or false. For example

```
LOGICAL :: ans
ans = .TRUE.
WRITE(UNIT=*,FMT='L5') ans
```

produces

```
bbbbT
```

11.2.4 Output layout edit descriptors

For output the effect of all the within-record positioning descriptors is the same as for input. The `X` and `TR` descriptors cause a tab right relative. If this results in tabbing to a position in the record that has not yet been filled with characters by the action of the `WRITE` statement and format then the new character positions tabbed over are filled with blanks. The `TL` descriptor causes the processing position to be tabbed left relative. This means that any subsequent processing which sends characters to the output record will replace those already placed in the record. The `T` descriptor causes a tab to an absolute position, with, if necessary, the output of blanks to fill any new character positions tabbed over.

The slash edit descriptor causes the transfer of characters to the current record to be ended and a new record to be started. If the file is connected for sequential access this new record becomes the last record of the file. For a direct access file this new record is the next record, the record with record number increased by one.

The inclusion of a character constant (a string of characters delimited by apostrophes or quotes) as an edit descriptor in an output format will when processed cause the enclosed string to be added to the output record. This is a way of adding annotation to output data. For example,

```
WRITE(UNIT=16,FMT=9000) hours,mins,secs
9000 FORMAT(' HOURS=',I3,'  MINS=',I3,'  SECS=',I3)
```

If the three values contained in the list variables were `1,17,38` then the execution of the `WRITE` statement and the associated format would produce,

```
bHOURS=bb1bbMINS=b17bbSECS=b38
```

11.2.5 Printing and formatted output

One of the least satisfactory features of the Fortran 77 standard, which unfortunately has not been corrected in Fortran 90, is its treatment of the idea of "printed output". Fortran formatted output was originally designed to handle output to a printer. In the late 1950s and early 1960s this was virtually the only way of obtaining human readable output from a computer. The printers available at that time used the first character of each record to control the movement of the paper. The effect of the first character was:

```
blank   -   start new line, single space
zero    -   skip one line, start a new line, double space
one     -   skip to start of new page, form feed
plus    -   do not advance paper, overprint same line
```

A convention thus developed in which the first character of any formatted output record was not considered to be part of the record but was used to determine *carriage control*. When formatted output began to be used to store data in machine readable and human readable form in disc files, the difficulty arose as to what to do about the carriage control character: store it in the record on the disc and only use it for carriage control if the record was actually printed; strip it off and insert the printer control information into the file in some other way; or assume that a disc file was not going to be printed using Fortran carriage control conventions and simply store all records as produced by the program.

The confusion that arose from all this has unfortunately not been clarified by Fortran 90. For formatted output to any device, or file, that the processor defines as "printing" the first character is not stored as part of the record but is stripped off and used to generate carriage control. Unfortunately the standard is unspecific about what should be considered to be "printing". So each implementation is free to define transfers as they see fit. Some therefore restrict the use of the first character of a record for carriage control to situations where a Fortran unit is connected directly to a real printer. On such systems when formatted output is sent to a disc file all the characters are stored as is. On others all formatted output whether it is to a disc file, the terminal or a real printer is defined as being "printing" and the data transferred so that the first character of each record is assumed to be carriage control and the external data is structured to reflect this. The first character of each record may not therefore appear in the file as such.

On any system it is likely that some strange behaviour will result if a record starts with a character other than one of the above four. It is therefore common to organise formats in such a way that the first character of every record is guaranteed to be one of the above. In most cases this is simply a blank to cause a new line to be taken if printed. A blank can be guaranteed by making each record begin with a descriptor that forces the first character to be one of the allowed control characters. This can be done by making each format list begin with one of the descriptors: `1X`, `TR1`, or `' '`.

11.2.6 Repeating a format

All the format lists we have used in examples so far have had one data value edit descriptor coresponding to each item of the input/output list. In some cases this was ensured by use of the convenient short-hand of indicating multiple consecutive occurences of the same descriptor by preceeding the descriptor with a repeat factor. The layout descriptors cannot be repeated in this fashion. However a whole format sub-list can be repeated. A format sub-list can be created by enclosing a section of the whole list in parentheses. This sub-list, called a group format, can be repeated by preceeding the opening left parenthesis with an integer constant which indicates how many times the whole group is to be repeated. For example,

```
READ(UNIT=4,FMT=9000) NVAL,VAL1,VAL2,VAL3,VAL4
9000 FORMAT(TR10,I5/4(TR10,F10.2))
```

would read an integer and four real numbers from two records skipping the intervening annotation. The data records might be as follows (the first line is included as a convenience for counting character positions).

```
1234567890123456789012345678901234567890......
 NUMBER = +1234 ANY OLD JUNK.....
FIRST VAL= -17.12345 SECOND IS   1234.45.......
```

Since the repeat factors must be literal constants we still have basically a fixed number of data values described in any format. This is not a problem when handling ordinary values since there is also a fixed number of items in any input/output list. However this would be impossibly restrictive for dealing with the input or output of arrays. The input/output list now may include a number of values which is dynamic; that is, determined by values calculated while the program is executed. Under such circumstances the fact that the format contains only items that are fixed when the program is written would make it impossible to handle array input/output adequately. This difficulty is overcome in a particularly simple way. If the end of the format list is reached before the input/output list has been fully processed the format list is re-scanned starting from the last opening left parenthesis in the format list. The final right parenthesis of any format list is also considered to act as an end-of-record indicator. That is whenever a format is re-scanned the re-scan always starts on a new record. For example suppose we wanted to read numbers into a real array and we knew that these were recorded eight per record each occupying 10 character fields. We could do this for any number of elements by,

```
READ(UNIT=8,FMT='(8F10.0)') (A(I), I=1,NVAL)
```

where we have assumed NVAL has been read in or calculated earlier. Each time eight values are read the last right parenthesis of the format is reached.

If all NVAL values have not yet been read the format is re-scanned from the first left parenthesis. The re-scan starts a new record each time it occurs. The process stops once NVAL values have been read. Eight values do not have to be read from the last record. This means that any number of values can be read in this way. The thing that matters is that they are all recorded eight to a record ten characters to each field.

Since NVAL determines the number of external records as well as the number of elements it is common for these to be recorded together and for them to be read together. This can be done with the statement and format,

```
READ(UNIT=8,FMT='(I5/(8F10.0))') NVAL,(A(I), I=1,NVAL)
```

This time the first record of the data file to be processed by the statement must contain the number of elements recorded in the subsequent records. The re-scan of this format now proceeds not from the initial left parenthesis but from the interior one.

Another common use of this capability is to put headings on tables of variable length. For example, suppose we needed to write out the class list of students. We might do this as,

```
CHARACTER(LEN=20) :: NAME(100)
INTEGER :: MKS(4,100), AVMKS(100), NST
    ...
    ...
WRITE(6,2000) (I,NAME(I),(MKS(J,I),J=1,4),AVMKS(I),I=1,NST)
2000 FORMAT('1', &
   'CLASS OF 1987 IN RANK ORDER OF AVERAGE MARKS'// &
   1X,' RANK',TR6,'NAME', &
      ' ENGLISH   MATHS  FRENCH', &
      ' PHYSICS AVERAGE'/(1X,I4,A10,5I6))
```

We are assuming this output is to be printed so that the first characters of each record are stripped off and used to control the printer carriage control. The first record will start a new page and will produce the appropriate title to identify the output. It will skip a line and put out the headings for the following table columns. We have assumed that the data has been sorted into rank order by the program so the table is written out in this way one line per student. Each line will consist of the ranking, the student name, the marks for each of the subjects and the overall average mark. The first few lines starting at the top of a page might look like,

```
CLASS OF 1987 IN RANK ORDER OF AVERAGE MARKS

RANK       NAME  ENGLISH  MATHS  FRENCH PHYSICS AVERAGE
   1       SMITH      87     95      82      91      89
   2       JONES      85     96      82      90      88
   3       BROWN      76     98      78      94      87
```

11.2.7 Variable formats

Fortran 90 provides a facility for storing a format description in a character variable. This can be useful in situations where the format of data to be read by a program is not known in advance. In this case the character string to be used as the format must be constructed by the program so as to be appropriate for the data to be read. A particularly important example of the use of this facility is when the data itself includes a representation of the format needed to read the data. Consider the following example:

```
CHARACTER(LEN=80) :: FORM
INTEGER :: NVAL
REAL :: A(1000)
      ...
! --READ THE FORMAT SPECIFICATION AND NUMBER OF VALUES
READ(UNIT=5,FMT='(A/I5)') FORM, NVAL
! --READ THE DATA IN THE FORMAT GIVEN IN FORM
READ(UNIT=5,FMT=FORM) (A(I), I=1,NVAL)
      ...
      ...
```

The input data for the above might look like,

```
(3F5.2)
   504
 3.54  .26  .35
-1.75 7.56-0.48
     ...
     ...
```

or it could be,

```
(F12.0,F8.0,F10.0)
  107
  -1.436E-12  1.1478  5.56E+21
   2.453E-11  1.1567 -5.78E+11
     ...
     ...
```

and so on.

Notice that in the second READ statement the character variable name FORM is given as the format list. The character variable, once any leading or trailing blanks are stripped off, must contain a valid format list. The format itself is specified in the data just as it would have been in the FORMAT statement.

11.3 Exercises

1. Declare variables and write list-directed input statements to read a person's name, age, height, marital status from the following record:

   ```
   LINCOLN, 10, 3.5, .FALSE.
   ```

   What exactly would the variable declared for the name contain after the READ had been performed.

2. What values would be read into the variables in the READ statement in the following:

   ```
   REAL     :: A,B,C
   REAL, DIMENSION(1:5) :: arr
   INTEGER :: I,J,K
   READ(*,*) A,B,C
   READ(*,*) I,J,K,arr
   ```

   given the input records:

   ```
   1.5 3.4 5.6 3 6 65
   2*0 45
   3*23.7 0 0
   ```

3. What values do the variables A, I, C1, C2 contain if the record,

   ```
   5.3,,,'Thank you'
   ```

   is read with the statements,

   ```
   READ(*,*) A, I, C1, C2
   ```

   where A is real, I is an integer and C1, C2 are character variables of length 10.

4. Given the statement:

```
READ(*,'(F10.3,A2,L10)') A,C,L
```

what would be read to A (a real), C (a character of length 2), L (a logical) from the following records?

a) `bbb5.34bbbNOb.TRUE.`
b) `5.34bbbbbbYbbFbbbbb`
c) `b6bbbbbb3211bbbbbbT`
d) `bbbbbbbbbbbbbbbbbbF`

5. Give the formats which would be suitable for use with the statements,

```
REAL          :: A
CHARACTER(LEN=12) :: B
INTEGER       :: C
READ(*,FORM) A,B,C
```

if the record to be read is,

```
bbb354bbINTRODUCTORYb1993
```

and values to be assigned to A, B, C are given in the following table:

A	B	C
35.4	INTRODUCTORY	1993
3.54	DUCT	93
.354	TROD	19
354.0	TORY	99

6. Given that A is an array declared with the statement,

```
INTEGER, DIMENSION(1:8) :: A
```

give a formatted input statement which will read in the values 1 to A(1), 2 to A(2), etc. from the following records:

```
12
34
56
78
```

7. A file `personnel.dat` contains records of people's name (up to 15 characters), age (3 digit integer), height (in metres to the nearest centimetre), telephone number (4 digit integer). Write a program to read the file and print out the details in the following format:

```
                           Height
     Name          Age   (metres)    Tel. No.
     ----          ---    ------    --------
Bloggs J. G.        45     1.80        3456
Clinton P. J.       47     1.75        6783
etc.
```

8. A file contains records in two groups with each group headed by a specification of the format in which the following data is to be read. Each group of data is terminated by the special value 99.9. Write a program to read in all the data.

   Example data:

```
'(3F6.4,I5)'
3.40  5.6  7.9     10
4.52  6.3  3.2     11
99.9    0    0      0
'(F6.1,I10)'
4.23        9
5.89        6
99.9        0
END
```

9. Give a `WRITE` statement which would write out the elements of a 10 x 10 real array in fields of 15 characters, with 10 elements on each line.

10. Give statements which would write out the elements of two real arrays of dimension 8, side by side, in two columns of width 10 with 3 figures of accuracy.

Chapter 12

Additional Features

The facilities described in previous chapters are sufficient for most purposes but there are a number of additional features provided in Fortran 90 that can be useful in special circumstances. The most important of these are: the `DOUBLE PRECISION` data type which can be used to specify that a higher numerical precision is required for certain variables; the `COMPLEX` data type which facilitates the expression of problems involving mathematical complex numbers in Fortran; and the `KIND=` parameter in type declarations which provides a portable method of specifying that alternative internal representations are to be used for variables of the intrinsic types. Several other topics of arguably lesser importance are also covered in this chapter.

12.1 Double precision data

This is an additional floating point data type. That is, it represents numbers in the same way as real data. The main difference is that double precision quantities are represented more accurately than default real quantities. The type name implies that they should be twice as accurate but the Fortran 90 standard does not actually require this, merely that they be more accurate. In fact, on most processors double precision is at least twice as precise and in many cases is substantially more accurate than this. For example a common form of processor has an effective decimal precision of six significant figures for real and 14 for double precision.

12.1.1 Double precision declarations

Objects may be declared to be double precision in the usual manner, for example,

```
DOUBLE PRECISION :: acc,sum,prod,diff(1:25,1:10)
```

This declares `acc`, `sum`, and `prod` to be scalar objects of type double precision, and `diff` to be a two-dimensional double precision array with `25 x 10` double precision elements. Note that the space between `DOUBLE` and `PRECISION` is optional, the two words together constitute the type-name but since this is made up of the two separate English words, an optional space is permitted.

12.1.2 Double precision constants

Double precision constants can be written in a similar way to floating point real constants. The only difference is that the letter D is used as the exponent letter instead of an E. Thus,

```
0.1D0, 0.1E0 and 0.1
```

represent the same constant value, `.1`, but the first of these will be stored in double precision and the other two in single precision. Since as we pointed out in Chapter 4, 0.1 is not normally represented exactly in a computer the difference could be significant. On a machine with precisions 6 and 16 the actual values represented might be nearer,

`0.100001`
and
`0.1000000000000001`

respectively, and the difference could have dramatic effects. If the accuracy requirements of the problem warrant the use of double precision at all then it is important to make sure that all constants are also in double precision. If it is thought likely that the precision of a program will be changed, this can be made very much easier and safer if all real constants are declared as symbolic using `PARAMETER` statements. Their precision can then be changed in the declaration statements rather than by having to search for every occurrence of a literal constant in the code to make the change.

12.1.3 Double precision expressions

All the operations of real arithmetic also apply to double precision so expressions can be written to calculate double precision results in the same way as for reals. Double precision quantities may be mixed quite freely in expressions with quantities of type integer and real. However prediction of the effects and results of such *mixed-mode* expressions needs a little thought.

If a double precision quantity and an integer are the operands of any arithmetic operation or comparison, the integer value is converted to the corresponding double precision value before the operation is performed. The result of the arithmetic operation will be of double precision. Similarly if one of the operands is real, it will be converted to double precision before performing the operation and the expression will produce a double precision result. However, it should be noted that when an integer is converted to double precision the result is accurate to double precision, or even exact, whereas if a real that is only initially accurate to single precision is converted then it will still only be accurate to single precision after the conversion. For example, if DVAR were a double precision variable then

```
DVAR*0.1
```

would produce a double precision result. However, as we saw above, 0.1 is likely to have an error in the least significant figure of the single precision, and this would propagate an error into the product to produce an error of similar magnitude in the result. For a system in which single precision was held to an accuracy of six figures and double precision to an accuracy of 16 we would have DVAR correct to 16 figures but DVAR*0.1 in error in all but the first six. To get a result correct to 16 figures we would have to write the expression as

```
DVAR*0.1D0
```

i.e. convert the constant to double precision.

Similar conversions occur when an integer or a real value is assigned to a double precision variable. If the value is of type integer or of type real it is converted to double precision before it is assigned. The same accuracy problem can occur in the real case. We also have the inverse assignment possibilities. A double precision expression value will be converted to an integer by truncation towards zero of any fractional part if it is assigned to a variable of type integer. Similarly a double precision value which is assigned to a real will be truncated, retaining only those significant figures that can be represented in the single precision real variable. The excess figures of accuracy are simply discarded before the assignment is made.

As was mentioned above, when mixing real and double precision quantities in the same expressions, it is important to be careful about how the errors will propagate. The most common reason for needing to use double precision is to allow certain critical steps of a calculation to be performed at a higher precision. In these circumstances real quantities are deliberately converted to double precision, the critical calculations carried out using the extra accuracy and the results returned back to single precision for the non-critical calculations. Such critical calculations are often such that, because of the precise sequence of operations and/or values of the operands, the generated errors become large if they are not limited in this way.

There are of course problems where the inherent accuracy required is simply greater than that possible with single precision. For example, there are numerous experimental quantities in physics that are measurable to accuracies of a few parts in ten or even one hundred thousand million, i.e. with the experimental errors in the 10th or the 11th significant figure. If one is writing programs to help in the analysis of such experiments it is not much use if the computer can only work to six figures. Such programs will need to have all their floating point data and operations in double precision.

Note, some computer systems provide three or more precisions of floating point numbers. We shall see later how such systems can be used with standard Fortran mechanisms for accessing the extra precisions.

12.1.4 Intrinsic functions

Most of the intrinsic functions which are defined for real arguments are also defined for double precision arguments. The definitions are "generic" with respect to precision. This means that there can be more than one actual function with the same generic name and the version of the function used on any particular invocation depends on the type of its arguments. For example,

```
REAL :: ra,rb,rc
DOUBLE PRECISION da,db,dc
 ra = SQRT(rb)
 da = SQRT(db)
 dc = SQRT(ra+db)
 ...
```

In this program fragment the first reference to the square root function `SQRT` has a single precision argument so the single precision version is invoked to calculate a single precision result. The second reference has a double precision argument and so the double precision version is invoked to produce the required double precision result. The third invocation is also of the double precision version since the argument expression evaluates to a double precision value.

There is one function that always returns a double precision result. This is the type conversion function `DBLE`. The arguments of `DBLE` may be of type integer, real or complex (see below), and the function returns the equivalent double precision value as result.

12.1.5 Double precision input/output

Double precision quantities may be written and read in closely analogous ways to those that apply to real quantities. A double precision quantity is simply treated as a numeric quantity in the input/output list. If default formatting is employed, the operation is list-directed (see Chapter 10). On input the next numeric value of any format in the input is converted into the double precision representation before storing it in the location indicated by the list variable. On output the double precision quantity is converted to a character string representing its value in either an F format or an E format depending on the value, exactly as for real values. The difference will be in the number of significant figures output. For explicitly formatted input/output the F, E, or G format edit descriptors used for real data may be used exactly as described in Chapter 11. Again the only difference is likely to be longer fields because of the higher precision.

In earlier versions of Fortran, double precision formatting required the use of a D edit descriptor which behaved exactly like the E descriptor. The data also had to be prepared with a D exponent letter and was written out with a `D`. This is no longer necessary and data with an E exponent or without an exponent at all can now be written and read from and to double precision quantities quite freely. Therefore the use of D formatting is not only non-essential, it is not desirable.

12.2 Complex data

This section will be of interest to those wanting to solve problems in subject areas, usually in science and engineering, where mathematical complex numbers are used. The non-mathematically minded reader can safely skip to the next section. Fortran is one of the few languages to include complex as an intrinsic data type and this can be a reason why it is chosen in preference to other languages.

Complex numbers are represented as a pair of real values. The first represents the real-part and the second the imaginary-part.

12.2.1 Complex object declaration

Objects of type complex are declared using the keyword `COMPLEX`. Single variables, names for constants, and arrays of complex numbers can be declared in the usual way. For example,

```
COMPLEX :: z,j,za(1:100)
```

declares the three names `z,j,za` to refer to objects that are of complex type. The first two refer to single complex numbers and the last declares an array of 100 complex numbers.

12.2.2 Complex constants

Constants of complex type can be written as a pair of real constants separated by a comma and enclosed in parentheses. For example,

```
(1.0,1.0)
(3.141,1.0E-9)
```

and symbolic constants can be created thus,

```
COMPLEX,PARAMETER :: ( i = (0.0,1.0) )
```

It is even allowable for a complex constant to have one, or both components written as integer constants. In this case the integer will be converted to the corresponding real value to represent the appropriate part of the complex constant.

12.2.3 Complex expressions

The operations of arithmetic are defined for complex operands producing complex results in the expected manner. These operations have the same natural precedence or order of evaluation as those involving real or integer operands. Real and integer operands can be mixed with complex operands quite freely. In this case if one of the two operands is complex but the other is integer or real, the non-complex argument is converted to a complex argument by adding a zero imaginary-part. Of course an integer is also first converted to the equivalent real value. It should be noted that the standard does not define a double precision complex type, but if such objects are required thay can be handled by the more general facilities for selecting numeric representation described later in Section 12.3.

12.2.4 Intrinsic functions

The set of mathematical intrinsic functions are also defined generically for complex arguments, where they will normally return a complex result unless, by definition, the result is real. For example, `SIN(z)` will calculate the complex function result as would be expected, namely,

```
Real part of      SIN(z)  = SIN(x)COSH(y)
Imaginary part of SIN(z)  = COS(x)SINH(y)
```

where `x` and `y` are the real and imaginary parts of `z`, respectively. However, the function `ABS(z)` would produce the real result

```
ABS(z)  = SQRT(x**2 + y**2)
```

(It should be noted that a good quality implementation is not likely to evaluate either function by a direct application of these expressions. Although the expressions are true mathematically the required functions are better evaluated by other methods in practice.)

The `REAL`, or `DBLE` functions applied to a complex argument return the real part of the complex value. The imaginary part can be obtained by the `AIMAG` function. Also a complex value can be constructed using the `CMPLX` function,

```
z = CMPLX(x,y)
```

assigns a complex value to `z` with real part equal to `x` and imaginary part equal to `y`.

12.2.5 Input/output of complex values

In general complex items are treated as two reals for input/output. For formatted input/output two `F` or `E` format descriptors are used to process each of the real values making up the parts of the complex value. For list-directed input/output both the input and the output forms for complex values are those of a complex constant, viz., a pair of real values enclosed in parentheses and separated by a comma.

12.3 Selection of data type by kind

We described above the use of the default double precision real type to select an alternative representation for data that approximates real number values. There is no such extra default type defined for integers, nor is there one for characters, logicals, or complex values and, as mentioned previously there is no default double precision complex type. Fortran 90 requires a processor to support at least one representation for integers, logicals, characters, and two representations for reals with different precisions. However, a processor may support more than this minimum. It may for instance provide two or even three representations for integers. There may be more than the default two representations for reals, and it might even be possible to manipulate more than one alphabet of characters. The available representations, default and non-default, may be selected and accessed by use of a KIND parameter associated with the type.

No matter what representations the processor has, it must associate a number, called the *kind number*, with each representation. There are no restrictions on the specific numbers a processor chooses for each representation except that the numbers chosen must be unique to each representation. No two representations for the same type may have the same kind number. These kind numbers may be used to select the representation to be used for particular objects.

12.3.1 Integer kind selection

Integer representations usually differ in the range of values that can be used. For example, we might have a processor which supported three integer representations, capable of handling numbers up to 100 (10^2), up to 10,000 (10^4) and up to 1,000,000,000,000 (10^{12}). These representations are said to have the decimal ranges of 2, 4, and 12 respectively and a processor might choose to use the kind numbers 1, 2, 4 for these representations.

12.3.1.1 Object declaration: Objects of a selected integer kind may be declared in the usual manner by use of the type-spec `INTEGER(KIND=n)`, where the number `n` specifies which of the available integer kinds is to be used. For example,

```
INTEGER(KIND=1) :: a,b,c
INTEGER(KIND=2) :: d,e,f
INTEGER(KIND=4) :: g,h,i
```

declares the objects `a,b,c` to be of type integer and selects the `KIND=1` representation. The second declaration selects the `KIND=2` representation for `d,e,f` and the third selects `KIND=4` for `g,h,i`. It should be noted that the keyword, `KIND=` may be omitted. The statement,

```
INTEGER(4) :: g,h,i
```

and the third statement above have exactly the same meaning.

Since the kind numbers are entirely arbitrary their use in this fashion may be highly non-portable. A different processor may use the same numbers for representations with very different characteristics, or the specific numbers might not even be used at all on some systems. A much more portable way of using kind values in a program is to parameterise the code.

```
INTEGER,PARAMETER :: short=1, medium=2, long=4
INTEGER(short)  :: a,b,c
INTEGER(medium) :: d,e,f
INTEGER(long)   :: g,h,i
```

These statements have the same declarative effect as the ones above. If throughout the program integers are always declared in this way using the appropriate parameter for the kind selector, then if the program is moved to a machine with different kind numbers it is a simple matter to change the value of the appropriate parameter.

It is also possible to find the kind number associated with a specific object. A generic intrinsic function called `KIND` is defined which returns the kind value used for the representation of its argument. For example, `KIND(a)`, `KIND(e)`, and `KIND(i)` would return the values `1`, `2` and `4`, respectively. In particular, `KIND(0)` returns the kind value chosen for the representation used for the default integer type on any processor. (N.B. there is no significance in the value `0` in this last example. Any integer constant written without explicit kind selection is a default integer constant.)

Even greater portability can be obtained by use of another intrinsic function that returns the kind value for a representation and which guarantees a specified range of integers can be handled. The function,

```
SELECTED_INT_KIND(r)
```

returns the kind value of the integer representation with the smallest range that is able to represent values, n, such that

$$-10^{r} < n < +10^{r}.$$

If no such representation exists the result is -1. Using this function we can write a portable program that chooses its integer representations according to the required ranges of values to be manipulated.

```
INTEGER,PARAMETER :: short  = SELECTED_INT_KIND(2),  &
                     medium = SELECTED_INT_KIND(4),  &
                     long   = SELECTED_INT_KIND(10)
INTEGER(short)    :: a,b,c
INTEGER(medium)   :: d,e,f
INTEGER(long)     :: g,h,i
```

would have the desired effect on our example system and would also work on any other system which had integer representations with a range of at least ten. Of course, on a system that could not represent a ten digit integer the program would fail since `long` would be negative and negative kinds are not permitted. This failure would occur at compile time and so very little programming effort or computer resources would have been expended in finding the limitation. This fully parameterised method of kind selection is the best way of using this facility. It provides maximum portability combined with maximum flexibility.

12.3.1.2 Integer constants of selected kind: It is possible for integer constants to be written with a kind selector. This forces the value to be represented using the indicated representation. The constant is written in the normal way for an integer constant but it is followed by an underscore and the required kind value. For example,

```
12_1, 1000_2, 12345678_4
```

are valid integer constants on our example machine. However,

```
1000_1, 12345678_2
```

would both be invalid because they request the use of integer kinds to represent values that are too large for the ranges supported by these kinds.

As with declarations the use of explicit values for the kind selector is likely to make the program highly machine specific. The best way to provide for portability is to use the parameters established by use of `SELECTED_INT_KIND` for use in the declaration of objects. The constants should then be written

```
12_short, 1000_medium, 12345678_long
```

If these parameters `short`, `medium` and `long` are used wherever an integer kind selection is required, then this guarantees that both constants and variables etc. will use the same representations where necessary and that these will be chosen independently of the processor being used.

12.3.1.3 Expression evaluation: If the two operands of any intrinsic operation have the same kind, then the result also has this kind. If the kinds are different, then the operand with the lower range is converted to the kind of the other operand before the operation is performed. For example, with the following declarations

```
INTEGER(short) :: members,attendees
INTEGER(long)  :: salaries,costs
```

in force, the expressions

```
members+attendees, salaries-costs, members*costs
```

have results of the kinds `short`, `long` and `long`, respectively.

It should be noted that the kind of an actual argument must match that of the corresponding dummy argument. It is, however, possible for kind values to distinguish which specific procedure of a generic overload set is to be invoked. It is therefore possible for the user to write procedures and operators which are generic over kind.

12.3.2 Real KIND selection

The representations for real numbers may differ both on the range of real numbers that can be represented and perhaps more importantly for reals, they can also differ on the precision to which they approximate real values. A typical machine may have three representations although there are machines in existence that actually have five or more, two or three are the most common. These could have precisions 6, 14, and 33 decimal digits and ranges of 38, 307 and 4915, where the range is again decimal and a range of R means that numbers with absolute values greater than 10^{-R} and less than 10^{+R} can be represented. A given compiler might assign the kind values 4,8 and 16, respectively, to these representations.

12.3.2.1 Object declaration: The form of object declaration is analogous to that used for integers. For example,

```
REAL(KIND=4)  :: x,y,z
REAL(KIND=8)  :: diff
REAL(KIND=16) :: critical_factor
```

would declare the objects `x,y,z` to be represented using the representation with kind equals 4, the object `diff` using the kind equals 8 representation, and the `critical_factor` would employ the high precision representation with kind equal to 16. Unfortunately, as with integers there is no restriction as to how a processor chooses to assign kind numbers. One processor might choose the values as above but a different processor, even one with the same hardware representations, might choose perversely to use the values 10, 6, and 4 instead of 4, 8 and 16. Again absolute kind values are specific to a processor and highly non-portable. As with integers, portability is gained by parameterisation.

It would be better to use declarations like

```
INTEGER,PARAMETER :: single=4, double=8, extended=16
REAL(single) :: x,y,z
REAL(double) :: diff
REAL(extended) :: critical_factor
```

Provided these parameters are used throughout a program to select the real representations, the kind of real used can be easily modified to work correctly on any processor with any choice of kind value assignment.

It should be noted that it would be quite likely that on a machine, like the one we are using for example purposes, the default REAL and DOUBLE PRECISION representations would in fact be those with kind values 4 and 8. Should we need to modify the program to run at higher precision it would be very much easier to do so if we had used this parameterised approach to kind selection than if we had simply used the default types.

As for integer kinds there are two kind-related intrinsic procedures for real kinds. These are the KIND function, which if it is called with an argument of real type, returns the kind value of its argument, and the SELECTED_REAL_KIND function. This latter function takes two arguments, P,R. These are both integers and both are optional, although one must be present. The value of P specifies the minimum required precision and R specifies the minimum required range. The result returned will be the kind value for the real representation that has the smallest precision and range that nevertheless exceed those specified by P and R. This means that for maximum portability when a program is known to require that real calculations be done with certain minimum approximation quality we should parameterise the program by, say,

```
INTEGER,PARAMETER :: single=SELECTED_REAL_KIND(5,20), &
                     double=SELECTED_REAL_KIND(10,40), &
                     extended=SELECTED_REAL_KIND(20,100)
REAL(single)      :: x,y,z
REAL(double)      :: diff
REAL(extended)    :: critical_factor
```

If all real quantities are declared using these parameters the program will automatically adjust to changing numerical environments when it is ported to another machine. Of course, if the target machine cannot provide a representation to meet the specified precision and range, the program will fail in compilation. If the target processor is unable to provide a representation with 20 digits precision, say, the parameter, extended, would be defined with a negative value, and all declarations with this as the kind parameter would fail.

12.3.2.2 Constants of selected real kind: As with integers real constants can select their representation by following the normal constant with an underscore and the kind value.

```
1.234_4, 3.14159_8, 0.1_16
```

or equivalently

```
1.234_single, 3.14159_double, 0.1_extended
```

causes the denoted real values to be represented in the selected real representation. Note, if an exponent form is used the kind selector is used to select the representation regardless of whether the `E` or `D` exponent letter is employed.

12.3.2.3 Real expression evaluation: Expression evaluation follows the usual pattern. If the operands have the same kind the result is also of this kind. If the operands are of different kind the operand of lower precision is converted to the kind of the other operand and the expression evaluated in this kind. If the precisions are the same then the kind with the larger range is used.

12.3.3 Complex KIND selection

There must be a complex data representation corresponding to each available real representation, and these are selected by the same kind parameter values as for real. For example,

```
COMPLEX(KIND=4)  :: z1
COMPLEX(KIND=8)  :: dz1
COMPLEX(KIND=16) :: ez1
```

declares complex variables of kinds in a similar way to declarations for real variables above. In this case the real representation to be used for each part of the complex value is selected.

Complex constants of selected kind are written in the normal way but now the kind of the real or imaginary part must be selected as above. If the kinds selected for the two parts are different the overall kind is selected in the same way as when determining the kind of an expression. That is, the kind with the higher precision or the higher range is chosen.

12.3.4 Character KIND selection

Every processor must support at least one default character set which must include the Fortran characters as part of that set. In addition, a processor might support other character sets. On a particular processor it may be possible to simultaneously work with Latin characters (the default kind of characters) and say Greek characters or perhaps more unusually, the characters of a non-alphabetic language like Japanese, where there might be many thousands of different values in the set. If they are supported, these different character sets are selected by a kind parameter. For example

```
CHARACTER(KIND=1) :: name,initials
CHARACTER(KIND=2) :: zeus,hebe
```

might be used to declare variables. The first using Latin characters (assumed to be selected by kind 1) and the second to hold the Greek character representation of the Gods (assuming that on this processor `KIND=2` selects the Greek character set).

The normal operations of character values apply to non-default character as well as to default ones, but characters of different kinds cannot be mixed. Only characters of the same kind can be concatenated, compared, and assigned. However, it is possible to include character variables or expressions of different kind in an input/output list. The effect of such a list is not only system dependent but may also be device dependent. Sending a mixture of standard Fortran default characters and Japanese (Kanji) characters to a printer that does not have the font facilities for printing the latter could have some very strange results.

Characters of non-default kind are essentially non-portable but the selected character kind facility means that wherever such data types are supported the sort of programming involved in manipulating them will be similar, if not identical. They can therefore be useful in a specific environment where both system and attached peripheral devices are properly set up to handle the same non-default characters.

12.3.5 Logical KIND selection

Objects of logical type can also be parameterised. A system is required to support at least one logical representation but it may support more. In which case the representation to be used for kinds of logical object is selected by the usual kind parameterisation. For example,

```
LOGICAL(KIND=4) :: yorn
LOGICAL(KIND=1),DIMENSION(1000,1000) :: mask
```

might declare a single variable `yorn` to be of default kind (assuming `KIND=4` means the default) and a large logical array to be of a non-default kind (assuing kind=1 selects a logical representation that uses much less storage, one byte instead of the more usual default of four). Of course there is no requirement that the numbers be one and four, they can as usual be any positive integral value.

The usual intrinsic function `KIND` if called with a logical argument returns the kind value for the argument. For example, `KIND(.TRUE.)` will return the kind value for default logical.

This is not a particularly useful facility unless the processor provides a non-default representation which is more storage efficient than the default. In this case it may be desirable for this to be used to represent the large logical arrays that frequently occur as mask arrays.

12.4 RETURN and STOP

So far we have described only one way for a program to terminate execution (apart from as the result of an error) or for a subprogram to return control to the program unit that invoked it. That is, by the execution of the final `END` statement of the program unit which when executed in a main program terminates the program and passes control back to the operating system, and when executed in a `FUNCTION` or `SUBROUTINE` returns control to the program unit that invoked it. The exclusive use of `END` to terminate program units has the merit that there is always one and only one place that every program unit passes to in order to terminate its processing. This is a useful restriction consistent with the idea of a disciplined structural approach to program design and implementation. There are occasions, however, where to follow this principle slavishly can lead to unnatural, difficult to read, and even somewhat inefficient code. The `RETURN` and `STOP` statements are other ways of forcing termination.

It may be the case that at some point many levels deep in nested control constructs an exceptional situation is detected which means that all the necessary results of a procedure can be determined without executing the rest of the code. For such a circumstance Fortran provides the `RETURN` statement which forces an immediate return of control to the invoking program. (Of course the same effect could be obtained by putting a label on the `END` statement and using a `GOTO` statement to pass control directly to this label.) The form of the `RETURN` statement is

```
RETURN
```

The situation with the `STOP` statement is similar but there are some significant differences. Execution of the `STOP` statement, no matter where it occurs in main program or subprogram causes the execution of the whole program to be terminated. The control of the computer is returned to the operating system. Because of this the `STOP` statement may be used to pass information to the operating system. The form of the STOP statement is

```
STOP
```
or
```
STOP n
```

where `n` is a literal integer constant of up to five digits or a character constant. When a `STOP` statement is executed the value of the parameter `n` is made available in some way to the operating system. This facility can be used to allow the operating system to distinguish between normal successful termination (executing the main program `END` or a `STOP` without argument) and an error termination.

12.5 Additional input/output statements

Fortran 90 allows a `PRINT` statement to be used as essentially an alternative spelling for the `WRITE` statement to the default unit. Thus the statement,

```
WRITE(UNIT=*,FMT=format-spec) iolist
```

can be written as

```
PRINT format-spec, iolist
```

and has identical effect. It "prints" on the default output unit. It hardly seems worth the trouble of using the less general form just to save specifying the `*` indicating the default unit, but a number of programmers like to use this old form so it will often be found in existing programs.

Other additional input/output statements are the three so-called "tape positioning" statements, `REWIND`, `BACKSPACE`, and `ENDFILE`. These three statements were originally introduced when it was common for programs to operate directly to devices like magnetic tape. The meaning of the statements is therefore directly related to the control of such devices. When working with sequential disc files they do still have some meaning but are not widely used.

The `REWIND` statement causes the processing position to return to the start of the file,

```
REWIND(UNIT=7)
```

would cause the file connected to unit seven to be repositioned before the first record of the file. On most systems when a file is connected to a unit by the execution of an OPEN statement the file is automatically positioned at the start, but on some systems this may not be the case. On a number of machines if a file is used then closed and re-opened it is not re-positioned but processing continues from the previous position. If there is any doubt whether the processing of a file will begin with the first record a REWIND for the appropriate unit will make sure of it.

The BACKSPACE statement causes the file to move its processing position back one record.

```
BACKSPACE(UNIT=4)
```

would cause the file connected to unit four to be positioned before the start of the last record read or written. It can then be reread or re-written. This is a relatively rare requirement with modern machines and the BACKSPACE statement is not used a great deal.

The ENDFILE statement forces an end-of-file to be written into the file. If the file had previously been one that was being read, any records remaining in the file past the current position would be destroyed. As most systems will automatically put an end-of-file after the last record written it is seldom necessary to explicitly use an ENDFILE statement.

12.6 Vector-valued subscripts

In certain applications, particularly those involving large sparse arrays whose elements are non-zero only at a small number of element locations, a very useful form of array reference can be made using *vector-valued subscript*. This facility allows a sub-array to be defined which consists, say, of only the non-zero elements. The example below is rather simple but does illustrate the point. Suppose the array A is declared as,

```
REAL,DIMENSION(1:20) :: A
```

and we wanted to access just the elements A(1), A(4), A(8), A(10), A(12). To do this we set up an integer array which contains the values of the subscripts of A at the required locations. For the example shown, if we set the elements of an array V (i.e. V(1), V(2) etc.) to 1, 4, 8, 10, and 12, we could reference the required elements of A as

```
A(V)
```

i.e `A(V)` is shorthand for `A(1)`, `A(4)`, `A(8)`, `A(10)`, and `A(12)`.

Such an array reference via a vector-valued subscript can be used more or less as can any other array section reference. For instance, to set these elements to 3.5 we would just require the statement

```
A(V) = 3.5
```

Vector-valued subscripts can be useful but must be used with care. Unlike all other array sections vector-valued subscript sections can specify many-to-one mappings. Such sections have vector subscripts with two or more elements having the same values. Thus if an array `B` contains the elements `(5.3,6.4,7.6,8.7,9.2)` and an array `V` contains `(1,2,2,5)` then the statement

```
A(1:4) = B(V)
```

would set the elements of `A` to `(5.3,6.4,6.4,9.2)`. The expression `B(V)` defines a many-to-one section since it refers to `B(2)` twice. However, it would be invalid to assign values to such a many-to-one section. We would then be attempting to assign more than once into the same array element with possibly different values and since there is no defined order for the element by element assignments the eventual result would be unpredictable. In a sense one-to-many assignment is valid but many-to-one is not.

12.7 Partial initialisation and the DATA statement

In Fortran 77 the only way to initialise variables was in `DATA` statements. The `DATA` statement has been retained in Fortran 90, but now its main use is to allow the initialisation of sections of arrays where the facilities of array constructors and assignment in the array declaration make this difficult. In all other circumstances the `DATA` statement is a much more clumsy and error prone construct than the direct initialisation during declaration. Consider the two sets of statements that follow. These are of equivalent effect.

```
INTEGER :: count=0, I=5, J=100
REAL :: inc=1.0E-05, max=10.0E+05, min=-10.0E+05
CHARACTER(LEN=5) :: light='Amber'
LOGICAL :: red=.TRUE., blue=.FALSE., green=.FALSE.

INTEGER :: count,I,J
REAL :: inc, max, min
CHARACTER(LEN=5) :: light
```

```
LOGICAL :: red, blue, green
DATA count/0/, I/5/, J/100/
DATA inc, max, min/1.0E-05, 10.0E+05, -10.0E+05/
DATA light/'Amber'/
DATA red/.TRUE./, blue, green/.FALSE.,.FALSE./
```

There is no advantage in the second form in these circumstances, but it may be found in old codes.

The DATA statement allows variables to be initialised individually or in groups. It is easier to see what is going on from the general form of the DATA statement. This is

```
DATA <varlist1>/<datalist1>/,<varlist2>/<datalist2>/,...
                ...<varlistn>/<datalistn>/
```

where <varlist> is a list of variable names of any type separated by commas and <datalist> is a list of constants of corresponding type separated by commas. The number of constants in each <datalist> must be equal to the number of variable names in the corresponding <varlist>. Each variable in a <varlist> is initially given the value specified by the corresponding constant in the <datalist>.

As a general rule we also recommend initialising arrays using array constructors in type declaration statements. However, there are problems which arise in practice where it is necessary to initialise parts of arrays with different values. In such cases the use of array constructors would become tedious if not impossible.

As an example consider initialising a 1000 by 1000 array with all the edge values equal to one and with the rest of the array zero. This could be done using a DATA statement to initialise the relevant sections of the array as follows:-

```
REAL, DIMENSION(1000,1000) :: matrix
DATA matrix( 1    , 1:1000 ) / 1000*1.0 /     ! top row
DATA matrix( 1000, 1:1000 ) / 1000*1.0 /      ! bottom row
DATA matrix( 2:999, 1 )     / 998*1.0 /       ! left column
DATA matrix( 2:999, 1000 )  / 998*1.0 /       ! right column
DATA matrix( 2:999, 2:999 )   / 996004*0.0 / ! interior
```

It would be difficult to achieve this concisely with a whole array assignment of a reshaped array constructor constant. Note the form of the datalist items

```
r*c
```

where `r` is an integer contant and `c` is a constant of the type required by the variable in the variable list. This form supplies the indicated number of constants to the data list.

Perhaps a more common example would be that of initialising a matrix to have a given constant value, say, 5.0 on the diagonal and zero everywhere else. To achieve this we can use the implied-do forms to specify the elements in the variable lists.

```
REAL,DIMENSION(100,100) :: diag
DATA (diag(i,i), i=1,100) / 100*5.0 /
                      ! sets diagonal elements.
DATA (diag(i,j),diag(j,i), i=1,99), j=i+1,100) / 9900*0.0 /
                      ! sets the upper and lower triangles
```

It requires substantial care and thought to ensure that such constructs actually do what is intended.

It is also possible with the DATA statement to initialise part of an array, or a component of a structure, while leaving the rest of the object undefined. In general this is a dangerous thing to do and should be avoided.

Chapter 13

Obsolescent and Undesirable Features

In this chapter we describe several obsolescent and redundant features of Fortran 90 which users of the language may encounter during their programming life. We do not recommend the use of such features but recognise that Fortran 90 programmers need to be aware of their existence since they might come across them in programs written by other people. Fortran 90 has carried forward the whole of Fortran 77 and also a number of features from existing Fortran compilers. This has been done to protect the investment in the millions of lines of code that have been written in Fortran since it was first developed. Inevitably, as modern features have been added, many of the older features have become redundant and programmers, especially those using Fortran 90 for the first time, need to be aware of the possible pit-falls in using them.

13.1 Obsolescent features

These are clearly identified in the Fortran 90 standard as being those features which were already redundant in Fortran 77 since features which provided better methods of programming had been provided in the Fortran 77 standard. The standards committee's intention is that these features of the language will be removed from the next revision of the language, probably in about the year 2000. Marking them as obsolescent is a clear guide to programmers to stop using them. Sensible Fortran 77 programmers were assumed to have stopped using these obsolescent features in new programs a long time ago. The reason that they have not been deleted from the Fortran 90 standard is that there are still so-called 'dusty deck' programs[1] still in use which were written prior to the Fortran 77 standard and which still contain obsolescent statements.

13.1.1 Arithmetic-IF

This relic of the original Fortran has been redundant since the early 1960s when the logical `IF` and computed `GOTO` were introduced. It is a three way branch statement of the form,

```
IF(<expression>) <label1>,<label2>,<label3>
```

[1] The term 'dusty deck' refers to the fact that early Fortran programs were stored on decks of punched cards.

where <expression> is any expression producing a result of type integer, real or double precision, and the three labels are statement labels of executable statements. If the value of the expression is negative, execution transfers to the statement labeled <label1>. If the expression is zero, transfer is to the statement labeled <label2>, and a positive result causes transfer to <label3>. The same label can be repeated.

Very old Fortran code is frequently dotted with structures like,

```
      IF(ICNT-100) 100,100,200
  100 ...
      ...
      GOTO 300
  200 ...
      ...
  300 ...
      ...
```

This is more readable when written as

```
IF(ICNT.LE.100)THEN
   ...
   ! 100 code
   ...
ELSE
   ...
   ! 200 code
   ...
ENDIF
! 300 code
...
```

If it was well written, the arithmetic IF could be replaced by a well-structured block of statements such as that above using the IF()THEN...ELSE...ENDIF construct. Unfortunately arithmetic-IFs were all too often used in an undisciplined way and were a major cause of unreadable logical "spaghetti" in programs.

Genuine three way choices, if they are needed, should be written as IF()THEN...ELSEIF()THEN...ELSE...ENDIF constructs, or should be coded using the SELECT CASE construct as was indicated in Chapter 5.

13.1.2 ASSIGN statement and assigned-GOTO

This facility is even more of an unused relic than the arithmetic-IF. Its origins lie back in the mists of time before Fortran supported subprograms. The ASSIGN statement and the associated assigned-GOTO provided a partial way of constructing something like a subroutine. The ASSIGN statement allows the value of a statement label to be assigned to an integer variable and the assigned-GOTO allows a branch to such a variable label. By putting a block of code at the bottom of a program it would be possible to assign an appropriate label to a variable, jump to this code and then branch back to this label using an assigned-GOTO. It would thus be possible to jump to this block of code from different places in the program and to return to the appropriate place once it had been executed. This is effectively what the procedure facility provides.

13.1.2.1 The ASSIGN statement: The `ASSIGN` statement has the form

```
ASSIGN <label> TO <integer-variable>
```

where `<label>` must be one that appears on a statement somewhere in the program unit containing the `ASSIGN` statement. The execution of such a statement causes the statement label value to be assigned to the integer variable. Once a statement label has been assigned to a variable that variable is not usable as an ordinary integer until it is redefined to contain an ordinary integer. A variable containing a statement label value may be used only as the transfer label in an assigned-GOTO or to reference the statement label of a `FORMAT` statement in a `READ` or `WRITE` statement.

It should be noted that a variable can only be assigned a statement label value by an `ASSIGN` statement. The two statements

```
IVAR = 1000
```

and

```
ASSIGN 1000 TO IVAR
```

have entirely different effects. In the first case the arithmetic value, 1000, is copied into the location called `IVAR`. In the second the address in memory of the code associated with the statement labelled 1000 is copied into the location called `IVAR`. Except as the most improbable of accidents these two values will be entirely different.

13.1.2.2 Assigned FORMAT specifiers: The `ASSIGN` statement can be used to assign a label to an integer which is subsequently referred to in an input/output statement as in the following example,

```
IF(A > 1.0E5)THEN
  ASSIGN 100 TO IFORM
ELSE
  ASSIGN 101 TO IFORM
```

```
    ENDIF
    ...
    WRITE(*,IFORM) A,B
100 FORMAT(2E10.3)
101 FORMAT(2F10.4)
```

The same functionality can be obtained through use of character variables to hold FORMAT specifications.

13.1.2.3 The assigned GOTO statement: The assigned GOTO statement has the form,

```
GOTO <integer-variable>
```

or

```
GOTO <integer-variable> ,(<label1>,<label2>,...)
```

When such a statement is executed the value of a statement label of an executable statement in the program unit containing the statement must have been previously assigned to the integer variable. The effect is to cause control to be transferred to the statement whose label is currently assigned to the integer variable. In the first form of the statement the label may be any label in the program unit. In the second form the assigned label must be one of the labels named in the list.

Use of the ASSIGN and assigned GOTO statements can all too easily result in totally unreadable code with no discernable logical structure.

13.1.3 Obsolescent DO-Loop options

The DO-loop as we have presented it always starts with a DO statement and ends with a corresponding ENDDO statement. The DO...ENDDO loop was introduced in Fortran 90 to replace the old DO loop which was terminated by a labelled executable statement. The old loop is exemplified by the following typical piece of code.

```
    DO 50 I=1,N
    ...
50  A(I) = A(I)+1.0
```

which differs from the new loop only in the way that the loop is terminated. The ENDDO statement of Fortran 90 is replaced by a label specification in the DO statement and the loop itself is terminated by an executable statement with this label. Other examples of the old style loop are,

```
      DO 100 K=1,N
      DO 100 J=1,N
      DO 100 I=1,N
      ...
  100 A(I,J,K)=A(I,J,K)/2.0
```

which shows a group of nested loops. Such loops were often written with a single terminating statement used for all the nested loops. This Fortran 77 style of writing loops often causes problems when programs are changed so that the loops do not logically end on a single statement any more. Confusion can also arise when a loop such as

```
    DO 10 I=1,NI
    IF(X.GT.Y) GOTO 10
    DO 10 J=1,NJ
    ...
10  A=A+1
```

is executed. When the `GOTO 10` is executed it is not clear which loop is iterated when the statement labelled `10` is completed. The `DO...ENDDO` avoids this sort of confusion.

13.1.3.1 Non-integral DO-loop indices: Fortran 77 allows the index of a `DO`-loop to be of type real or double precision as well as integer. This feature can hardly be called a relic as it was introduced into Fortran in the Fortran 77 standard. However subsequent practice and experience has shown that use of the facility can be dangerous and is often distinctly non-portable.

Because real numbers of either precision are not exact (they are subject to round-off errors) this leads to loops with unpredictable iteration counts. For example, consider the following DO statement,

```
      DO 10 X = 0.0, pi/2.0, pi/20.0
```

(assuming `pi` is a real parameter with the value `3.1415926`)

The obvious intention of such a loop is to process the loop body with the index variable set to `0.0, pi/20, 2pi/20, 3pi/20, 4pi/20, ... , 10pi/20`. However, because real arithmetic is subject to round-off the value calculated for `pi/2.0` on some machines may actually be slightly less than `10pi/20.0`. On such machines the loop iteration count will be `10` not the expected `11` and so the loop will not be executed for the last required value `pi/2`. On other machines which use a different representation and rounding strategy the number of iterations carried out could be different.

When a loop over a sequence of real values is needed it is much better to construct it in terms of integral indices and to calculate the required real values inside the loop.

```
      DO 10 I = 0,10
        X = I*PI/20.0
        ...
```

This has essentially the same effect but has an entirely predictable iteration behaviour on all machines.

13.1.4 PAUSE statement

The `PAUSE` statement was used in previous versions of Fortran to suspend a program and wait for operator action. The form of the statement is

```
    PAUSE <stop code>
```

where the <stop code> is either a character constant or a string of up to five digits.

On multi-user systems, which today are often run without any operators in attendance, the system may not be actually able to pause, or the pause may require, not the operator, but the user to input some system specific information to resume the execution. The action of pause has become distinctly non-portable. The same functionality, in a more portable way, can be obtained through use of a `READ` statement preceded by a `WRITE` statement. Thus

```
    WRITE(*,*) <stop code>
    READ(*,*) I
```

would have the same effect as a `PAUSE` statement.

13.1.5 Hollerith constants

Statements of the form,

```
       WRITE(*,100)
100    FORMAT(16HTITLE OF PROGRAM)
```

which output, for example, the literal string `TITLE OF PROGRAM` were common in early Fortran programs. This so-called Hollerith string, which required the programmer to specify explicitly the number of characters in the string, was completely replaced in Fortran 77 by the character constant as in,

```
      WRITE(*,100)
100   FORMAT('TITLE OF PROGRAM')
```

13.2 Undesirable features

These features are those whose use is considered by the authors to be generally undesirable. In most cases such features are unnecessary. Their effect can be better programmed using other Fortran 90 features. In the following a brief description of each feature will be given followed by a recommendation on which Fortran 90 feature should be used in preference.

13.2.1 Fixed format source statements

Up until the introduction of Fortran 90, all standard Fortran programs had to adhere to a strict format which was designed to aid the transfer of the source code on to punched cards. This source form is totally unsuitable for current environments where programs are entered via VDUs and so a free source form, described in Chapter 3 has been introduced.

The fixed source form, which is still an albeit redundant part of Fortran 90, requires that Fortran statements occupy positions 1 to 72 of a record. Positions 1 to 5 are used for statement labels. Any character apart from blank in column 6 is used to signify that the record is a continuation of the previous record. The main statement has to occupy columns 7 to 72. Any characters that spill over into columns 73 or above are ignored.

Comment statements are identified by either the letter 'C' or '*' in position 1 of a record. Blanks can be used to space out statements and they have no significance except in character strings.

This old source form and the new free-form layout are not compatible. They cannot be mixed in a single program unit. A processor must have some way of deciding which form is to be used for a particular program before it can compile it. A common convention is to use the suffix, `.F90` on the filename of a Fortran program written in free-form and to assume that a program in fixed-form will use the old suffix, `.FOR`.

13.2.2 Implicit declaration and typing

Implicit declaration and typing of variables has been widely used by many, if not most, casual Fortran programmers. The assumption is that by default all variables that are not explicitly declared take their type according to the first letter of the variable name (i.e. those that have variable names starting with I,J,K,L,M,N are of default type INTEGER and those that start with any other letter are of type REAL). This has been a feature of Fortran from its conception. It is therefore somewhat rare to find Fortran programs with all their variables declared explicitly as we have advocated in previous chapters. The ability simply to create variables when they are needed without prior declaration, and to have them implicitly typed is very convenient especially when a quick prototype program is being written. It is however most definitely dangerous.

Every program of any size or complexity will have residual bugs. This is practically a law of nature like the second law of thermodynamics. Detailed analyses of many large running Fortran programs and the bugs they have been found to contain, has shown that by far the largest number of these, 60% or more, are due to use of implicitly declared variables. It is therefore clear that the simple precaution of always declaring variables explicitly will significantly reduce the likelihood of programs containing bugs. The use of IMPLICIT NONE as described in Chapter 4 is a useful aid which will ensure that a compiler will flag any variables that are undeclared and its use is recommended.

13.2.2.1 The IMPLICIT Statement: Implicit declaration and typing can be extended to apply to the other types by use of an IMPLICIT statement. If it occurs, an IMPLICIT statement must be the first statement, other than possibly PARAMETER or USE statements, following the program unit header and it establishes the associations between types and letters that are to be used to determine the type of any variable not explicitly declared. For example,

```
IMPLICIT CHARACTER*8(C),DOUBLE PRECISION(D),COMPLEX(U-W,Z)
```

associates the letter C with CHARACTER*8, D with DOUBLE PRECISION, and U,V,W,Z with COMPLEX. Any variables or symbolic constants not explicitly declared whose names start with any of these letters will be assumed to be of the associated type. Note, all the letters not explicitly associated with a type by an IMPLICIT statement retain their default association.

The general form of the IMPLICIT statement is

```
IMPLICIT <type>(<letter range>),<type>(<letter range>)...
```

where <type> can be any of the Fortran data types, intrinsic or derived, and <letter range> (of which one must be present), must be either a single letter or a range of letters. A range is indicated by an initial letter and a final letter separated by a minus. A range means all the letters in the alphabetic sequence from the initial to the final letter.

At least one type(letter) association must be specified on any IMPLICIT statement and no letter must be associated more than once with a type.

13.2.3 Storage association

The Fortran 90 language is defined in such a way that programs can be written without the programmer needing to be aware of the relationship or association between variables and the actual storage units they occupy. This design has great advantages for those writing programs which they require to be portable between machines, particularly to new computer architectures since it means that compiler writers for such machines can transparently (to the programmer) take advantage of new possibilities for optimisation. Fortran 90 contains Fortran 77 as a sub-set so it has inevitably carried forward many features which depend on storage association which were part of Fortran 77.

Fortran 90 defines three kinds of *storage unit*, the character storage unit, the numeric storage unit and the unspecified storage unit. Each data type is associated with one or more storage units. Real, integer and logical variables are defined to occupy one numeric storage unit. Character variables of length one are defined to occupy one character storage unit. Arrays as declared, and lists of variables specified to be part of a COMMON block (see below) establish a sequence of storage units. Such a sequence is called a *storage sequence*. There are various ways in which two storage sequences may be overlapped or associated. Such *storage association* can allow the same data object to be known by different names in the same program unit, or may permit different program units to access the same object in different program units, possibly with different names.

13.2.3.1 The COMMON statement: The only way in Fortran 77 to specify that data was to be globally available to several subprograms was to use a COMMON block. Variables and arrays which were required to be globally available had to be declared in COMMON statements in each subprogram in which they were required to be accessible. A simple Fortran 77 program illustrates this.

```
PROGRAM SHARE
 REAL A(50), B(20), C
 COMMON/Block1/A,B,C
 ...
```

```
  ...
  CALL Sub1
  CALL Sub2
  ...
END
SUBROUTINE Sub1
  REAL A(50), B(20), C
  COMMON/Block1/A,B,C
  ...
  ...
END
SUBROUTINE Sub2
  REAL A(50), B(20), C
  COMMON/Block1/A,B,C
  ...
  ...
END
```

The above example would make the arrays A and B and the real variable C accessible in the main program and the two subroutines via the COMMON block Block1. The COMMON block establishes a block of storage that is, in this case 71 numeric storage units long that is storage associated between the program units that declare it. It would be possible for the block to be declared differently in each program unit.

```
SUBROUTINE Sub2
REAL X,Y
INTEGER Z
COMMON/Block1/ X(10),Y,Z(60)
```

would also be a valid declaration, even though not all the variables are of the same type. The only requirement is that the common block has the same length and sequence of storage units.

The problem with use of this feature is that it is all to easy to get it wrong by accident. To be safe, COMMON statements and their associated type declaration statements have to define the same variables as well as storage sequence in each subprogram that they are used. Since it is all too easy to miss out or mis-spell a variable in a COMMON block list it is therefore very easy to introduce bugs which are very hard to find into programs . The fact that COMMON works by establishing a storage sequence which requires memory to be structured in a linear fashion is a feature that inhibits optimisation on any system that does not naturally organise its memory this way.

Fortran 90 allows the use of global data sharing through the Module facility. As described in Chapter 8, global data need only be specified once in a module and then the module can be USEd in each subprogram that it is required. Since the data has only to be specified once, this mechanism is far less prone to error and therefore should be strongly preferred to the use of COMMON. No storage sequence is implied or required by global data declared in a module. The system can employ its available memory in ways that are optimal.

13.2.3.2 The EQUIVALENCE statement: The misuse of EQUIVALENCE has been well known as a major source of bugs in Fortran 77 programs and also a major cause of difficulty in transporting programs from one machine to another. This has been particularly so when EQUIVALENCE has interacted with the use of the COMMON statement. The COMMON facility causes the set of data occupying a specific sequence of storage units to be shared between a number of different routines. The EQUIVALENCE facility allows a specific set of storage units to be referred to by various different names in the same program unit. If the names made equivalent happen to be part of storage sequences, the whole storage sequences are also made to overlap in the process.

The form of the EQUIVALENCE statement is

```
EQUIVALENCE (<var list>),(<var list>),...
```

where <var list> is a list of names for variables that are required to occupy the same storage unit. Note, character variables may not be EQUIVALENCEd with anything other than other character variables. An EQUIVALENCE statement is a non-executable statement and must appear with the specification statements, before any executable statement.

The <var list> establishes a storage unit which can be referred to by more than one name. If these names happen to be part of a storage sequence then the association of the whole sequence is by implication also established. For example,

```
REAL A(100),B(100)
COMPLEX Z(50)
EQUIVALENCE(A(1),Z(1)),(A(2),B(1))
```

ties together the sequences of storage referred to by the arrays A,B,Z. The first list makes A(1) and the real part of Z(1) refer to the same location. That is the two sequences are made to start at the same point. So A(1) refers to the real part of Z(1) and A(2) refers to the imaginary part of Z(1), and so on; every even numbered A refers to the imaginary part of the elements in the complex array and every odd numbered A refers to a real part. The second equivalence associates the B array sequence with the A sequence but with the B sequence starting at the second location of the A. This by implication associates odd numbered B elements with the imaginary parts of Z.

If a set of complex values was stored in Z it would be possible to refer to its parts by way of the real arrays. Strictly speaking this is the only case when sequences of objects of different types that are associated can legally be defined by way of one type and referenced by way of another. However as few, if any, compilers check this, EQUIVALENCE, which was originally introduced as a memory saving device, is most often used in practice as a way of changing types without having to go through a conversion routine. The type conversion routines change the bit patterns representing the value so as to preserve the value. Storing a value in a variable as one type then taking it out of a variable of a different type that is EQUIVALENCEd to the first does not change the bit pattern, merely its interpretation. The values represented by the "input" pattern and the "output" will usually be very different in this case.

In Fortran 90, the EQUIVALENCE statement is redundant since the main uses of it by Fortran 77 programmers, i.e. aliasing and type conversion, can now be achieved using pointer data types and the intrinsic TRANSFER function.

13.2.3.3 Assumed size array arguments: The old way of passing variable size of arrays as arguments was based on the idea that an array was always a linear sequence of storage units; the array was assumed to occupy a linear and contiguous sequence of storage units organised in array element order. An array could be passed as an argument by indicating that what was to be passed was merely the starting address of such a sequence. To do this the dummy array would be declared with its last dimension specified as an asterisk. Such dummy arguments are called *assumed-size*. In the following,

```
SUBROUTINE subsize(as)
REAL :: as(*)
...
```

the dummy argument, as, assumes its size from the size of the storage sequence of the associated actual argument. The actual argument may be an array name (meaning the first element in the array) or an array element name. The size of as will be that of the storage sequence defined by the actual array from the actual element to the end of the array. The ranks of actual and dummy arrays do not have to be the same, merely the lengths of storage sequences so associated. These assumed-size arrays are fairly easy to use when both are rank one, but if either is multi-dimension working out exactly which subset of the elements is which is very tricky and error prone, particularly if the ranks do not agree. Consider the following,

```
SUBROUTINE assm(nda)
REAL :: nda(10,30,*)
...
```

If this were called with an actual argument that was the first element of a rank 3 array which had its first two dimensions declared also as (10,30), it would be quite easy to work out which elements of the actual array corresponded to which of the dummy. If on the other hand the actual argument is an element 2,3 from an array of rank, say 2, declared with dimensions (40,40) it would be much more difficult to work out how the elements of the actual array map on to those of the dummy array.

Assumed-size arrays may only be manipulated via array element references. They may not be sectioned nor may they be used in whole array expressions. Given their complexity and lack of utility compared with assumed-shape arrays there is no reason for their continued use.

13.2.3.4 Sequence structures

The introduction of derived types in Fortran 90 inevitably raised the question of how this feature should react with some of the older features of the language. Derived types as presented in Chapter 4 are defined such that there is no storage association of components. Thus there is no requirement in the language that the components of a structure should occupy contiguous storage units or that they should be stored in the order given in the definition of the derived type. For example, consider the following derived type definition,

```
TYPE PERSON
CHARACTER(LEN=30)  :: name
CHARACTER(LEN=3)   :: sex
REAL               :: height
ENDTYPE PERSON
```

and the variable declared as,

```
TYPE(PERSON) :: man1
```

In general, there is no requirement that the structure defined by `man1` should have its `name`, `sex`, and `height` occupying adjacent storage units in that order. Objects of such a derived type cannot be included in any storage sequence, nor can they become associated with any other object by storage association. However, in order to use a structure such as `man1` in a storage association context (e.g. in a `COMMON` block), a storage sequence must be defined for the type and the variable. To enable this, the `SEQUENCE` statement is provided which, when specified in a type definition, overrides the general rule and causes the definition and subsequent declaration of a derived type variable to have a storage sequence. Thus the type, `PERSON`, could be declared as,

```
TYPE PERSON
SEQUENCE
CHARACTER(LEN=30) :: name
CHARACTER(LEN=3)  :: sex
REAL              :: height
ENDTYPE PERSON
```

and then the declaration,

```
TYPE(PERSON) :: man1
```

would require that the `man1%name`, `man1%sex` and `man1%height` were stored in contiguous storage units in the correct order. Such an object can be included in a storage sequence such as a common block where it contributes 33 character storage units followed by a single numeric storage unit.

We believe that that the `SEQUENCE` statement and functionality should be avoided. It suffers from all the problems of storage asssociation in general and adds a number of complications of its own. The non-`SEQUENCE` data type can and should be used in preference to these sequenced types.

13.2.3.5 The BLOCK DATA subprogram

A `COMMON` block must be declared independently in each routine that needs to access it. This means that variables in a `COMMON` block cannot be initialised in the same manner as ordinary local or global variables. It would be all too easy for two routines to initialise a variable in common to different values. The initial value would then depend on the order in which these were loaded. Since this order has no defined relationship to execution order and is different for different processors there has to be some other

special mechanism for initialising variables in common. The BLOCK DATA subprogram is a program unit specifically for this purpose.
A BLOCK DATA subprogram contains no executable statements and cannot be called whilst a program is running. The only statements allowed are the declaration and specification statements necessary to declare a common block and to specify initial values for its variables. An example BLOCK DATA subprogram is shown below.

```
BLOCK DATA INICOM
 INTEGER N,NSQ
 PARAMETER ( N = 100, NSQ = N*N )
 REAL A,B
 COMMON/BLOCK1/A(N,N), B(N)
 DATA A, B / NSQ*0.0, N*0.0/
END
```

This BLOCK DATA subprogram initialises the arrays A and B, declared to be in the COMMON block BLOCK1, to zero. Notice that the subprogram has a name, INICOM. If there are multiple BLOCK DATA subprograms in a program, they must each have a unique name. If more than one BLOCK DATA subprogram is used, any particular common block must not be declared in more than one such BLOCK DATA subprogram.

In Fortran 90 the BLOCK DATA subprogram is redundant since all global data can be defined and initialised in a module.

13.2.4 ENTRY statement

This feature was also introduced officially in Fortran 77, although it had long been a common extension. The problem with ENTRY statements is their effect on structure and readability when used in an undisciplined way.

An ENTRY statement is a non-executable statement. It has the form of a subprogram header statement and it allows a subprogram to be referenced by an entry name and allows execution to start at some intermediate place in the executable code of the subprogram. The main advantage of this is that the ENTRY statement allows the data defined in one procedure to be accessible from a different procedure.

A classic example of disciplined use of ENTRY statements is shown by the following program fragment,

```
FUNCTION FITDAT(N,X,Y)
 INTEGER N
 REAL X(N),Y(N),FITDAT,INTERP
 REAL A,B,C,D,E
 SAVE A,B,C,D,E
```

```
  ...
   perform the calculation to determine A-E and calculate
   the residual least square sum which gives a measure of
   the accuracy of the fit to be returned as the function
   result
  ...
  RETURN
  ENTRY INTERP(ARG)
  INTERP =(((E*ARG + D)*ARG + C)*ARG + B)*ARG + A
END
```

The function `FITDAT` can be invoked once , say, to calculate a least squares fit of a polynomial to a set of data. In the above the coefficients of the 4th order polynomial are calculated as `A, B, C, D, E`. Subsequent invokations of `INTERP` will then have access to these coefficients for the purposes of evaluating the polynomial.

Use of `ENTRY` statements in this way is reasonably clear and effective. Note however that the functionality provided by the `ENTRY` statement as described above has been completely replaced in Fortran 90 by the `MODULE/USE` facility. The above example as a module would be,

```
MODULE Fit_Polynomial
  REAL,SAVE :: A,B,C,D,E
CONTAINS
  FUNCTION FITDAT(X,Y)
   INTEGER   :: N
   REAL      :: X(:),Y(:),FITDAT
   ...
   perform the calculation to determine A-E and calculate the
   residual least square sum which gives a measure of the
   accuracy of the fit to be returned as the function result
   ...
  ENDFUNCTION
  FUNCTION INTERP(ARG)
   INTERP =(((E*ARG + D)*ARG + C)*ARG + B)*ARG + A
  ENDFUNCTION
ENDMODULE
```

The above module could be `USE`d in any procedure that required to access either function. Any invocation of `FITDAT` would make the coefficients `A-E` accessible to `INTERP`.

13.2.5 Statement functions

Statement functions were used in Fortran 77 as a convenient short-hand to avoid having to code frequently used one-line formulae as external functions. In the following code,

```
PROGRAM Example_Function
  REAL F,X,Y
  F(X,Y) = X**2 + Y**2
  ...
  Z1 = F(U1,V1)
  ...
  Z2 = F(U2,V2)
  ...
ENDPROGRAM Example_Function
```

F is defined by a single statement and is a statement function. This is a very restricted form of internal procedure. It did not generalise readily to the more extensive type and array facilities of Fortran 90.

It is far better in practice to avoid such use and to code the above example as an internal procedure. Thus,

```
PROGRAM Example_Function
 REAL :: F
 REAL :: Z1,Z2,U1,U2
 ...
 Z1 = F(U1,V1)
 ...
 Z2 = F(U2,V2)
 ...
CONTAINS
 FUNCTION F(X,Y)
  REAL F,X,Y
  F = X**2 + Y**2
 ENDFUNCTION F
ENDPROGRAM Example_Function
```

13.2.6 Computed GOTO

The computed GOTO statement in Fortran 77 provides a means of implementing a multi-way branch. The dangers of using it in an undisciplined manner are fairly obvious and its use is not recommended. However, in the past careful use of the facility provided a means of implementing a SELECT CASE structure. The following code illustrates this,

```
GOTO( 100,101,102 ), I
    ...
    ! code for default case I<1 or I>3
    ...
    GOTO 200
100 CONTINUE
    ...
    ! code for I=1 case
    ...
    GOTO 200
```

```
101 CONTINUE
    ...
    ! code for I=2 case
    ...
    GOTO 200
102 CONTINUE
    ...
    ! code for I=3 case
    ...
    ...
200 CONTINUE
    ...
```

Depending on the value of `I` a jump is made to the appropriate piece of code. However the labelled statements may be anywhere in the program unit. The possibilities for structural nightmares are immense.

The following code which uses the Fortran 90 `SELECT CASE` construct is much safer and clearer,

```
SELECT CASE (I)
  CASE DEFAULT
    ...
    ! code for default case I<1 or I>3
    ...
  CASE(1)
    ...
    ! code for I=1 case
    ...
  CASE(2)
    ...
    ! code for I=2 case
    ...
  CASE(3)
    ...
    ! code for I=3 case
    ...
ENDSELECT
```

13.2.7 Alternate RETURN

The alternate `RETURN` facility is an extension of the `RETURN` statement which can be illustrated by the following example,

```
    PROGRAM ALT_RETURN
    ...
    CALL SUB1(x,y,*98,*99)
    ...
 98 CONTINUE
    ...
 99 CONTINUE
    ...
```

```
END PROGRAM

SUBROUTINE SUB1(X,Y,*,*)
...
RETURN 1
...
RETURN 2
END
```

The facility allows a calling subprogram to specify labels as arguments to a called subprogram as shown. The called subprogram can then return control to different points in the calling subprogram by specifying an integer parameter to the RETURN statement which corresponds to a set of labels specified in the argument list.

The above method of coding which was often used to specify error exits from subprograms is, in general, considered to be bad practice and is better replaced by the use of an integer return code argument to the subroutine and a case statement following the call statement as in the following example,

```
CALL SUBROUTINE sub1(x, y, ierr)
SELECT CASE(ierr)
 CASE(1)
  code for case when ierr=1
 CASE(2)
  code for case when ierr=2
 ...
END SELECT CASE
```

13.2.8 The INCLUDE statement

This statement has been included in Fortran 90 in an attempt to standardise a common facility provided by many Fortran compilers. The statement takes the form,

```
INCLUDE <character literal constant>
```

For example,

```
INCLUDE 'subs.f'
```

and the effect is that the contents of the file subs.f are included in the current program at the point where the INCLUDE statement appears.

This facility was and can be used to partially overcome some of the problems associated with specifying common blocks in different subprograms. Thus a set of common blocks can be specified in a single file and then included in programs wherever required. This avoids problems of mis-spelling or inconsistent specification in different subprograms but does not avoid possible side effects caused by specification statements which precede the `INCLUDE` statement. For example, if we had an include file called `FRED.COM` containing the common block

```
COMMON/FRED/ I,J,K(1000)
```

and this was included into two program units

```
PROGRAM FIRST
INTEGER :: I,J,K
INCLUDE 'FRED.COM'
...
ENDPROGRAM FIRST
SUBROUTINE SECOND
REAL I,J,K
INCLUDE 'FRED.COM'
...
ENDSUBROUTINE SECOND
```

we would have a legal program but one where the meaning of the included common block was different in the two program units. The simple, indeed simplistic textual substitution nature of `INCLUDE` can result in a number of problems like this because the meaning of Fortran statements is sensitive to the context in which they appear.

The same functionality is provided in a much safer way by use of the `MODULE/USE` facility.

13.2.9 The DO WHILE loop

The `DO WHILE` loop is provided in Fortran 90 since many Fortran 77 compilers provided it as an extension. It is a special case of the more general conditional exit loop described in Chapter 5. In fact the example,

```
DO WHILE( I <= 0 )
  ...
ENDDO
```

is functionally identical to,

```
DO ; IF( I > 0) EXIT
  ...
ENDDO
```

The second spelling is, in our opinion, preferable to the first since it is much clearer that the loop is terminated only at the start of the first iteration after I becomes greater than 0. It is also merely a special case of the more general conditional exit form of loop. The DO WHILE form often causes confusion to new programmers since it can be mistakenly assumed that the loop is terminated as soon as I becomes 1, regardless of where in the loop this happens.

13.2.10 The NAMELIST Statement

The NAMELIST statement allows groups of variables to be treated in a special way for input/output. The detailed rules of the facilities provided are fairly complex and we believe the feature is best avoided. However to give some idea of what the namelist facility provides we present the following example which is taken from the Fortran 90 standard.

```
INTEGER                :: I
REAL, DIMENSION(8)     :: X
CHARACTER(LEN=11)      :: P
COMPLEX                :: Z
LOGICAL                :: G
NAMELIST/TODAY/ G,I,P,Z,X
...
READ(*, NML = TODAY)
...
```

The above statements define a namelist group called TODAY in an obvious way. The READ statement initiates input of a data record which might look like,

```
&TODAY  I=12345,  X(1)=12345,  X(3:4)=2*1.5,  P="ISN'T  BOBS",
Z=(123,0)/
```

The values taken by the variables are shown in Table 13.1.

The NAMELIST facility allows a group of variable names to be specified as belonging to a named list. Input or output of these variables can be initiated by a read or write which specifies this namelist. The input record must start with &<namelist name>. It is then made up of a sequence of <variable reference name> = <set of values> items, and the input group is terminated by a /. The variables referenced must belong to the namelist group in question and they specify to which of the variables the following data values apply. If a variable is not included in the input record its value is not changed.

Variable	**Value**
I	12345
X(1)	12345.0
X(2)	unchanged
X(3)	1.5
X(4)	1.5
X(5) to X(8)	unchanged
P	ISN'T BOB'S
Z	(123.0, 0.0)
G	unchanged

Table 13.1

Namelist groups can also be used in output statements and the effect is to produce output records which look similar to the input record. A record output by a namelist-write is suitable for subsequent namelist-read.

There are a great many complicated subtleties which we will not cover further, but which tend to detract from the facility. Simple namelist I/O such as that above could be useful but in most cases it is hardly much more difficult to handle the I/O in conventional ways. It seems an unnecessary additional facility with too many tricky rules to bother learning.

Appendix A

Intrinsic Procedures

A.1 Introduction

Fortran 90 has increased the number of intrinsic procedures available from just under 40 in Fortran 77 to well over 100. The language now provides a rich set of features to support the new facilities covered by the language especially in the areas of numerical programming and array handling. Users of Fortran need to be aware of these intrinsic procedures since, apart from saving time spent in coding unnecessary functions, use of them will ensure that programs will be optimised for any machine on which they run. Compiler vendors take great care to ensure that the intrinsic procedures are carefully optimised for the target hardware since this will evidently help sell their product.

This chapter is intended mainly as a reference aid for programmers. It has been based closely on the relevant section of the Fortran 90 standard, (ISO/IEC 1539 : 1991, "Programming Language Fortran").

A.1.1 Types of procedure

There are four types of intrinsic procedure:

inquiry functions whose results depend on the properties of their principal arguments. For example, `LEN(C)` which returns the length of the character variable `C`, or `SIZE(A)` which returns the size of the array `A`.

elemental functions which are defined for scalar (non-array) arguments but can also be applied to arrays. Thus `SIN(X)` returns the mathematical sine of the scalar variable `X` whereas `SIN(A)`, where `A` is an array, will return an array whose elements are the sines of the elements of the array `A`.

transformational functions which usually take array arguments and return results which are scalars or arrays. Examples are: `SUM(A)` which returns a scalar which is the sum of all the elements of the array `A`, and `TRANSPOSE(A)` which returns an array which is the transpose of the array `A`.

subroutines which are invoked by a `CALL` statement.

A.1.2 Positional arguments or argument keywords

All intrinsic procedures may be invoked with either positional arguments or argument keywords. The descriptions given below give the keyword names and positional sequence. A keyword is required for an argument only if a preceding optional argument is omitted.

A.2 Argument presence inquiry function

PRESENT(A)

Determine whether an optional argument, A, *is present.*

The result has the value true if A is present and otherwise has the value false.

A.3 Numeric Functions

All the functions in this section are elemental. All arguments specified with a KIND keyword are optional and must be an integer scalar initialisation expression. If present, a KIND argument specifies the kind type parameter of the result, otherwise the result has the same kind as the principal argument.

ABS(A)

Absolute value of A.

The result type and type parameter is the same as A, except that if A is complex, the result is real.

If A is of type integer or real, the value of the result is |A|. If A is complex with value (x,y), the result is equal to a processor-dependent approximation to $\sqrt{(x^2+y^2)}$.

Example : ABS((3.0,4.0)) has the value 5.0 (approximately).

AIMAG(Z)

Imaginary part of a complex number, Z.

The result is real with the same kind type parameter as Z. If Z has the value (x,y), the result has value y.

Example : AIMAG((2.0,3.0)) has the value 3.0.

AINT(A,KIND)

Truncation of a real number, A, *to a whole real number.*

If |A|<1, AINT(A) has the value 0; if |A|>1, AINT(A) has a value equal to the integer whose magnitude is the largest integer that does not exceed the magnitude of A and whose sign is the same as the sign of A.

Examples: AINT(2.783) has the value 2.0. AINT(-2.783) has the value -2.0.

ANINT(A,KIND)

Nearest real whole number to a real number A.

If A>0, ANINT(A) has the value AINT(A+0.5); if A<=0, ANINT(A) has the value AINT(A-0.5).

Examples: ANINT(2.783) has the value 3.0, ANINT(-2.783) has the value -3.0.

CEILING(A)

Returns the least integer greater than or equal to a real number A.

The result is undefined if the processor cannot represent this value in the default integer type.

Examples: CEILING(3.7) has the value 4. CEILING(-3.7) has the value -3.

CMPLX(X,Y,KIND)

Convert to complex type.

Y and KIND are optional arguments. X must be of type integer, real, or complex. Y, if present, must be of type integer or real. Y must not be present if X is of type complex. If Y is absent and X is not complex, it is as if Y were present with the value zero. If Y is absent and X is complex, it is as if Y were present with the value AIMAG(X). CMPLX(X,Y,KIND) has the complex value whose real part is REAL(X,KIND) and whose imaginary part is REAL(Y,KIND).
Example : CMPLX(-3) has the value (-3.0,0.0).

CONJG(Z)

Conjugate of a complex number, Z.

If Z has the value (x,y), the result has the value (x,-y).
Example : CONJG((2.0,3.0)) has the value (2.0,-3.0).

DBLE(A)

Convert to double precision type.

Case i) : If A is of type double precision DBLE(A)=A.
Case ii) : If A is of type integer or real, the result is the value A rounded as necessary to double precision.
Case iii) : If A is of type complex, the result is the real part of A rounded as necessary to double precision.

Example : DBLE(-3) has the value -3.0D0.

DIM(X,Y)

The difference X-Y *if it is positive, otherwise zero.*

X must be of type integer or real. Y must be of the same type and kind type parameter as X.
Example : DIM(-3.0,2.0) has the value 0.0.

DPROD(X,Y)

Double precision real product of reals X *and* Y.

The result has a value equal to the double precision product of real values X and Y.
Example : DPROD(-3.0,2.0) has the value -6.0D0.

FLOOR(A)

Returns the greatest integer less than or equal to its real argument, A.

The result is undefined if the processor cannot represent this value in the default integer type.
Examples: FLOOR(3.7) has the value 3. FLOOR(-3.7) has the value -4.

INT(A,KIND)

Convert to integer type.

A must be of type integer, real, or complex.

Case i) : If A is of type integer, INT(A)=A.
Case ii) : If A is of type real and |A|<1, INT(A)=0.
Case iii) : If A is of type real and |A|>=1, INT(A) is the integer whose magnitude is the largest integer that does not exceed the magnitude of A and whose sign is the same as the sign of A.
Case iv) : If A is of type complex, INT(A)=INT(REAL(A)).

If KIND is present the result is an integer of this kind, otherwise it is of default integer type. The result is undefined if the processor cannot represent the result in the specified integer type.

Examples: INT(3.7) has the value 3. INT(-3.7) has the value -3.

MAX(A1,A2,A3,...)

Maximum value of a set of integers or a set of real numbers.

The arguments A3,... are optional.

Example : MAX(-9.0,7.0,2.0) has the value 7.0.

MIN(A1,A2,A3,...)

Minimum value of a set of integers or a set of real numbers.

The arguments A3,... are optional.

Example : MIN(-9.0,7.0,2.0,-5.0) has the value -9.0.

MOD(A,P)

Remainder function.

A and P must be of the same type (integer or real) and kind type parameter.

If P is non-zero, the value of the result is A-INT(A/P)*P.

If P is zero, the result is processor dependent.

Examples: MOD(3.0,2.0) has the value 1.0 (approximately). MOD(8,5) has the value 3. MOD(-8,5) has the value -3. MOD(8,-5) has the value 3. MOD(-8,-5) has the value -3.

MODULO(A,P)

Modulo function.

A and P must be of the same type (integer or real) and kind type parameter.

Case i) : If A is of type integer and P>0, MODULO(A,P) has the value R such that A=QxP+R, where Q is an integer and 0<R<P.
Case ii) : If A is of type integer and P<0, MODULO(A,P) has the value R such that A=QxP+R, where Q is an integer and 0>R>P.
Case iii) : If A is of type real and P is non-zero, MODULO(A,P)=A-FLOOR(A/P)*P.

In all cases if P is zero, the result is processor dependent.

Examples: MODULO(8,5) has the value 3. MODULO(-8,5) has the value 2. MODULO(8,-5) has the value -2. MODULO(-8,-5) has the value -3.

NINT(A, KIND)

Nearest integer to a real A.

If A>=0, NINT(A) has the value INT(A+0.5); if A<0, NINT(A) has the value INT(A-0.5). The result is undefined if the processor cannot represent the result in the specified integer type. If KIND is present the result is an integer of this kind, otherwise it is of default integer type.

Example : NINT(2.783) has the value 3.

REAL(A,KIND)

Convert integer, real or complex data to real type.

If KIND is present, the result is a real of this kind. If KIND is not present then, the result is of default real type if A is of type integer or real, and is of the same kind as A if A is of complex type.

Case i) : If A is of type integer or real, the result is a real valued approximation to A.

Case ii) : If A is of type complex. the result is a real valued approximation to the real part of A.

Examples: REAL(-3) has the value -3.0. REAL(Z) has the same kind type parameter and the same value as the real part of the complex variable Z.

SIGN(A,B)

Absolute value of A *times the sign of* B.

A must be of type integer or real. B must be of the same type and kind as A.

The result is |A| if B>=0 and -|A| if B<0.

Example : SIGN(-3.0,2.0) has the value 3.0.

A.4 Mathematical Functions

All the functions in this section are elemental.

ACOS(X)

Arccosine (inverse cosine) in radians of a real X (|X|<=1).

The result lies in the range 0<=ACOS(X)<=π.

Example : ACOS(0.54030231) has the value 1.0 (approximately).

ASIN(X)

Arcsine (inverse sine) in radians of a real X (|X|<=1).

The result lies in the range -π/2<ASIN(X)<π/2.

Example : ASIN(0.84147098) has the value 1.0 (approximately).

ATAN(X)

Arctangent (inverse tangent) in radians of a real X.

The result lies in the range -π/2<=ATAN(X)<=π/2.

Example : ATAN(1.5574077) has the value 1.0 (approximately).

ATAN2(Y,X)

Arctangent (inverse tangent) function.

Y and X must be of type real and of the same kind. If Y has the value zero, X must not have the value zero.
The result is of the same type and kind as the arguments. It is an approximation to the principal value of the argument of the complex number (X,Y), expressed in radians. It lies in the range -π< ATAN2(Y,X) <=π and this is equal to an approximation to $\tan^{-1}$(Y/X) if X/=0. If Y>0, the result is positive. If Y=0, the result is zero for X>0 and π for X<0. If Y<0, the result is negative. If X=0, the absolute value of the result is π/2.
Examples: ATAN2(1.5574077,1.0) has the value 1.0 (approximately).

COS(X)

Cosine of real or complex number, X.

The argument is a value in radians.
The result is of the same type and kind as the argument.
Example : COS(1.0) has the value 0.54030231 (approximately).

COSH(X)

Hyperbolic cosine of a real number, X.

The result is of the same kind as the argument.
Example : COSH(1.0) has the value 1.5430806 (approximately).

EXP(X)

Exponential (e^x) of a real or complex number, X.

If X is of type complex, its imaginary part is regarded as a value in radians.
The result is of the same type and kind as the argument.
Example : EXP(1.0) has the value 2.7182818 (approximately).

LOG(X)

Natural logarithm ($\log_e(x)$)of a real (X>0) *or complex number* (X/=0).

The result is of the same type and kind as the argument.
A result of type complex is the principal value with imaginary part w in the range -π<w<=π. The imaginary part of the result is π only when the real part of the argument is less than zero and the imaginary part of the argument is zero.
Example : LOG(10.0) has the value 2.3025851 (approximately).

LOG10(X)

Common logarithm ($\log_{10}(x)$) of a real (X>0).

Example : LOG10(10.0) has the value 1.0 (approximately).

SIN(X)

Sine of a real or complex number, X.

The argument is a value in radians.
The result is of the same type and kind as the argument.

Example : `SIN(1.0)` has the value 0.84147098 (approximately).

SINH(X)

Hyperbolic sine of a real number, `X`.

The result is of the same kind as the argument.

Example : `SINH(1.0)` has the value 1.1752012 (approximately).

SQRT(X)

Square root of a real number `X`, `(X>0)` *or complex number,* `X`.

The result is of the same type and kind as the argument.

A result of type complex is the principal value with the real part greater than or equal to zero. When the real part of the result is zero, the imaginary part is greater than or equal to zero.

Example : `SQRT(4.0)` has the value 2.0 (approximately).

TAN(X)

Tangent of a real number, `X` *(in radians).*

The result is of the same kind as the argument.

Example : `TAN(1.0)` has the value 1.5574077 (approximately).

TANH(X)

Hyperbolic tangent of a real number, X.

The result is of the same kind as the argument.

Example : `TANH(1.0)` has the value, 0.76159416 (approximately).

A.5 Character Functions

All functions in this section are elemental except for `REPEAT` and `TRIM` which are transformational.

ACHAR(I)

Returns the character in a specified position of the ISO 646:1983 (ASCII) collating sequence.

`I` must be of type integer.

If `0<=I<=127`, the result is the character in the Ith position in the ISO 646:1983 (ASCII) collating sequence, provided the processor is capable of representing that character; otherwise, the result is processor dependent. If the processor is not capable of representing both upper and lower-case letters and `I` corresponds to a letter in a case that the processor is not capable of representing, the result is the letter in the case that the processor is capable of representing. Note, `ACHAR(IACHAR(C))` must have the value `C` for any character `C` capable of representation in the processor.

Example : `ACHAR(88)` has the value `'X'`.

ADJUSTL(STRING)

Adjust to the left, removing leading blanks and inserting trailing blanks.
STRING must be of type character.
Example : `ADJUSTL('    WORD')` has the value `'WORD    '`

ADJUSTR(STRING)

Adjust to the right, removing trailing blanks and inserting leading blanks.
STRING must be of type character.
Example : `ADJUSTR('WORD    ')` has the value `'    WORD'`.

CHAR(I,KIND)

Returns the character in position I *of the processor collating sequence associated with the specified kind.*
If KIND is absent, the default character kind is used.
I must be of type integer with a value in the range `0<=I<=n-1`, where n is the number of characters in the collating sequence associated with the specified kind. `ICHAR(CHAR(I,KIND(C)))` must have the value I for `0<=I<=n-1` and `CHAR(ICHAR(C),KIND(C))` must have the value C for any character C capable of representation in the processor.
Example : `CHAR(88)` has the value `'X'` on a processor using the ISO 646:1983 (ASCII) collating sequence as default.

IACHAR(C)

Returns the position of a character in the ISO 646:1983 (ASCII) collating sequence as a default integer.
C must be of type default character and of length one.
If C is in the collating sequence defined by the codes specified in ISO 646:1983 (International Reference Version of the coding standard commonly known as ASCII), the result is the position of C in that sequence and satisfies the inequality `0<=IACHAR(C)<=127`. A processor-dependent value is returned if C is not in the ASCII collating sequence. The results are consistent with the LGE, LGT, LLE, and LLT lexical comparison functions. For example, if `LLE(C,D)` is true, `IACHAR(C).LE.IACHAR(D)` is true.
Example : `IACHAR('X')` has the value 88.

ICHAR(C)

Returns the position of a character in the processor collating sequence.
C must be a character of length one capable of representation in the processor.
The result is an integer in the range `0<=ICHAR(C)<=n-1`, where n is the number of characters in the collating sequence. For any characters C and D capable of representation in the processor, `C<D` is true if and only if `ICHAR(C)<ICHAR(D)` is true, and `C==D` is true if and only if `ICHAR(C)==ICHAR(D)` is true.
Example : `ICHAR('X')` has the value 88 on a processor using the ASCII collating sequence for the default character type.

INDEX(STRING,SUBSTRING,BACK)

Returns an integer which is the starting position of a substring within a string. STRING and SUBSTRING must be of type character and both of the same kind. BACK, which is optional, must be of type logical.

Case i) : If BACK is absent or is present with the value false, the result is the minimum positive value of I such that STRING(I:I+LEN(SUBSTRING)-1)=SUBSTRING, or zero if there is no such value. Zero is returned if LEN(STRING)<LEN(SUBSTRING), and one is returned if LEN(SUBSTRING)=0.

Case ii) : If BACK is present with the value true, the result is the maximum value of I less than or equal to LEN(STRING)-LEN(SUBSTRING)+1 such that STRING(I:I+LEN(SUBSTRING)-1)-SUBSTRING, or zero if there is no such value. Zero is returned if LEN(STRING)<LEN(SUBSTRING), and LEN(STRING)+1 is returned if LEN(SUBSTRING)=0.

Examples: INDEX('FORTRAN','R') has the value 3. INDEX('FORTRAN','R',BACK=.TRUE.) has the value 5.

LEN_TRIM(STRING)

Returns the length of the character argument without counting trailing blank characters.

If the argument contains no non-blank characters, the result is zero.

Examples: LEN_TRIM('TABB ') has the value 4 and LEN_TRIM(' ') has the value 0.

LGE(STRING_A,STR1NG_B)

Test whether a string is lexically greater than or equal to another string, based on the ASCII collating sequence.

STRING_A and STRING_B must be of type default character.

If the strings are of unequal length, the comparison is made as if the shorter string were extended on the right with blanks to the length of the longer string. If either string contains a character not in the ASCII character set, the result is processor dependent. The result is true if the strings are equal or if STRING_A follows STRING_B in the ASCII collating sequence; otherwise, the result is false. Note that the result is true if both STRING_A and STRING_B are of zero length.

Example : LGE('ONE','TWO') has the value false.

LGT(STRING_A,STR1NG_B)

Test whether a string is lexically greater than another string, based on the ASCII collating sequence.

STRING_A and STRING_B must be of type default character. If the strings are of unequal length, the comparison is made as if the shorter string were extended on the right with blanks to the length of the longer string. If either string contains a character

not in the ASCII character set, the result is processor dependent. The result is true if STRING_A follows STRING_B in the ASCII collating sequence; otherwise, the result is false. Note that the result is false if both STRING_A and STRING_B are of zero length.
Example : `LGT('ONE','TWO')` has the value false.

LLE(STRING_A,STRING_B)

Test whether a string is lexically less than or equal to another string, based on the ASCII collating sequence.

STRING_A and STRING_B must be of type default character.
If the strings are of unequal length, the comparison is made as if the shorter string were extended on the right with blanks to the length of the longer string. If either string contains a character not in the ASCII character set. the result is processor dependent. The result is true if the strings are equal or if STRING_A precedes STRING_B in the ASCII collating sequence; otherwise, the result is false. Note that the result is true if both STRING_A and STRING_B are of zero length.
Example : `LLE('ONE','TWO')` has the value true.

LLT(STRING_A,STRING_B)

Test whether a string is lexically less than another string, based on the ASCII collating sequence.

STRING_A and STRING_B must be of type default character.
If the strings are of unequal length, the comparison is made as if the shorter string were extended on the right with blanks to the length of the longer string. If either string contains a character not in the ASCII character set, the result is processor dependent. The result is true if STRING_A precedes STRING_B in the ASCII collating sequence; otherwise, the result is false. Note that the result is false if both STRING_A and STRING_B are of zero length.
Example : `LLT('ONE','TWO')` has the value true.

REPEAT(STRING,NCOPIES)

Concatenate several copies of a string.

This is a transformational function.
STRING must be scalar and of type character. NCOPIES must be scalar and of type integer. Its value must not be negative.
The result is a character produced by concatenating NCOPIES of STRING.
Examples: `REPEAT('H',2)` has the value `'HH'`. `REPEAT('XYZ',0)` has the value of a zero-length string.

SCAN(STRING,SET,BACK)

Scan a string for any one of the characters in a set of characters.

SET and STRING must be of type character of the same kind. BACK, which is optional, must be of type logical.

Case i) : If `BACK` is absent or is present with the value false and if `STRING` contains at least one character that is in `SET`, the result is the position of the leftmost character of `STRING` that is in `SET`.

Case ii) : If `BACK` is present with the value true and if `STRING` contains at least one character that is in `SET`, the result is the position of the rightmost character of `STRING` that is in `SET`.

Case iii) : The result is zero if no character of `STRING` is in `SET` or if the length of `STRING` or `SET` is zero.

Examples:

Case i) : `SCAN('FORTRAN','TR')` has the value 3.

Case ii) : `SCAN('FORTRAN','TR',BACK=.TRUE.)` has the value 5.

Case iii) : `SCAN('FORTRAN','BCD')` has the value 0.

TRIM(STRING)

Returns the the characters of the scalar argument with trailing blanks removed.

`TRIM` is a transformational function.

If `STRING` contains no non-blank characters, the result has zero length.

Example : `TRIM('TABB  ')` has the value `'TABB'`.

VERIFY(STRING,SET,BACK)

Verifies that a set of characters contains all the characters in a string by returning an integer identifying the position of the first character in the string that does not appear in the set.

`SET` and `STRING` must be of type character and of the same kind. `BACK`, which is optional, must be of type logical.

Case i) : If `BACK` is absent or present with the value false and if `STRING` contains at least one character that is not in `SET`, the result is the position of the leftmost character of `STRING` that is not in `SET`.

Case ii) : If `BACK` is present with the value true and if `STRING` contains at least one character that is not in `SET`, the result is the position of the rightmost character of `STRING` that is not in `SET`.

Case iii) : The result is zero if each character in `STRING` is in `SET` or if `STRING` has zero length.

Examples:

Case i) : `VERIFY('ABBA','A')` has the value 2.

Case ii) : `VERIFY('ABBA','A',BACK=.TRUE.)` has the value 3.

Case iii) : `VERIFY('ABBA','AB')` has the value 0.

A.6 Character Inquiry Function

`LEN` is an elemental function.

LEN(STRING)

Returns the integer length of a scalar or array-valued character entity.

Example : If `C` is declared by the statement

```
CHARACTER(LEN=11) :: C(100)
```

then `LEN(C)` has the value 11.

A.7 Kind Functions

In this section, `KIND` is an inquiry function, `SELECTED_INT_KIND` and `SELECTED_REAL_KIND` are transformational.

`KIND(X)`

Returns the value of the kind type parameter of any entity `X` *of an intrinsic type.*

Example : `KIND(0.0)` has the kind type parameter value of default real.

`SELECTED_INT_KIND(R)`

Returns the kind type parameter of an integer type that has at least the specified range.

R must be an integer initialization expression.

The result is the value of the kind type parameter for the integer type of least range that represents all values n in the range $-10^R<n<10^R$, or if no such kind type parameter is available on the processor, the result is -1.

Example : `SELECTED_INT_KIND(6)` has the value `KIND(0)` on a machine that supports a default integer representation method with radix = 2 and which represents 31 digits.

`SELECTED_REAL_KIND(P,R)`

Returns the kind type parameter of a real data type with decimal precision of at least `P` *digits and a decimal exponent range of at least* `R`.

`P` and `R` are both optional but at least one argument must be present. Both must be integer initialization expressions.

The result is an integer scalar and is the value of the kind type parameter of a real data type with decimal precision, as returned by the function `PRECISION` of at least `P` digits and a decimal exponent range, as returned by the function `RANGE`, of at least `R`, or, if no such kind type parameter is available on the processor, the result is -1 if the precision is not available, -2 if the exponent range is not available, and -3 if neither is available. If more than one kind type parameter value meets the criteria, the value returned is the one with the smallest decimal precision, unless there are several such values, in which case the smallest of these kind values is returned.

Example : `SELECTED_REAL_KIND(6,30)` has the value `KIND(0.0)` on a machine that supports a default real approximation method with radix = 2, 24 digits in the significand, and exponents ranging from -127 to +127.

A.8 Logical Function

`LOGICAL(L,KIND)`

Converts between kinds of logical.

The value of the result is that of `L`. The result is of type logical and with the kind as specified by the `KIND` argument. If the `KIND` argument is absent the result is of default logical type.

Example : `LOGICAL(L.OR..NOT.L)` has the value true and is of type default logical, regardless of the kind of the logical variable `L`.

A.9 Numeric Manipulation and Inquiry Functions

All functions in this section are elemental. The numeric manipulation and inquiry functions are described in terms of a model for the representation and behaviour of numbers on a processor. The model has parameters which are determined so as to make the model best fit the machine on which the executable program is executed.

A.9.1 Models for integer and real data

The model set for integer i is defined by:

$$i = s \times \sum_{k=1}^{q} w_k \times r^{k-1}$$

where r is an integer exceeding one, q is a positive integer, each w_j is a non-negative integer less than r, and s is +1 or -1.

The model set for real x is defined by:

$$x = \begin{cases} 0 \text{ or} \\ s \times b^e \times \sum_{k=1}^{p} f_k \times b^{-k} \end{cases}$$

where b and p are integers exceeding one; each f_k is a non-negative integer less than b, with f_1 nonzero; s is +1 or -1; and e is an integer that lies between some integer maximum e_{max} and some integer minimum e_{min} inclusively. For x = 0, its exponent e and digits f_k are defined to be zero. The integer parameters r and q determine the set of model integers and the integer parameters b, p, e_{min}, and e_{max} determine the set of model floating point numbers. The parameters of the integer and real models are available for each integer and real data type implemented by the processor. The parameters characterise the set of available numbers in the definition of the model. The numeric manipulation and inquiry functions provide values related to the parameters and other constants related to them. Examples of these functions in this section use the models:

$$i = s \times \sum_{k=1}^{31} w_k \times 2^{k-1}$$

and

$$x = \begin{cases} 0 \ or \\ s \times 2^e \times \left(\frac{1}{2} + \sum_{k=2}^{24} f_k \times 2^{-k}\right), & -126 \le e \le 127 \end{cases}$$

A.9.2 Floating-point manipulation functions

In the following functions real arguments are named `X` and integer arguments are named `I`. Unless otherwise indicated these may be of any kind. Normally the kind of the result is determined by that of the argument.

EXPONENT(X)

Returns the exponent part, e, of the real argument when represented as a model number.

The result is undefined if the processor cannot represent e in the default integer type. The result is zero if X is zero.

Examples: `EXPONENT(1.0)` has the value 1 and `EXPONENT(4.1)` has the value 3 for reals whose model is as at the end of A.9.1.

FRACTION(X)

Returns the fractional part of the model representation of the real argument value.

The result has the value `X` x b^{-e}, where b and e are as defined in A.9.1 for the model representation of `X`. If `X` has the value zero, the result has the value zero.

Example : `FRACTION(3.0)` has the value 0.75 for reals whose model is defined in A.9.1.

NEAREST(X,S)

Returns the machine representable number distinct from a real `X` *and nearest to it in the direction of the infinity with the same sign as* `S (S/=0)`.

Example : `NEAREST(3.0,2.0)` has the value $3+2^{-22}$ on a machine whose representation is that of the model at the end of A.9.1.

RRSPACING(X)

Returns the reciprocal of the relative spacing of model numbers near the real argument value `X`.

The result has the value |`X`| x b^{-e} x b^p, where b, e, and p are as defined in A.9.1 for the model representation of `X`.

Example : `RRSPACING(-3.0)` has the value 0.75 x 2^{24} for reals whose model is as at the end of A.9.1.

SCALE(X,I)

Scales the exponent of the real argument, X, *by the integer,* I.

The result is `X x` b^I, where `b` is the base in the model representation of `X`. If the result is not within range, it is processor dependent.

Example : `SCALE(3.0,2)` has the value 12.0 for reals whose model is as at the end of A.9.1.

`SET_EXPONENT(X,I)`

Sets the exponent of the real argument, `X`, *to the integer,* `I`.

The result is X x b^{I-e}, where b and e are as defined in A.9.1 for the model representation of X.

The result must be within range; if not, the result is processor dependent. If X has value zero, the result has value zero.

Example : `SET_EXPONENT(3.0,1)` has the value 1.5 for reals whose model is as at the end of A.9.1.

`SPACING(X)`

Returns the absolute spacing of model numbers near the real argument value.

The result is 1.0 x b^{e-p}, where b, e, and p are as defined in A.9.1 for the model representation of X. The result must be within range; otherwise, the result is `TINY(X)`.

Example : `SPACING(3.0)` has the value 2^{-22} for reals whose model is as at the end of A.9.1.

A.9.3 Numeric Inquiry Functions

`DIGITS(X)`

Returns the value q if `X` *is of type integer and p if* `X` *is of type real.*

The values q and p are as defined in A.9.1 for the model representing numbers of the same type and kind as X.

Example : `DIGITS(X)` has the value 24 for real X whose model is as at the end of A.9.1.

`EPSILON(X)`

Returns the value b^{1-p} *(that is almost negligible compared to unity) in the model representing numbers of the same type and kind as the real,* `X`.

Example : `EPSILON(X)` has the value 2^{-23} for real X whose model is as at the end of A.9.1.

`HUGE(X)`

Returns the largest representable number of the same type and kind as `X`.

The result has the value r^{q-1} if X is of type integer and $(1 - b^{-p})b^{e_{max}}$ if X is of type real, where r, q, b, p, and e_{max} are as defined in A.9.1.

Example : `HUGE(X)` has the value $(1 - 2^{-24}) \times 2^{127}$ for real X whose model is as at the end of A.9.1.

MAXEXPONENT(X)

Returns the value e_{max}, as defined in A.9.1 for the model representing numbers of the same type and kind as the real argument X.

Example : `MAXEXPONENT(X)` has the value 127 for real X whose model is as at the end of A.9.1.

MINEXPONENT(X)

Returns the value e_{min} as defined in A.9.1 for the model representing numbers of the same type and kind as the real argument X.

Example : `MINEXPONENT(X)` has the value -126 for real X whose model is as at the end of A.9.1.

PRECISION(X)

Returns the effective decimal precision of the real representation with the same type and kind as the argument X.

The result is `INT((p-1)*LOG10(b))+k`.

b and p are as defined in A.9.1 for the model representing real numbers with the same value for the kind as the real or complex argument X, and where k is 1 if b is an integral power of 10 and 0 otherwise.

Example : `PRECISION(X)` has the value 6 for real X whose model is as at the end of A.9.1.

RADIX(X)

Returns the value r if X *is of type integer and the value b if* X *is of type real.*

The values r and b are as defined in A.9.1 for the model representing numbers of the same type and kind as the integer or real argument X.

Example : `RADIX(X)` has the value 2 for real X whose model is as at the end of A.9.1.

RANGE(X)

Returns the decimal exponent range in the model representing integer or real numbers with the same kind as the integer, real or complex argument X.

Case i) : For an integer argument. the result has the value `INT(LOG10(HUGE(X)))`.

Case ii) : For a real or complex argument, the result has the value `INT(MIN(LOG10(HUGE(X)),-LOG10(TINY(X))))`.

Example : `RANGE(X)` has the value 38 for real X whose model is as at the end of A.9.1.

TINY(X)

Returns the smallest representable value of the same kind as the real argument X.

The result is 1.0 x $b^{e_{min}-1}$, where b and e_{min} are as defined in A.9.1 for the model representing numbers of the same type and kind as the real argument X.

Example : `TINY(X)` has the value 2^{-127} for real X whose model is as at the end of A.9.1.

A.10 Bit Inquiry and Manipulation Functions

The bit manipulation procedures consist of a set of ten functions and one subroutine. Logical operations on bits are provided by the functions `IOR`, `IAND`, `NOT`, and `IEOR`; shift operations are provided by the functions `ISHFT` and `ISHFTC`; bit subfields may be referenced by the function `IBITS` and by the subroutine `MVBITS`; single-bit processing is provided by the functions `BTEST`, `IBSET`, and `IBCLR`.

For the purposes of these procedures, a bit is defined to be a binary digit w located at position k of a non-negative integer scalar object based on a model non-negative integer defined by

$$j = \sum_{k=0}^{s-1} w_k \times 2^k$$

and for which w_k may have the value 0 or 1. An example of a model number compatible with the examples used in A.9.1 would have s = 32, thereby defining a 32-bit integer.

An inquiry function `BIT_SIZE` is available to determine the parameter s of the model. The value of the argument of this function need not be defined. It is not necessary for a processor to evaluate the argument of this function if the value of the function can be determined otherwise.

Effectively, this model defines an integer object to consist of s bits in sequence numbered from right to left from 0 to s-1. This model is valid only in the context of the use of such an object as the argument or result of one of the bit manipulation procedures. In all other contexts, the model defined for an integer in A.9.1 applies. In particular, whereas the models are identical for $w_{s-1} = 0$, they do not correspond for $w_{s-1} = 1$ and the interpretation of bits in such objects is processor dependent.

`BIT_SIZE(I)`

Returns the number of bits s defined above.

`I` must be of type integer. The result is the number of bits s in the model integer for bit manipulation contexts.

Example : `BIT_SIZE(1)` has the value 32 if s in the model is 32.

`BTEST(I,POS)`

Tests a bit of an integer value.

`POS(>=0)` must be of type integer. It must be less than `BIT_SIZE(I)`.

The result has the value true if bit `POS` of `I` has the value 1 and has the value false if bit `POS` of `I` has the value 0.

Examples: `BTEST(8,3)` has the value true.

If `A` has the value $\begin{bmatrix} 1 & 2 \\ 3 & 4 \end{bmatrix}$

the value of BTEST(A,2) is $\begin{bmatrix} \textit{false} & \textit{false} \\ \textit{true} & \textit{false} \\ \textit{false} & \textit{true} \end{bmatrix}$

and the value of BTEST(2,A) is $\begin{bmatrix} \textit{true} & \textit{false} \\ \textit{false} & \textit{false} \end{bmatrix}$

IAND(I,J)

Performs a bitwise logical conjunction (AND).

I and J must be of type integer. The result has the value obtained by combining I and J bit-by-bit according to the following truth table:

I	J	IAND(I,J)
1	1	1
1	0	0
0	1	0
0	0	0

Example : IAND(1,3) has the value 1.

IBCLR(I,POS)

Clears one bit to zero.

POS and I must be of type integer. POS must be non-negative and less than BIT_SIZE(I).

The result has the value of the sequence of bits of I, except that bit POS of I is set to zero.

Examples: IBCLR(14,1) has the result 12. If V has the value [1,2,3,4], the value of IBCLR(POS=V,I=31) is [29,27,23,15].

IBITS(I,POS,LEN)

Extracts a sequence of bits.

All arguments must be integers. POS and LEN must be non-negative and POS+LEN must be less than or equal to BIT_SIZE(I).

The result is the sequence of LEN bits in I beginning at bit POS right-adjusted and with all other bits zero.

Example : IBITS(14,1,3) has the value 7.

IBSET(I,POS)

Sets one bit to one.

Both arguments must be integers. POS must be non-negative and less than BIT_SIZE(I).

The result is the sequence of bits of `I`, with bit `POS` of `I` is set to one.
Examples: `IBSET(12,1)` has the value 14. If `V` has the value [1,2,3,4], the value of `IBSET(POS=V,I=0)` is [2,4,8,16].

`IEOR(I,J)`

Performs a bitwise exclusive OR.

Both arguments must be integers of the same kind. The result has the value obtained by combining `I` and `J` bit-by-bit according to the following truth table:

I	J	IEOR(I,J)
1	1	0
1	0	1
0	1	1
0	0	0

Example : `IEOR(1,3)` has the value 2.

`IOR(I,J)`

Performs a bitwise inclusive OR.

Both arguments must be integers of the same kind. The result has the value obtained by combining `I` and `J` bit-by-bit according to the following truth table:

I	J	IOR(I,J)
1	1	1
1	0	1
0	1	1
0	0	0

Example : `IOR(1,3)` has the value 3.

`ISHFT(I,SHIFT)`

Performs a logical shift.

Both arguments must be integers. The absolute value of `SHIFT` must be less than or equal to `BIT_SIZE(I)`.
The result has the value obtained by shifting the bits of `I` by `SHIFT` positions. If `SHIFT` is positive, the shift is to the left; if `SHIFT` is negative, the shift is to the right. Bits shifted out from the left or from the right, as appropriate, are lost. Zeros are shifted in from the opposite end.
Example : `ISHFT(3,1)` has the result 6.

ISHFTC(I,SHIFT,SIZE)

Performs a circular shift of the rightmost bits.

All arguments must be of type integer.

The absolute value of SHIFT must be less than or equal to SIZE. SIZE which is optional must be 0<SIZE<BIT_SIZE(I). If SIZE is absent, a default value of BIT_SIZE(I) is used.

The result has the value obtained by shifting the SIZE rightmost bits of I circularly by SHIFT positions. If SHIFT is positive, the shift is to the left; if SHIFT is negative, the shift is to the right. No bits are lost. The unshifted bits are unaltered.

Example : ISHFTC(3,2,3) has the value 5.

NOT(I)

Performs a bitwise logical complement.

The result has the value obtained by complementing I bit-by-bit according to the following truth table:

I	NOT(I)
1	0
0	1

Example : if I is represented by the string of bits 01010101, NOT(I) has the binary value 10101010.

A.11 Transfer Function

TRANSFER(SOURCE,MOLD,SIZE)

Transfers a given object from one type and kind interpretation to another without changing the physical representation.

Returns a result with a physical representation identical to that of SOURCE but interpreted with the type and type parameters of MOLD.

SOURCE and MOLD may be of any type and may be scalar or array valued. SIZE which is optional must be scalar and of type integer. The corresponding actual argument must not be an optional dummy argument.

Case i) : If MOLD is a scalar and SIZE is absent, the result is a scalar.

Case ii) : If MOLD is array valued and SIZE is absent, the result is array valued and of rank one. Its size is as small as possible such that its physical representation is not shorter than that of SOURCE.

Case iii) : If SIZE is present, the result is array valued of rank one and size SIZE. If the physical representation of the result has the same length as that of SOURCE. the physical representation of the result is that of SOURCE. If the physical representation of the result is longer than that of SOURCE, the physical representation of the leading part is that of SOURCE and the remainder is undefined. If the physical representation of the result is shorter than that of SOURCE, the physical representation of the result is the leading part of SOURCE. If D and E are scalar variables such that the physical representation of D is as long as or longer than that of E, the value of TRANSFER(TRANSFER(E,D),E) must be the value of E. If D is an array and E is an array of rank one, the value of TRANSFER(TRANSFER(E D),E,SIZE(E)) must be the value of E.

Examples:

Case i) : TRANSFER(1082130432,0.0) has the value 4.0 on a processor that represents the values 4.0 and 1082130432 as the string of binary digits 0100 0000 1000 0000 0000 0000 0000 0000.

Case ii) : TRANSFER((/1.1,2.2,3.3 /),(/(0.0,0.0)/)) is a complex rank-one array of length two whose first element has the value (1.1,2.2) and whose second element has a real part with the value 3.3. The imaginary part of the second element is undefined.

Case iii) : TRANSFER((/1.1,2.2,3.3 /),(/(0.0,0.0)/),1) has the value (1.1,2.2).

A.12 Vector and Matrix Multiply Functions

DOT_PRODUCT(VECTOR_A,VECTOR_B)

Performs dot-product multiplication of numeric or logical vectors.

VECTOR_A must be of numeric type (integer. real, or complex) or of logical type. It must be array valued and of rank one.

VECTOR_B must be of numeric type if VECTOR_A is of numeric type or of type logical if VECTOR_A is of type logical. It must be array valued and of rank one and of the same size as VECTOR_A.

If the arguments are of numeric type, the type and kind of the result are those of the expression VECTOR_A*VECTOR_B. If the arguments are of type logical, the result is of type logical with the kind of the expression VECTOR_A.AND.VECTOR_B.

Case i) : If VECTOR_A is of type integer or real, the result has the value SUM(VECTOR_A*VECTOR_B). If the vectors have size zero, the result has the value zero.

Case ii) : If VECTOR_A is of type complex, the result has the value SUM(CONJG(VECTOR_A)*VECTOR_B). If the vectors have size zero, the result has the value zero.

Case iii) : If VECTOR_A is of type logical, the result has the value ANY(VECTOR_A.AND.VECTOR_B). If the vectors have size zero, the result has the value false.

Example : DOT_PRODUCT((/1,2,3/),(/2,3,4/)) has the value 20.

MATMUL(MATRIX_A,MATRIX_B)

Performs matrix multiplication of numeric or logical matrices.

MATRIX_A must be of numeric type (integer, real, or complex) or of logical type. It must be array valued and of rank one or two.

`MATRIX_B` must be of numeric type if `MATRIX_A` is of numeric type and of logical type if `MATRIX_A` is of logical type. It must be array valued and of rank one or two. At least one of `MATRIX_A` and `MATRIX_B` must have rank two. The size of the first (or only) dimension of `MATRIX_B` must equal the size of the last (or only) dimension of `MATRIX_A`.

The type and kind of the result is determined by the same rule as for the dot product. The shape of the result depends on the shapes of the arguments as follows:

Case i) : If `MATRIX_A` has shape (n,m) and `MATRIX_B` has shape (m,k), the result has shape (n,k).

Case ii) : If `MATRIX_A` has shape (m) and `MATRIX_B` has shape (m,k), the result has shape (k).

Case iii) : If `MATRIX_A` has shape (n,m) and `MATRIX_B` has shape (m), the result has shape (n).

Results Values:

Case i) : Element (i,j) of the result has the value `SUM(MATRIX_A(i,:)* MATRIX_B(:,j))` if the arguments are of numeric type and has the value `ANY(MATRIX_A(i,:).AND.MATRIX_B(:,j))` if the arguments are of logical type.

Case ii) : Element (j) of the result has the value `SUM(MATRIX_A(:)*MATRIX(:,j))` if the arguments are of numeric type and has the value `ANY(MATRIX_A(:).AND.MATRIX_B(:,j))` if the arguments are of logical type.

Case iii) : Element (i) of the result has the value `SUM(MATRIX_A(i,:)*MATRIX_B(:))` if the arguments are of numeric type and has the value `ANY(MATRIX_A(i,:).AND.MATRIX_B(:))` if the arguments are of logical type.

Examples: Let `A` and `B` be the matrices $\begin{bmatrix}1 & 2 & 3\\2 & 3 & 4\end{bmatrix}$ and $\begin{bmatrix}1 & 2\\2 & 3\\3 & 4\end{bmatrix}$

Let `X` and `Y` be the vectors [1,2] and [1,2,3].

Case i) : The result of `MATMUL(A,B)` is the matrix-matrix product with the value $\begin{bmatrix}14 & 20\\20 & 29\end{bmatrix}$

Case ii) : The result of `MATMUL(X,A)` is the vector-matrix product with the value [5,8,11].

Case iii) : The result of `MATMUL(A,Y)` is the matrix-vector product with the value [14,20].

A.13 Array Reduction Functions

The array reduction functions SUM, PRODUCT, MAXVAL, MINVAL, COUNT, ANY and ALL perform numerical, logical, and counting operations on arrays. They may be applied to the whole array to give a scalar result or they may be applied over a given dimension to yield a result of rank reduced by one. By use of a logical mask that is conformable with the given array, the computation may be confined to any subset of the array (for example, the positive elements).

In this section MASK denotes a logical array argument which is optional unless otherwise indicated. DIM denotes an integer scalar with a value in the range 1<=DIM<=n where n is the rank of the principal argument. DIM is optional in all cases.

ALL(MASK,DIM)

Determine whether all values are true in MASK *along dimension* DIM. The argument MASK must be present. The result is of the same logical type and kind as MASK. It is scalar if DIM is absent or MASK has rank one; otherwise, the result is an array of rank n-1 and of shape $(d_1, d_2, , \ldots, d_{DIM-1}, d_{DIM+1}, \ldots, d_n)$ where $(d_1, d_2, \ldots, d_n)$ is the shape of MASK.

Case i) : The result of ALL(MASK) has the value true if all elements of MASK are true or if MASK has size zero, and the result has value false if any element of MASK is false.

Case ii) : If MASK has rank one, ALL(MASK,DIM) has a value equal to that of ALL(MASK). Otherwise, the value of element $(s_1, s_2, \ldots, s_{DIM-1}, s_{DIM+1}, \ldots, s_n)$ of ALL(MASK,DIM) is equal to ALL(MASK($s_1, s_2, \ldots s_{DIM-1}, :, s_{DIM+1}, \ldots, s_n$)).

Examples:

Case i) : The value of ALL((/.TRUE.,.FALSE.,.TRUE./)) is false.

Case ii) : If B is the array $\begin{bmatrix}1 & 3 & 5\\ 2 & 4 & 6\end{bmatrix}$ and C is the array $\begin{bmatrix}0 & 3 & 5\\ 7 & 4 & 8\end{bmatrix}$ then ALL(B/=C,DIM=1) is [true,false,false] and ALL(B/=C,DIM=2) is [false,false].

ANY(MASK,DIM)

Determine whether any value is true in MASK *along dimension* DIM. This function is essentially the complement of ALL above.

Examples:

Case i) : The value of ANY((/.TRUE.,.FALSE.,.TRUE./)) is true.

Case ii) : If B is the array $\begin{bmatrix}1 & 3 & 5\\ 2 & 4 & 6\end{bmatrix}$ and C is the array $\begin{bmatrix}0 & 3 & 5\\ 7 & 4 & 8\end{bmatrix}$ ANY(B/=C,DIM=1) is [true,false,true] and ANY(B/=C,DIM=2) is [true,true].

COUNT(MASK,DIM)

Count the number of true elements of MASK *along dimension* DIM.

The arguments are similar to those above.

Examples:

Case i) : The value of `COUNT((/.TRUE.,.FALSE.,.TRUE./))` is 2.

Case ii) : If B is the array $\begin{bmatrix}1 & 3 & 5\\2 & 4 & 6\end{bmatrix}$ and C is the array $\begin{bmatrix}0 & 3 & 5\\7 & 4 & 8\end{bmatrix}$

`COUNT(B/=C,DIM=1)` is [2,0,1] and `COUNT(B/=C,DIM=2)` is [1,2].

MAXVAL(ARRAY,DIM,MASK)

Maximum value of the elements of ARRAY *along dimension* DIM *corresponding to the true elements of* MASK.

ARRAY must be an array of type integer or real. The result is of the same type and kind as ARRAY. It is scalar if DIM is absent or ARRAY has rank one; otherwise, the result is an array of rank n-1 and of shape $(d_1, d_2, ..., d_{DIM-1}, d_{DIM+1}, ..., d_n)$ where $(d_1,d_2,...,d_n)$ is the shape of ARRAY.

Case i) : The result of `MAXVAL(ARRAY)` has a value equal to the maximum value of all the elements of ARRAY or has the value of the negative number of the largest magnitude supported by the processor for numbers of the type and kind of ARRAY if ARRAY has size zero.

Case ii) : The result of `MAXVAL(ARRAY,MASK=MASK)` has a value equal to the maximum value of the elements of ARRAY corresponding to true elements of MASK or has the value of the negative number of the largest magnitude supported by the processor for numbers of the type and kind of ARRAY if there are no true elements.

Case iii) : If ARRAY has rank one, `MAXVAL(ARRAY,DIM[,MASK])` has a value equal to that of `MAXVAL(ARRAY[,MASK=MASK])`. Otherwise, the value of element $(s_1, s_2, ..., s_{DIM-1}, s_{DIM+1}, ..., s_n))$ of `MAXVAL(ARRAY,DIM[,MASK])` is equal to `MAXVAL(ARRAY(`$s_1, s_2, ..., s_{DIM-1}, s_{DIM+1}, ..., s_n$`),&`
`[,MASK=MASK(`$s_1, s_2, ..., s_{DIM-1}, s_{DIM+1}, ..., s_n$`)])`.

Examples:

Case i) : The value of `MAXVAL((/1,2,3/))` is 3.

Case ii) : `MAXVAL(C,MASK=C<0.0)` finds the maximum of the negative elements of C.

Case iii) : If B is the array $\begin{bmatrix}1 & 3 & 5\\2 & 4 & 6\end{bmatrix}$, `MAXVAL(B,DIM=1)` is [2,4,6] and

`MAXVAL(B,DIM=2)` is [5,6].

MINVAL(ARRAY,DIM,MASK)

Minimum value of all the elements of `ARRAY` *along dimension* `DIM` *corresponding to true elements of* `MASK`.

This function is the opposite operation and is similar in specification to `MAXVAL` above.

Examples:

Case i) : The value of `MINVAL((/1,2,3/))` is 1.

Case ii) : `MINVAL(C,MASK=C>0.0)` forms the minimum of the positive elements of `C`.

Case iii) : If `B` is the array $\begin{bmatrix} 1 & 3 & 5 \\ 2 & 4 & 6 \end{bmatrix}$, `MINVAL(B,DIM=1)` is [1,3,5] and `MINVAL(B,DIM=2)` is [1,2].

PRODUCT(ARRAY,DIM,MASK)

Product of all the elements of `ARRAY` *along dimension* `DIM` *corresponding to the true elements of* `MASK`.

This function is similar in specification to `MAXVAL` above.

Examples:

Case i) : The value of `PRODUCT((/1,2,3/))` is 6.

Case ii) : `PRODUCT(C,MASK=C>0.0)` forms the product of the positive elements of `C`.

Case iii) : If `B` is the array $\begin{bmatrix} 1 & 3 & 5 \\ 2 & 4 & 6 \end{bmatrix}$, `PRODUCT(B,DIM=1)` is [2,12,30] and `PRODUCT(B,DIM=2)` is [15,48].

SUM(ARRAY,DIM,MASK)

Sum all the elements of `ARRAY` *along dimension* `DIM` *corresponding to the true elements of* `MASK`.

This function is similar in specification to `MAXVAL` above.

Examples:

Case i) : The value of `SUM((/1,2,3/))` is 6.

Case ii) : `SUM(C,MASK=C>0.0)` forms the arithmetic sum of the positive elements of `C`.

Case iii) : If `B` is the array $\begin{bmatrix} 1 & 3 & 5 \\ 2 & 4 & 6 \end{bmatrix}$, `SUM(B,DIM=1)` is [3,7,11] and `SUM(B,DIM=2)` is [9,12].

A.14 Array Inquiry Functions

The function ALLOCATED returns the allocation status of an array. The functions SIZE, SHAPE, LBOUND, and UBOUND return, respectively, the size of the array, the shape, and the lower and upper bounds of the subscripts along each dimension. The values of the array arguments to these functions need not be defined, merely the attribute that determines the value of the function.

ALLOCATED(ARRAY)

Indicate whether or not an allocatable array is currently allocated.
The result has the value true if ARRAY is currently allocated and has the value false if ARRAY is not currently allocated. The result is undefined if the allocation status of the array is undefined.

LBOUND(ARRAY,DIM)

Returns all the lower bounds or a specified lower bound of an array.
The result is scalar if DIM is present; otherwise, the result is an array of rank one and size n, where n is the rank of ARRAY.

Case i) : For an array section or for an array expression, other than a whole array or array structure component, LBOUND(ARRAY,DIM) has the value 1; otherwise, it has a value equal to the lower bound for subscript DIM of ARRAY. It has the value 1 if dimension DIM has size zero.

Case ii) : LBOUND(ARRAY) has a value whose i^{th} component is equal to LBOUND(ARRAY,i), for i=1,2,...,n, where n is the rank of ARRAY.

Examples: If A is declared by the statement
REAL :: A(2:3,7:10) then LBOUND(A) is [2,7] and LBOUND(A,DIM=2) is 7.

SHAPE(SOURCE)

Returns the shape of an array or a scalar as a default integer array of rank one whose size is equal to the rank of SOURCE.

Examples: The value of SHAPE(A(2:5,-1:1)) is [4,3]. The value of SHAPE(3) is the rank-one array of size zero.

SIZE(ARRAY,DIM)

Returns the extent of an array along a specified dimension or the total number of elements in the array.

Examples: The value of SIZE(A(2:5,-1:1),DIM=2) is 3. The value of SIZE(A(2:5,-1:1)) is 12.

UBOUND(ARRAY,DIM)

Returns all the upper bounds of an array or a specified upper bound. The result is scalar if DIM is present; otherwise, the result is an array of rank one and size n, where n is the rank of ARRAY.

Examples: If A is declared by the statement
REAL :: A(2:3,7:10) then UBOUND(A) is [3,10] and UBOUND(A,DIM=2) is 10.

A.15 Array Construction Functions

The functions `MERGE`, `SPREAD`, `PACK`, and `UNPACK` construct new arrays from the elements of existing arrays. `MERGE` combines two conformable arrays into one array by an element-wise choice based on a logical mask. `SPREAD` constructs an array from several copies of an actual argument (`SPREAD` does this by adding an extra dimension, as in forming a book from copies of one page). `PACK` and `UNPACK` respectively gather and scatter the elements of a one dimensional array from and to positions in another array where the positions are specified by a logical mask.

MERGE(TSOURCE,FSOURCE,MASK)

Merge two arrays under a logical mask.

`TSOURCE` and `FSOURCE` must have same type and type parameters. The result is the corresponding element from `TSOURCE` if `MASK` is true and that from `FSOURCE` otherwise.

Examples: If `TSOURCE` is the array $\begin{bmatrix} 1 & 6 & 5 \\ 2 & 4 & 6 \end{bmatrix}$, `FSOURCE` is the array $\begin{bmatrix} 0 & 3 & 2 \\ 7 & 4 & 8 \end{bmatrix}$ and

`MASK` is the array $\begin{bmatrix} \textit{true} & \textit{false} & \textit{true} \\ \textit{false} & \textit{false} & \textit{true} \end{bmatrix}$ then

`MERGE(TSOURCE,FSOURCE,MASK)` is $\begin{bmatrix} 1 & 3 & 5 \\ 7 & 4 & 6 \end{bmatrix}$.

The value of `MERGE(1.0,0.0,K>0)` is 1.0 for `K=5` and 0.0 for `K=-2`.

PACK(ARRAY,MASK,VECTOR)

Pack an array of any rank into an array of rank one, under the control of a mask.

`ARRAY` may be of any type. It must not be scalar. `VECTOR`, which is optional, must be a rank one array of the same type and type parameters as `ARRAY`. `VECTOR` must have at least as many elements as there are true elements in `MASK`. If `MASK` is scalar with the value true, `VECTOR` must have at least as many elements as there are in `ARRAY`.

The result is an array of rank one with the same type and type parameters as `ARRAY`. If `VECTOR` is present, the result size is that of `VECTOR`; otherwise, the result size is the number t of true elements in `MASK` unless `MASK` is scalar with the value true, in which case the result size is the size of `ARRAY`.

Element `i` of the result is the element of `ARRAY` that corresponds to the `i`th true element of `MASK`, taking elements in array element order, for `i`=1,2,...,t. If `VECTOR` is present and has size n>t, element `i` of the result has the value `VECTOR(i)`, for `i`=t+1,...,n.

Examples: The non-zero elements of an array M with the value $\begin{bmatrix} 0 & 0 & 0 \\ 9 & 0 & 0 \\ 0 & 0 & 7 \end{bmatrix}$ may be "gathered" by the function PACK. The result of PACK(M,MASK=M/=0) is [9,7] and the result of PACK(M,M/=0,VECTOR=(/2,4,6,8,10,12/)) is [9,7,6,8,10,12].

SPREAD(SOURCE,DIM,NCOPIES)

Replicates an array by adding a dimension.

Broadcasts several copies of SOURCE along a specified dimension (as in forming a book from copies of a single page) and thus forms an array of rank one greater than SOURCE. SOURCE may be scalar or array valued. The rank of SOURCE must be less than 7. NCOPIES must be scalar and of type integer.

The result is an array of the same type and type parameters as SOURCE and of rank n+1, where n is the rank of SOURCE. If SOURCE is scalar, the shape of the result is (MAX(NCOPIES,0)). If SOURCE is array valued with shape $(d_1, d_2, \ldots, d_n)$, the shape of the result is $(d_1, d_2, \ldots, d_{DIM-1}$, MAX(NCOPIES,0), $d_{DIM}, \ldots, d_n)$. If SOURCE is scalar, each element of the result has a value equal to SOURCE. If SOURCE is array valued, the element of the result with subscripts $(r_1, r_2, \ldots r_{n+1})$ has the value SOURCE $(r_1, r_2, \ldots r_{DIM-1}, r_{DIM+1}, \ldots, r_{n+1})$.

Example : If A is the array [2,3,4], SPREAD(A,DIM=1,NCOPIES=NC) is the array

$\begin{bmatrix} 2 & 3 & 4 \\ 2 & 3 & 4 \\ 2 & 3 & 4 \end{bmatrix}$ if NC has the value 3 and is a zero-sized array if NC has the value 0.

UNPACK(VECTOR,MASK,FIELD)

Unpack an array of rank one into an array of any rank under the control of a mask.

VECTOR may be of any type. It must have rank one. Its size must be at least t where t is the number of true elements in MASK. FIELD must be of the same type and type parameters as VECTOR and must be conformable with MASK.

The result is an array of the same type and type parameters as VECTOR and the same shape as MASK. The element of the result that corresponds to the ith true element of MASK, in array element order, has the value VECTOR(i) for i=1,2,...,t where t is the number of true values in MASK. Each other element has a value equal to FIELD if FIELD is scalar or to the corresponding element of FIELD if it is an array.

Examples: Specific values may be "scattered" to specific positions in an array by using UNPACK. If M is the array $\begin{bmatrix} 1 & 0 & 0 \\ 0 & 1 & 0 \\ 0 & 0 & 1 \end{bmatrix}$, V is the array [1,2,3], and Q is the logical mask $\begin{bmatrix} \mathit{false} & \mathit{true} & \mathit{false} \\ \mathit{true} & \mathit{false} & \mathit{false} \\ \mathit{false} & \mathit{false} & \mathit{true} \end{bmatrix}$ then the result of UNPACK(V,MASK=Q,FIELD=M) has the value $\begin{bmatrix} 1 & 2 & 0 \\ 1 & 1 & 0 \\ 0 & 0 & 3 \end{bmatrix}$ and the result of UNPACK(V,MASK=Q,FIELD=0) has the value $\begin{bmatrix} 0 & 2 & 0 \\ 1 & 0 & 0 \\ 0 & 0 & 3 \end{bmatrix}$

A.16 Array Reshape Function

RESHAPE(SOURCE,SHAPE,PAD,ORDER)

Constructs an array of a specified shape from the elements of a given array. SOURCE may be of any type, and must be an array. If PAD is absent or of size zero, the size of SOURCE must be greater than or equal to PRODUCT(SHAPE), which is the size of the result. SHAPE must be of type integer, and rank one. Its size must be positive and less than 8. It must not have an element whose value is negative. PAD, which is optional, must be an array of the same type and type parameters as SOURCE. ORDER, which is optional, must be of type integer, must have the same shape as SHAPE, and its value must be a permutation of (1,2,...,n), where n is the size of SHAPE. If absent, the default is (1,2,...,n).

The result is an array of shape SHAPE (that is, SHAPE(RESHAPE(SOURCE,SHAPE,PAD,ORDER)) is equal to SHAPE) with the same type and type parameters as SOURCE. The elements of the result, taken in permuted subscript order ORDER(1), . . . , ORDER(n), are those of SOURCE in normal array element order followed if necessary by those of PAD in array element order, followed if necessary by additional copies of PAD in array element order.

Examples: `RESHAPE((/1,2,3,4,5,6/),(/2,3/))` has the value $\begin{bmatrix}1 & 3 & 5\\ 2 & 4 & 6\end{bmatrix}$.

`RESHAPE((/1,2,3,4,5,6/),(/2,4/),(/0,0/),(/2,1/))` has the value $\begin{bmatrix}1 & 2 & 3 & 4\\ 5 & 6 & 0 & 0\end{bmatrix}$.

A.17 Array Manipulation Functions

The functions TRANSPOSE, EOSHIFT, and CSHIFT manipulate arrays. TRANSPOSE performs the matrix transpose operation on a two-dimensional array. The shift functions leave the shape of an array unaltered but shift the positions of the elements parallel to a specified dimension of the array. These shifts are either circular (CSHIFT), in which case elements shifted off one end reappear at the other end, or end-off (EOSHIFT), in which case specified boundary elements are shifted into the vacated positions.

CSHIFT(ARRAY,SHIFT,DIM)

Perform a circular shift on an array of rank one or perform circular shifts on all the rank one sections along a given dimension of an array of rank two or greater.
Elements shifted out at one end of a section are shifted in at the other end. Different sections may be shifted by different amounts and in different directions. ARRAY may be of any type. It must not be scalar. SHIFT must be of type integer and must be scalar if ARRAY has rank one; otherwise, it must be scalar or of rank n-1 and of shape $(d_1, d_2, \ldots, d_{DIM-1}, d_{DIM+1}, \ldots, d_n)$ where $(d_1, d_2, \ldots, d_n)$ is the shape of ARRAY.
The result is of the type and type parameters of ARRAY, and has the shape of ARRAY.

Case i) : If ARRAY has rank one, element i of the result is ARRAY(1+MODULO(i+SHIFT-1,SIZE(ARRAY))).

Case ii) : If ARRAY has rank greater than one, section $(s_1, s_2, \ldots, s_{DIM-1} : s_{DIM+1}, \ldots, s_n)$ of the result has a value equal to CSHIFT(ARRAY$(s_1, s_2, \ldots, s_{DIM-1} : s_{DIM+1}, \ldots, s_n)$,1,sh), where sh is SHIFT or SHIFT$(s_1,s_2,\ldots,s_{DIM-1}:s_{DIM+1},\ldots,s_n)$.

Examples:

Case i) : If V is the array [1,2,3,4,5,6], the effect of shifting V circularly to the left by two positions is achieved by CSHIFT(V,SHIFT=2) which has the value [3,4,5,6,1,2]; CSHIFT(V,SHIFT=-2) achieves a circular shift to the right by two positions and has the value [5,6,1,2,3,4].

Case ii) : The rows of an array of rank two may all be shifted by the same amount or by different amounts. If `M` is the array $\begin{bmatrix} 1 & 2 & 3 \\ 4 & 5 & 6 \\ 7 & 8 & 9 \end{bmatrix}$ the value of `CSHIFT(M,SHIFT=-1,DIM=2)` is $\begin{bmatrix} 3 & 1 & 2 \\ 6 & 4 & 5 \\ 9 & 7 & 8 \end{bmatrix}$ and the value of `CSHIFT(M,SHIFT=(/-1,1,0/),DIM=2)` is $\begin{bmatrix} 3 & 1 & 2 \\ 5 & 6 & 4 \\ 7 & 8 & 9 \end{bmatrix}$.

`EOSHIFT(ARRAY,SHIFT,BOUNDARY,DIM)`

Perform an end-off shift on an array of rank one or perform end-off shifts on all the rank-one sections along a given dimension of an array of rank two or greater. Elements are shifted off at one end of a section and copies of a boundary value are shifted in at the other end. Different sections may have different boundary values and may be shifted by different amounts and in different directions. `ARRAY` may be of any type. It must not be scalar. `SHIFT` must be of type integer and must be scalar if `ARRAY` has rank one; otherwise, it must be scalar or of rank n-1 and of shape $(d_1, d_2, \ldots, d_{DIM-1}, d_{DIM+1}, \ldots, d_n)$ where $(d_1, d_2, \ldots, d_n)$ is the shape of `ARRAY`. `BOUNDARY`, which is optional, must be of the same type and type parameters as `ARRAY` and must be scalar if `ARRAY` has rank one; otherwise, it must be either scalar or of rank n-1 and of shape $(d_1, d_2, \ldots, d_{DIM-1}, d_{DIM+1}, \ldots, d_n)$. `BOUNDARY` may be omitted for the data types in the following table and, in this case, it is as if it were present with the scalar value shown.

Type of ARRAY	Value of BOUNDARY
Integer	0
Real	0.0
Complex	(0.0,0.0)
Logical	false
Character(*len*)	*len* blanks

`DIM`, which is optional, must be a scalar and of type integer with a value in the range `1<=DIM<=n` where `n` is the rank of `ARRAY`. If `DIM` is omitted, it is as if it were present with the value 1.

The result has the type, type parameters, and shape of `ARRAY`. Element $(s_1, s_2, \ldots, s_n)$ of the result has the value `ARRAY`$(s_1, s_2, \ldots, s_{DIM-1}, s_{DIM+sh}, s_{DIM+1}, \ldots, s_n)$ where sh is `SHIFT` or `SHIFT`$(s_1, s_2, \ldots, s_{DIM-1}, s_{DIM+1}, \ldots, s_n)$ provided the inequality `LBOUND(ARRAY,DIM)`$<=s_{DIM+sh}<=$`UBOUND(ARRAY,DIM)` holds and is otherwise `BOUNDARY` or `BOUNDARY`$(s_1, s_2, \ldots, s_{DIM-1}, s_{DIM+1}, \ldots, s_n)$.

Examples:

Case i) : If `V` is the array [1,2,3,4,5,6], the effect of shifting `V` end-off to the left by 3 positions is achieved by `EOSHIFT(V, SHIFT=3)` which has the value [4,5,6,0,0,0]; `EOSHIFT(V,SHIFT=-2,BOUNDARY=99)` achieves an end-off shift to the right by 2 positions with the boundary value of 99 and has the value [99,99,1,2,3,4].

Case ii) : The rows of an array of rank two may all be shifted by the same amount or by different amounts and the boundary elements can be the same or different. If `M` is the array $\begin{bmatrix} A & B & C \\ D & E & F \\ G & H & I \end{bmatrix}$ then the value of

`EOSHIFT(M,SHIFT=-1,BOUNDARY='*',DIM=2)` is $\begin{bmatrix} * & A & B \\ * & D & E \\ * & G & H \end{bmatrix}$

and the value of `EOSHIFT(M,SHIFT=(/-1,1,0/), &`

`BOUNDARY=(/'*','/','?'/),DIM=2)` is $\begin{bmatrix} * & A & B \\ E & F & / \\ G & H & I \end{bmatrix}$.

TRANSPOSE(MATRIX)

Transpose an array of rank two.

The result is an array of the same type and type parameters as `MATRIX` and with rank two and shape (n,m) where (m,n) is the shape of `MATRIX`.

Element `(i,j)` of the result has the value `MATRIX(j,i)`, `i=1,2,...,n`; `j=1,2,...,m`.

Example : If `A` is the array $\begin{bmatrix} 1 & 2 & 3 \\ 4 & 5 & 6 \\ 7 & 8 & 9 \end{bmatrix}$ then `TRANSPOSE(A)` has the value

$$\begin{bmatrix} 1 & 4 & 7 \\ 2 & 5 & 8 \\ 3 & 6 & 9 \end{bmatrix} .$$

A.18 Array Location Functions

The functions `MAXLOC` and `MINLOC` return the location (subscripts) of an element of an array that has a maximum and minimum value, respectively. By use of an optional logical mask that is conformable with the given array, the reduction may be confined to any subset of the array.

`MAXLOC(ARRAY,MASK)`

Determine the location of the first element of an array having the maximum value of the elements, optionally under control of a mask.

`ARRAY` must be of type integer or real. It must not be scalar.

The result is of type default integer; it is an array of rank one and of size equal to the rank of `ARRAY`.

Case i) : If `MASK` is absent, the result is a rank-one array whose element values are the values of the subscripts of an element of `ARRAY` whose value equals the maximum value of all the elements of `ARRAY`. The `i`th subscript returned lies in the range 1 to e, where e is the extent of the `i`th dimension of `ARRAY`. If more than one element has the maximum value, the element whose subscripts are returned is the first such element, taken in array element order. If `ARRAY` has size zero, the value of the result is processor dependent.

Case ii) : If `MASK` is present, the result is a rank-one array whose element values are the values of the subscripts of an element of `ARRAY`, corresponding to a true element of `MASK`, whose value equals the maximum value of all such elements of `ARRAY`. The `i`th subscript returned lies in the range 1 to e, where e, is the extent of the `i`th dimension of `ARRAY`. If more than one such element has the maximum value, the element whose subscripts are returned is the first such element taken in array element order. If there are no such elements (that is, if `ARRAY` has size zero or every element of `MASK` has the value false), the value of the result is processor dependent.

An element of the result is undefined if the processor cannot represent the value as a default integer.

Examples:

Case i) : The value of `MAXLOC((/2,6,4,6/))` is [2].

Case ii) : If A has the value $\begin{bmatrix} 0 & -5 & 8 & -3 \\ 3 & 4 & -1 & 2 \\ 1 & 5 & 6 & -4 \end{bmatrix}$, `MAXLOC(A,MASK=A<6)` has the value [3,2]. Note that this is true even if A has a declared lower bound other than 1.

MINLOC(ARRAY,MASK)

Determine the location of the first element of an array having the minimum value of the elements optionally under control of a mask.

ARRAY must be of type integer or real. It must not be scalar.

The result is of type default integer; it is an array of rank one and of size equal to the rank of ARRAY.

This function is similar in specification to MAXLOC above except the minimum is located rather than the maximum.

Examples:

Case i) : The value of `MINLOC((/4,3,6,3/))` is [2].

Case ii) : If A has the value $\begin{bmatrix} 0 & -5 & 8 & -3 \\ 3 & 4 & -1 & 2 \\ 1 & 5 & 6 & -4 \end{bmatrix}$, `MINLOC(A,MASK=A>-4)` has the value [1,4]. Note that, this is true even if A has a declared lower bound other than 1.

A.19 Pointer Association Status Inquiry Function

The function ASSOCIATED tests whether a pointer is currently associated with any target, with a particular target, or with the same target as another pointer.

ASSOCIATED(POINTER,TARGET)

Returns the association status of its pointer argument or indicates the pointer is associated with the target.

The POINTER association status must not be undefined. TARGET, which is optional, must be a pointer or target. If it is a pointer, its pointer association status must not be undefined.

The result is of type default logical.

Case i) : If TARGET is absent, the result is true if POINTER is currently associated with a target and false if it is not.

Case ii) : If TARGET is present and is a target, the result is true if POINTER is currently associated with TARGET and false if it is not.

Case iii) : If TARGET is present and is a pointer, the result is true if both POINTER and TARGET are currently associated with the same target, and is false otherwise. If either POINTER or TARGET is disassociated, the result is false.

Examples: `ASSOCIATED(CURRENT,HEAD)` is true if `CURRENT` points to the target `HEAD`. After the execution of

```
A_PART=>A(:N)
```

`ASSOCIATED(A_PART,A)` is true if `N` was equal to `UBOUND(A)`. After the execution of

```
NULLIFY(CUR); NULLIFY(TOP)
```

`ASSOCIATED(CUR,TOP)` is false.

A.20 Intrinsic Subroutines

The subroutines `DATE_AND_TIME` and `SYSTEM_CLOCK` return data from the date and real-time clock. The time returned is local, but there are facilities for finding out the difference between local time and Coordinated Universal Time. (Note that CUT is defined by CCIR Recommendation 460-2 and is a more precise version of the time standard more commonly but incorrectly known as Greenwich Mean Time).

`DATE_AND_TIME(DATE,TIME,ZONE,VALUES)`

Returns data on the real-time clock and date in a form compatible with the representations defined in ISO 8601:1988.

`DATE`, which is optional, must be scalar and of type default character, and must be of length at least 8 in order to contain the complete value. It is an `INTENT(OUT)` argument. Its leftmost 8 characters are set to a value of the form CCYYMMDD, where CC is the century, YY the year within the century, MM the month within the year, and DD the day within the month. If there is no date available, they are set to blank.

`TIME`, which is optional, must be scalar and of type default character, and must be of length at least 10 in order to contain the complete value. It is an `INTENT(OUT)` argument. Its leftmost 10 characters are set to a value of the form hhmmss.fff, where hh is the hour of the day, mm is the minutes of the hour, and ss.fff is the seconds and fractions of the second in milliseconds. If there is no clock available, they are set to blank.

`ZONE`, which is optional, must be scalar and of type default character, and must be of length at least 5 in order to contain the complete value. It is an `INTENT(OUT)` argument. Its leftmost 5 characters are set to a value of the form +-hhmm, where hh and mm are the time difference with respect to Coordinated Universal Time (CUT) in hours and parts of an hour expressed in minutes, respectively. If there is no clock available, they are set to blank.

`VALUES`, which is optional, must be of type default integer and of rank one. It is an `INTENT(OUT)` argument. Its size must be at least 8. The values returned in `VALUES` are as follows:

`VALUES(1)` the year (for example, 1990), or `-HUGE(0)` if there is no date available;

`VALUES(2)` the month of the year, or `-HUGE(0)` if there is no date available;

`VALUES(3)` the day of the month, or `-HUGE(0)` if there is no date available;

`VALUES(4)` the time difference with respect to Coordinated Universal Time (CUT) in minutes, or `-HUGE(0)` if this information is not available;

`VALUES(5)` the hour of the day, in the range of 0 to 23, or `-HUGE(0)` if there is no clock;

VALUES(6) the minutes of the hour, in the range 0 to 59, or -HUGE(0) if there is no clock;
VALUES(7) the seconds of the minute, in the range 0 to 60, or -HUGE(0) if there is no clock;
VALUES(8) the fraction of the second in milliseconds, in the range 0 to 999, or -HUGE(0) if there is no clock.
Example :

```
INTEGER :: DATE_TIME(8)
CHARACTER(LEN=10) :: BIG_BEN(3)
CALL DATE_AND_TIME(BIG_BEN(1),BIG_BEN(2), &
                   BIG_BEN(3),DATE_TIME)
```

if called in Geneva, Switzerland on 1985 April 12 at 15:27:35.5 would have assigned the characters 19850412 to BIG_BEN(1), 152735.500 to BIG_BEN(2), and +0100 to BIG_BEN(3), and the following values to DATE_TIME: [1985,4,12,60,15,27,35,500].

SYSTEM_CLOCK(COUNT,COUNT_RATE,COUNT_MAX)

Returns integer values from a real-time clock.

COUNT, which is optional, must be scalar and of type default integer. It is an INTENT(OUT) argument. It is set to a processor-dependent value based on the current value of the processor clock or to -HUGE(0) if there is no clock. The processor-dependent value is incremented by one for each clock count until the value COUNT_MAX is reached and is reset to zero at the next count. It lies in the range 0 to COUNT_MAX if there is a clock.

COUNT_RATE, which is optional, must be scalar and of type default integer. It is an INTENT(OUT) argument. It is set to the number of processor clock counts per second, or to zero if there is no clock.

COUNT_MAX, which is optional, must be scalar and of type default integer. It is an INTENT(OUT) argument. It is set to the maximum value that COUNT can have, or to zero if there is no clock.

Example : If the processor clock is a 24-hour clock that registers time in 1-second intervals, at 11:30 A.M. the reference

```
CALL SYSTEM_CLOCK(COUNT=C,COUNT_RATE=R, &
                  COUNT_MAX=M)
```

sets C=11x3600+30x60=41400, R=1, and M=24x3600-1=86399.

A.21 Bit Copy Subroutine

MVBITS(FROM,FROMPOS,LEN,TO,TOPOS)

Copies a sequence of bits from one data object to another.

FROM must be of type integer. It is an INTENT(IN) argument. FROMPOS must be of type integer and non-negative. It is an INTENT(IN) argument. FROMPOS+LEN must be less than or equal to BIT_SIZE(FROM). The model for the interpretation of an integer value as a sequence of bits is in A.12. LEN must be of type integer and non-negative. It is an INTENT(IN) argument. TO must be a variable of type integer with the same kind value as FROM and may be the same variable as FROM. It is an INTENT(INOUT) argument. TO is set by copying the sequence of bits of length LEN, starting at position FROMPOS of FROM to position TOPOS of TO. No other bits of TO are altered. On return, the LEN bits of TO starting at TOPOS are equal to the value that the LEN bits of FROM starting at FROMPOS had on entry. TOPOS must be of type integer and non-negative. It is an INTENT(IN) argument. TOPOS+LEN must be less than or equal to BIT_SIZE(TO).

Example : If TO has the initial value 6, the value of TO after the statement CALL MVBITS(7,2,2,TO,0) is 5.

A.22 Pseudorandom Numbers

The subroutine RANDOM_NUMBER returns a pseudorandom number or an array of pseudorandom numbers. The subroutine RANDOM_SEED initializes or restarts the pseudorandom number sequence.

RANDOM_NUMBER(HARVEST)

Returns one pseudorandom number or an array of pseudorandom numbers from the uniform distribution over the range 0<=X<1.

HARVEST must be of type real. It is an INTENT(OUT) argument. It may be a scalar or an array variable. It is set to contain pseudorandom numbers from the uniform distribution in the interval 0<=X<1.0

Examples:

```
REAL :: X, Y(10,10)
! Initialise X with a pseudorandom number
CALL RANDOM_NUMBER(HARVEST=X)
CALL RANDOM_NUMBER(Y)
! X and Y contain uniformly distributed random numbers
```

RANDOM_SEED(SIZE,PUT,GET)

Restarts or queries the pseudorandom number generator used by RANDOM_NUMBER.

There must either be exactly one or no arguments present. SIZE, which is optional, must be scalar and of type default integer. It is an INTENT(OUT) argument. It is set to the number N of integers that the processor uses to hold the value of the seed. PUT, which is optional, must be a default integer array of rank one and size greater than or equal to N. It is an INTENT(IN) argument. It is used by the processor to set the seed value. GET, which is optional, must be a default integer array of rank one and size greater than or equal to N. It is an INTENT(OUT) argument. It is set by the processor to the current value of the seed.

If no argument is present, the processor sets the seed to a processor-dependent value.

Examples:

```
CALL RANDOM_SEED                    ! Processor initialization
CALL RANDOM_SEED(SIZE=K)                ! Sets K=N
CALL RANDOM_SEED(PUT=SEED(1:X))         ! Set user seed
CALL RANDOM_SEED(GET=OLD(1:K))          ! Read current seed
```

Appendix B

Answers to Exercises

Chapter 1

Exercise 1.1:
A suitable algorithm would be:

1. Start
2. Reserve storage for years, weeks and days
3. Read in values for years and weeks
4. days = years x 365 + weeks x 7
5. Print out the value of days (with a suitable message)
6. End

Exercise 1.2:

```
PROGRAM Exercise1_2
 INTEGER :: years,weeks,days
  READ(UNIT=*,FMT=*)years,weeks
  days = years*365 + weeks*7
  WRITE(UNIT=*,FMT=*)'Number of days = ',days
END PROGRAM
```

Exercise 1.3:
The algorithm and program are exact analogues of those given in the text.

Exercise 1.4:
The algorithm and program are exact analogues of those given in the text.

Chapter 2

Exercise 2.1:
The algorithm is contained in the answer to exercise 2.2.

Exercise 2.2:

1. set count = 0
2. Start loop
3. Read in the three values (first, second, third)
4. If first < 0 exit loop
5. Put minimum = first
6. if second < minimum, put minimum = second
7. if third < minimum, put minimum = third
8. Print out minimum
9. Add minimum to cumulative sum
10. increment count
11. End of loop

12. average = cumulative sum divided by count
13. print out the average
14. End of program

Exercise 2.3:

```
PROGRAM Exercise2_3
  REAL :: first, second, third, average, minimum
  INTEGER :: count
  count=0
  DO
    READ(*,*) first,second,third
    IF(first<0)EXIT
    minimum = first
    IF(second<minimum)minimum=second
    IF(third<minimum)minimum=third
    WRITE(*,*)'Minimum = ',minimum
    sum = sum + minimum
    count=count+1
  ENDDO
  average = sum/count
  WRITE(*,*)'Average minimum = ',average
END PROGRAM
```

Exercise 2.4:

1. Read in the three values (val1,val2,val3)
2. If val1 < val2 put first = val1 else put first = val2
3. If val3 < first put first = val3

Chapter 3

Exercise 3.1:

X, c, $, %, *, ", ' are all valid.
£, @ are invalid but can appear in character strings.

Exercise 3.2:

a) invalid
b) valid
c) invalid - commas must be used to separate variable names and a variable called I1I2I3 (which is permissible) must not contain spaces in its name.
d) valid - spaces may be used for layout and are not needed around operators in expressions.

Exercise 3.3:

a) There should be a continuation character i.e.

```
A = B + C + &
            D
```

b) `WRITE(*,*) A ! the sum of three numbers, B,C,D`

c) `INTEGER A,B,C`

Exercise 3.4:

```
PROGRAM MAIN
  INTEGER :: degreesfahrenheit, degreescentigrade
  READ(UNIT=*,FMT=*) degreesfahrenheit
  degreescentigrade = 5 * (degreesfahrenheit -32)/9
  WRITE(UNIT=*,FMT=*) degreescentigrade
END
```

Exercise 3.5:
All valid apart from Filename.Ext which contains an invalid full stop.

Chapter 4

Exercise 4.1:
-1 and 30 are integer constants
.500, 6.35, 2E-5, and .123E+12 are real constants
'Have a nice day' and '   ' are character constants
.TRUE. is a logical constant

Exercise 4.2:
3.0 (real), 6.0 (real), 2.25 (real), 0 (integer), 1 (integer), 0 (integer), 21.0 (real), 12 (integer), 0.0 (real), 0 (integer), 0 (integer)

Exercise 4.3:
Assume the phrases will be no longer than 30 characters long and they will be read off separate lines.

```
PROGRAM Exercise4_3
  CHARACTER(LEN=30) :: phrase1, phrase2
  CHARACTER(LEN=60) :: sentence
  READ(*,*) phrase1
  READ(*,*) phrase2
  sentence = TRIM(phrase1) //','//phrase2
! The intrinsic function TRIM (in the Appendix) returns
! a string containing phrase1 with the trailing blanks
! removed
  WRITE(*,*) sentence
  N= INDEX(sentence,',')
  WRITE(*,*)'Position of comma = ',N
END
```

Two sample lines of data might be:

```
'This is the first phrase'
'and this is the second'
```

Exercise 4.4:
The intrinsic function `INDEX` is available. Thus,

```
INDEX( sentence,',')
```

would return the position of the comma.

Exercise 4.5:
`red_or_not1` is `.FALSE.` since the first logical expression in the brackets is `.TRUE.` and the second is `.FALSE.` Therefore the `.AND.` combination is `.FALSE.`

`red_or_not2` is `.TRUE.` since the first logical expression in the brackets is `.TRUE.` and the second is `.FALSE.` Therefore the `.OR.` combination is `.TRUE.`

Exercise 4.6:
`colour` is a named constant and cannot be changed in the program. `hue` is a character variable initialised to `'Blue'` but can be subsequently changed in the program.

Exercise 4.7:
```
PROGRAM Exercise4_7
 REAL :: pi=3.141592
 REAL :: rad1,rad2,area
 READ(*,*)rad1,rad2
! Use ABS to take account of case rad1 < rad2
 area=ABS(pi*(rad1**2-rad2**2))
 WRITE(*,*)' Area between circles = ', area
END
```

Exercise 4.8:
```
REAL :: time=0.0, height=5.6
REAL, PARAMETER :: half = 0.5
CHARACTER(LEN=4) :: name = 'Rush'
CHARACTER(LEN=*), PARAMETER :: club = 'Liverpool'
LOGICAL, PARAMETER :: stat = .TRUE.
INTEGER :: turns = 500
```

Exercise 4.9:
```
PROGRAM Exercise4_9
TYPE student_marks
  CHARACTER(LEN=32) :: name
  LOGICAL :: part_time
  INTEGER :: Eng, Mat, Sci
END TYPE

TYPE(student_marks) :: Tom, Dick, Harry
```

```
Harry%name = 'Harold Brown'
Harry%part_time = .TRUE.
Harry%Eng = 34
Harry%Mat = 76
Harry%Sci = 64

WRITE(*,*)Harry

Tom%Eng = 34

IF(Harry%Eng == Tom%Eng)THEN
  WRITE(*,*)'Harry and Tom have the same mark in English'
ELSE
  WRITE(*,*)'Harry and Tom have different marks in English'
ENDIF
END PROGRAM
```

Chapter 5

Exercise 5.1:
See the answer to exercise 5.2.

Exercise 5.2:
```
PROGRAM Exercis5_2
INTEGER :: I,upper
READ(*,*)upper
IF(upper <= 100)THEN
 I=0
 DO
   I=I+1
   IF(I>upper)EXIT
   cube=I**3
   WRITE(*,*)I,cube
 ENDDO
ELSE
 WRITE(*,*)'Upper limit too large - must be < 100'
ENDIF
END PROGRAM
```

Exercise 5.3:
```
PROGRAM Exercis5_3
INTEGER :: sum,I,n
sum=0
READ(*,*)n
DO I=1,n
  sum=sum+I
ENDDO
WRITE(*,*)'Sum of first ', n, 'integers = ',sum
END PROGRAM
```

Exercise 5.4:
See answer to exercise 5.5.

Exercise 5.5:
For certain values of a,b,c the value of b**2-4*a*c will be negative and an attempt to calculate the SQRT would cause the program to fail. In such a case the equation has complex roots and a simple solution is to stop the program and print a suitable message as shown below. The more confident reader might like to write the program to print out the complex roots.

```
PROGRAM Exercise5_5
 REAL :: a,b,c,root1,root2
 DO
   READ(*,*)a,b,c
   IF(a==999.9)EXIT
   IF(b**2>4*a*c)THEN
     root1=(-b+SQRT(b**2-4*a*c))/(2*a)
     root2=(-b-SQRT(b**2-4*a*c))/(2*a)
     WRITE(*,*)'The roots are ',root1,root2
   ELSE
     WRITE(*,*)' There are no real roots'
   ENDIF
 ENDDO
END PROGRAM
```

Note in the above program that it would be more efficient to calculate b**2 - 4*a*c (called the discriminant) once and then use this in subsequent statements. This would be at the expense of having to declare an extra variable to hold the value. Thus,

```
READ(*,*) a, b, c
IF(a == 999.)EXIT
discr = b**2 - 4*a*c
IF( discr > 0.)THEN
  root1 = (-b + SQRT(discr) )/ (2*a)
  root2 = (-b - SQRT(discr) )/ (2*a)
  ...etc...
```

Exercise 5.6:
The program is given for red and green only for brevity.

```
PROGRAM Exercise5_6
  INTEGER :: num_red=0,num_green=0,num_unknown=0
  CHARACTER(LEN=10) :: colour ! assume max of 10 characters
  DO
   READ(*,*)colour
   IF(colour == 'blank')EXIT
   SELECT CASE (colour)
     CASE('red')
       num_red=num_red+1
```

```
                    _green+1

          own=num_unknown+1
    END SELECT
  ENDDO
  WRITE(*,*)'Number of reds = ',num_red
  WRITE(*,*)'Number of greens = ',num_green
  WRITE(*,*)'Number of unknowns = ',num_unknown
END PROGRAM
```

Exercise 5.7:

```
PROGRAM Exercise5_7
  INTEGER :: fives, num
  fives=0
  DO I=1,10
    READ(*,*)num
    IF(num<0)CYCLE
    IF(num-(num/5)*5 == 0)fives=fives+1
  ENDDO
  WRITE(*,*)fives
END PROGRAM
```

Exercise 5.8:

The iteration count is the integer part of (the end value minus the start value divided by the increment). The answers are therefore:

a) 1 b) 3 c) 44

Chapter 6

Exercise 6.1:

```
PROGRAM Exercise6_1
  INTEGER, DIMENSION(8,8) :: board

  board=0
! odd rows
  DO I=1,8,2
    DO J=1,8,2
      board(I,J)=1
    ENDDO
  ENDDO
! even rows
  DO I=2,8,2
    DO J=2,8,2
      board(I,J)=1
    ENDDO
  ENDDO
  DO I=1,8
    WRITE(*,*) board(I,1:8)
```

```
  ENDDO
END PROGRAM
```

Exercise 6.2:

```
INTEGER, DIMENSION(8,16,2)

BED(7,5,2)
```

Exercise 6.3:

TWO and FOUR are conformable since they both have rank 2 and shape (2,6).

Exercise 6.4:

The array element order of the arrays TWO and THREE are,

```
TWO(1,0), TWO(2,0), TWO(1,1), TWO(2,1), TWO(1,2), TWO(2,2)
etc...
THREE(-1,1,1), THREE(0,1,1), THREE(1,1,1), THREE(-1,2,1),
THREE(0,2,1), THREE(1,2,1), THREE(-1,3,1), THREE(0,3,1),
THREE(1,3,1), etc...
```

Exercise 6.5:

BOXES = (/1,4,6,12,23/)

Exercise 6.6:

```
REAL,DIMENSION(3,2) :: A=RESHAPE( (/2.1,3.2,7.4,&
                                5.3,6.5,8.9/),(/3,2/) )
```

Exercise 6.7:

All are valid except `A(3.0)`.

Exercise 6.8:

In array element notation, the main body of the program will look like:

```
PROGRAM Exercise6_8
  IMPLICIT NONE
  INTEGER, DIMENSION(:,:), ALLOCATABLE :: matrix
  INTEGER :: largest=-HUGE(0), dim1, dim2
  INTEGER :: num_zero=0,num_pos=0, sum_pos=0, I, J
! Note the use of HUGE(0) which returns the largest integer
! available on the machine.
  READ(*,*) dim1,dim2
  ALLOCATE(matrix(1:dim1,1:dim2))
  READ(*,*) matrix
  WRITE(*,*) matrix
  DO J=1,dim2
    DO I=1,dim1
      WRITE(*,*)matrix(I,J)
      IF(matrix(I,J) > largest)largest=matrix(I,J)
      IF(matrix(I,J) == 0)num_zero = num_zero+1
```

```
      IF(matrix(I,J) >  0)THEN
        num_pos  = num_pos + 1
        sum_pos  = sum_pos + matrix(I,J)
      ENDIF
    ENDDO
  ENDDO
  WRITE(*,*)'largest,num_zero,num_pos,sum_pos = ',&
             largest,num_zero,num_pos,sum_pos
! Using the whole array intrinsics we would have:

  largest  = MAXVAL(matrix)
  num_zero = COUNT(matrix == 0)
  num_pos  = COUNT(matrix > 0)
  sum_pos  = SUM( matrix, MASK = matrix > 0)
  WRITE(*,*)'largest,num_zero,num_pos,sum_pos = ',&
             largest,num_zero,num_pos,sum_pos
END PROGRAM
```

Exercise 6.9:
Using array element notation:

```
PROGRAM Exercise6_9
  INTEGER,PARAMETER :: n_miles=20, stretch=5
  REAL :: maxcost=TINY(0.0),cost5
  REAL, DIMENSION(n_miles) :: cost = &
  (/6.3, 7.6, 9.2, 3.4, 5.6, 7.23, 9.76, 6.83, 5.45, 4.56,
&
    4.86, 5.8, 6.4, 7.43, 7.8, 8.6, 9.25, 8.9, 8.4, 7.23/)
  INTEGER :: start
  DO I=1,n_miles-stretch+1
    cost5 = 0
    DO J=I,I+stretch-1
      cost5 = cost5 + cost(J)
    ENDDO
    IF(cost5 > maxcost)THEN
      maxcost=cost5
      start = I
    ENDIF
  ENDDO
  WRITE(*,*) &
   ' The most expensive ',stretch,' mile stretch is', &
   ' from ',start,' to ',start+stretch,' and costs
',maxcost
END PROGRAM
```

Or, using whole array notation:

```
PROGRAM Exercise6_9p1
  INTEGER,PARAMETER :: n_miles=20, stretch=5
  INTEGER, PARAMETER :: n_stretches = n_miles-stretch+1
```

```
  INTEGER, DIMENSION(1) :: start  ! needed for result of
MAXLOC
  REAL :: maxcost
  REAL, DIMENSION(n_stretches) :: cost5
  REAL, DIMENSION(n_miles) :: cost = &
  (/6.3, 7.6, 9.2 ,3.4, 5.6, 7.23 ,9.76, 6.83, 5.45, 4.56,
&
    4.86, 5.8, 6.4, 7.43, 7.87, 8.6, 9.25, 8.9, 8.4, 7.23/)
  DO I=1,n_stretches
    cost5(I) = SUM(cost(I:I+stretch-1))
  ENDDO
  maxcost = MAXVAL(cost5)
  start = MAXLOC(cost5)
  WRITE(*,*) &
   ' The most expensive ',stretch,' mile stretch is', &
   ' from ',start,' to ',start+stretch,' and costs
',maxcost
END PROGRAM
```

Note that the whole array solution involves the extra storage for the array cost5.

Exercise 6.10:
The program uses nested loops to investigate all possible permutations which do not have repeated visits.

```
PROGRAM Exercise6_10
  IMPLICIT NONE
  INTEGER :: I,J,K,L,M
  INTEGER :: dist_travelled, min_dist=HUGE(0)
  INTEGER, PARAMETER :: n_towns=5
  INTEGER, DIMENSION(6) :: route
  CHARACTER, DIMENSION(5) :: towns = &
  (/'A','B','C','D','E'/)
  INTEGER, DIMENSION(n_towns,n_towns) :: dist= &
  RESHAPE( &
    (/  0,120,180,202,300, &
      120,  0,175,340,404, &
      180,175,  0, 98, 56, &
      202,340, 98,  0,168, &
      300,404, 56,168,  0 /), (/5,5/) )
LI:  DO I=1,n_towns
LJ:    DO J=1,n_towns
         IF(J==I)CYCLE
LK:      DO K=1,n_towns
           IF(K==J .OR. K==I)CYCLE
LL:        DO L=1,n_towns
             IF(L==J .OR. L==K .OR. L==I )CYCLE
LM:          DO M=1,n_towns
               IF(M==L .OR. M==K .OR. M==J .OR. M==I)CYCLE
               dist_travelled = dist(I,J) + dist(J,K) +
dist(K,L) + &
```

```
                              dist(L,M) + dist(M,I)
              IF(dist_travelled < min_dist) THEN
                min_dist=dist_travelled
                route(1)=I
                route(2)=J
                route(3)=K
                route(4)=L
                route(5)=M
                route(6)=I
              ENDIF
          ENDDO LM
        ENDDO LL
      ENDDO LK
    ENDDO LJ
  ENDDO LI
  WRITE(*,*)'Shortest route travelled is :'
  DO I=1,n_towns+1
    WRITE(*,*)towns(route(I))
  ENDDO
  WRITE(*,*)'Distance travelled = ',min_dist
END PROGRAM
```

Note that the above solution is not optimum in that the program uses more memory than necessary. It is not strictly necessary to store the whole array of distances since it is symmetric. The program also does more computation than necessary since it looks twice at routes that are known to involve the same distance such as those with I,J,K,L,M,I taking values of 1,2,3,4,5,1 and 1,5,4,3,2,1. Optimisation of the program to take these factors into account is left as a further exercise for the reader.

Chapter 7

Exercise 7.1:
V1 and V2 are arguments. V3 and V4 are local variables.

Exercise 7.2:
Internal procedures are defined within a host procedure following a CONTAINS statement. They inherit the environment of the host and are therefore useful for implementing auxiliary routines which need only be called from the host.

Exercise 7.3:
A should not be assigned a value since it has INTENT(IN). Note that a good compiler would flag this as an error but compilers are not compelled to do so.

Exercise 7.4:

```
SUBROUTINE Shaded_Circle(Radius, Colour)
  REAL :: Radius
  CHARACTER(LEN=*), OPTIONAL :: Colour
  IF(.NOT. PRESENT(Colour) ) Colour = "GREEN"
```

```
  CALL Circle(Radius)
  CALL Shade_Circle(Colour)
END
```

Exercise 7.5:

```
INTERFACE
  SUBROUTINE Shaded_Circle(Radius, Colour)
    REAL :: Radius
    CHARACTER(LEN=*), OPTIONAL :: Colour
  END
END INTERFACE
```

Exercise 7.6:

A, B and C are assumed shape.
E and F are automatic.

Exercise 7.7:

```
PROGRAM Test
INTERFACE
 FUNCTION Std_Dev(x)
   REAL :: Std_Dev
   REAL, DIMENSION(:) :: x
 END
ENDINTERFACE
 REAL, DIMENSION(10) :: s = &
 (/.1,.2,.3,.4,.5,.6,.7,.8,.9,0.0/)
 WRITE(*,*) Std_Dev(s)
END PROGRAM

FUNCTION Std_Dev(x)
  REAL :: Std_Dev
  REAL, DIMENSION(:) :: x
! local variables
  INTEGER :: n,i
  REAL :: mean,total
!
  n = SIZE(x)
  mean = SUM(x)/n
  total=0.
  DO i=1, n
    total = total + (x(i)-mean)**2
  ENDDO
  Std_Dev = SQRT(total/n)
END FUNCTION
```

Exercise 7.8:

```
PROGRAM test
INTEGER throw_dice,th
DO I=1,100
 th= throw_dice()
 WRITE(*,*) 'total throw= ', th
```

```
ENDDO
END PROGRAM
FUNCTION throw_dice()
  INTEGER :: throw_dice
  INTEGER :: throw1,throw2
  CALL RANDOM_NUMBER(r)
! r is returned 0 <= r <= 1
! NINT(r*5) gives an integer between 1 and 5
  throw1 = 1 + NINT(r * 5)
  WRITE(*,*) 'throw1= ',throw1
  CALL RANDOM_NUMBER(r)
  throw2 = 1 + NINT(r * 5)
  WRITE(*,*) 'throw2= ',throw2
  throw_dice = throw1 + throw2
END FUNCTION
```

Notice that the function has no argument but that the brackets must be included in the function header.

Exercise 7.9:
An algorithm for the binary cut is as follows:

> Start
> Let i and j be the indices of the low and high marks.
> Initially set i = 1 and j = n (the number in the list)
> Assume k is the number we are trying to find
> Do
>   if(i >= j)exit
>   determine the half way point (ihalf = i+(j-i)/2)
>   if k is above ihalf put i = ihalf+1
>   Otherwise put j = ihalf
> END Do
> j will now point at the number k
> Finish

A program calling a function which implements the above algorithm is as follows:

```
PROGRAM search
  INTERFACE
   FUNCTION  binary_cut(k,list)
    INTEGER :: binary_cut
    INTEGER, DIMENSION(:) :: list
   END FUNCTION
  ENDINTERFACE
  INTEGER :: index
  INTEGER, PARAMETER :: K = 13    ! Test data
  INTEGER, DIMENSION(10) ::
list=(/2,4,6,6,12,13,13,24,32,32/)
  index = binary_cut(K,list)
```

```
  DO i=1,10
   WRITE(*,*) i , list(i)
  ENDDO
  WRITE(*,*)' The number ',K, ' is at position ', index, &
            ' in the list'
END PROGRAM

FUNCTION  binary_cut(k,list)
  INTEGER :: binary_cut
  INTEGER, DIMENSION(:) :: list
  INTEGER :: k
  INTEGER :: n,i=1,j,ihalf
  n=SIZE(list)
  j=n
  DO
    IF(i >= j)EXIT
    ihalf = i+(j-i)/2;
    WRITE(*,*) 'ihalf,i,j = ',ihalf,i,j
    IF(list(ihalf) >= k)THEN
      j = ihalf
      WRITE(*,*)'bottom half'
    ELSE
      i = ihalf+1
      WRITE(*,*)'top half'
    ENDIF
  ENDDO
  binary_cut = j
  WRITE(*,*)'K at position ',i,j
END FUNCTION
```

Exercise 7.10:

```
PROGRAM Exercise7_10
 INTEGER :: which
 CHARACTER(LEN=3) :: day
 READ(*,*)which
 WRITE(*,*)day(which)
END PROGRAM

FUNCTION day(i)
  CHARACTER(LEN=3) :: day
  INTEGER :: i
  CHARACTER(LEN=3), DIMENSION(7) :: names = &
  (/'Sun','Mon','Tue','Wed','Thu','Fri','Sat'/)
  IF(i >= 1 .AND. i <= 7) THEN
    day = names(i)
  ELSE
    day = '???'
  ENDIF
END FUNCTION
```

Exercise 7.11:

```
PROGRAM Exercise7_11
 INTEGER :: year
 INTEGER :: N_Feb
 LOGICAL :: leap
 READ(*,*)year
 IF(leap(year))THEN
  WRITE(*,*)'Leap year'
  N_Feb=29
 ELSE
  WRITE(*,*)' Not Leap Year'
 ENDIF
END PROGRAM

FUNCTION leap(year)
  INTEGER :: year
  LOGICAL :: leap
  leap = .FALSE.
  IF( (year-1900)/4 * 4 == year-1900)leap=.TRUE.
END FUNCTION
```

Chapter 8

Exercise 8.1:

Global data is data that is accessible by all units in a program. It is set up by defining the data in a module and then USEing this module in any program unit that requires access to it.

Exercise 8.2:

Many of the facilities of Fortran 90 require the use of explicit interfaces. To avoid having to specify interfaces explicitly in every relevant subprogram, subprograms which call each other can be defined together in a module in which case they have access to each other's interfaces.

Exercise 8.3:

A derived type can be defined in a module in such a way that, although the derived type itself is accessible by using the module, the details of the structure of the derived data type are not accessible to the programmer. This is defined using the PRIVATE statement in the derived type definition. For example:

```
MODULE example
TYPE pair
  PRIVATE
  REAL :: part1,part2
END TYPE
END MODULE
```

If the above module was USEd in a subprogram unit then although the programmer could declare objects of type pair he/she could not use expressions like object%part1. The writer of the module would have to provide facilities for the programmer to access the components of the type via procedures defined in the module.

Exercise 8.4:
When an operator can be used to operate on different data types it is said to be overloaded. The arithmetic operator + is overloaded since it can be used to add two reals or two integers or even an integer and a real. An example of a user-defined operator overload is given at the end of section 8.4 by the .CROSSES. operator which tests whether a line crosses a circle.

Exercise 8.5:
```
MODULE generic_sort
  INTERFACE gsort
   MODULE PROCEDURE int_sort, rea_sort
  END INTERFACE
CONTAINS
  SUBROUTINE int_sort(A)
  ! This subroutine implements a bubble-sort
    INTEGER, DIMENSION(:) :: A
    INTEGER :: temp
    INTEGER :: N
    LOGICAL :: swapped
    N=SIZE(A)
    i=1
    swapped = .TRUE.
  ! flag is used to signify whether a swap takes place.
  ! If one doesn't then the algorithm has finished.
    DO
      IF(i > N .or. .not. swapped)EXIT
      swapped = .false.
      DO j=1,N-i
        IF(A(j) > A(j+1))THEN  ! swap values
          temp   = A(j)
          A(j)   = A(j+1)
          A(j+1) = temp
          swapped = .true.
        ENDIF
      ENDDO
      i = i + 1
    ENDDO
  END SUBROUTINE
  SUBROUTINE rea_sort(A)
  ! This subroutine implements a bubble-sort
    REAL, DIMENSION(:) :: A
    REAL :: temp
    INTEGER :: N
    LOGICAL :: swapped
    N=SIZE(A)
```

```
    i=1
    swapped = .TRUE.
  ! flag is used to signify whether a swap takes place.
  ! If one doesn't then the algorithm has finished.
    DO
      IF(i > N .or. .not. swapped)EXIT
      swapped = .false.
      DO j=1,N-i
        IF(A(j) > A(j+1))THEN  ! swap values
          temp   = A(j)
          A(j)   = A(j+1)
          A(j+1) = temp
          swapped = .true.
        ENDIF
      ENDDO
      i = i + 1
    ENDDO
  END SUBROUTINE
END MODULE
PROGRAM Test
  USE generic_sort
  REAL, DIMENSION(6) :: R = (/4.1,1.2,5.5,2.3,6.7,3.6/)
  INTEGER, DIMENSION(6) :: I = (/4,1,5,2,6,3/)
  CALL gsort(R)
  CALL gsort(I)
  WRITE(*,*) 'Real array =  ', R
  WRITE(*,*) 'Integer array ', I
END PROGRAM
```

Exercise 8.6:

```
MODULE array_sorter
 USE generic_sort  ! from exercise 5
 INTERFACE sort_array
   MODULE PROCEDURE sort_1D, sort_2D
 END INTERFACE
CONTAINS
 SUBROUTINE sort_1D(A)
   INTEGER, DIMENSION(:) :: A
   CALL int_sort(A)
 END SUBROUTINE
 SUBROUTINE sort_2D(A)
   INTEGER, DIMENSION(:,:) :: A
   INTEGER, DIMENSION(SIZE(A)) :: D
   D = RESHAPE(A,(/SIZE(A)/))
   CALL int_sort(D)
   A = RESHAPE( D, (/ SIZE(A,DIM=1),SIZE(A,DIM=2) /) )
 END SUBROUTINE
 END MODULE array_sorter

 PROGRAM TestEx8_6
 USE array_sorter
 INTEGER, DIMENSION(5) :: arr1=(/1,5,3,4,2/)
```

```
 INTEGER, DIMENSION(3,2)  :: arr2= &
    RESHAPE((/5,3,6,3,8,4/), (/3,2/) )
 CALL sort_1D(arr1)
 CALL sort_2D(arr2)
 WRITE(*,*) arr1
 WRITE(*,*) arr2
 END
```

Exercise 8.7:

```
MODULE circles
! Type definitions
  TYPE POINT
   PRIVATE      ! the structure of the type
                ! will not be visible
   REAL :: x,y
  ENDTYPE POINT
  TYPE CIRCLE
   PRIVATE
   TYPE(POINT) :: centre
   REAL :: radius
  ENDTYPE CIRCLE
! Interface definitions
  INTERFACE OPERATOR (.CROSSES.)
    MODULE PROCEDURE circle_crosses
  END INTERFACE
! The following input/output routines must be provided
! since the type CIRCLE is private. The bodies of the
! routines are given after the CONTAINS statement
  INTERFACE read_circles     ! the public name
    MODULE PROCEDURE input_circles
  END INTERFACE
  INTERFACE write_circles    ! the public name
    MODULE PROCEDURE output_circles
  END INTERFACE
PRIVATE circle_crosses, input_circle, output_circle
CONTAINS
   FUNCTION circle_crosses( c1,c2 )
   LOGICAL :: circle_crosses
   TYPE(CIRCLE), INTENT(IN) :: c1,c2
   REAL :: d

   d = (c1%centre%x - c2%centre%x)**2 + &
       (c1%centre%y - c2%centre%y)**2

   IF( d < (c1%radius + c2%radius)**2 .OR.   &
       d > (c1%radius - c2%radius)**2 ) THEN
       circle_crosses = .TRUE.
   ELSE
       circle_crosses = .FALSE.
   ENDIF
  ENDFUNCTION circle_crosses
```

```
   SUBROUTINE input_circles(c)
    TYPE(CIRCLE), INTENT(OUT), DIMENSION(8) :: c
    DO i=1,8
     READ(1,*) c(I)%centre%x, c(I)%centre%y, c(I)%radius
    END DO
   END SUBROUTINE
   SUBROUTINE output_circles(c)
    TYPE(CIRCLE), INTENT(OUT), DIMENSION(8) :: c
    DO i=1,8
     WRITE(*,'(3f10.1)') c(I)%centre%x, c(I)%centre%y,
c(I)%radius
    END DO
   END SUBROUTINE

ENDMODULE circles

PROGRAM Example
  USE circles  ! Pull in the module
   TYPE(CIRCLE), DIMENSION(8) :: c
   INTEGER :: crossings=0

   OPEN(UNIT=1, FILE='circles.d')
   call read_circles(c)
   WRITE(*,*) "circles read in"
   call write_circles(c)

l1: DO I= 1,8
l2:  DO J = 1, I-1
      IF( c(I) .CROSSES. c(J) ) THEN
        WRITE(*,*) I, ' crosses ', J
        crossings = crossings + 1
      ENDIF
     END DO l2
    END DO l1

    WRITE(*,*) "Number of circles which cross = ",
crossings
END PROGRAM
```

Sample data for the program:

10 10 30
10 10 40
15 10 23
16 10 15
14.5 15.5 34
5 5 23
4 4 32
3 3 45
5 5 78

10 3 23

Chapter 9

Exercise 9.1:

```
TYPE list
  INTEGER :: data
  TYPE(list), POINTER :: next
  TYPE(list), POINTER :: previous
END TYPE
```

Exercise 9.2:

```
PROGRAM Exercise9_1

TYPE list
  INTEGER :: data
  TYPE(list), POINTER :: next
  TYPE(list), POINTER :: previous
END TYPE
TYPE(list), TARGET :: head
TYPE(list), POINTER :: current, new
INTEGER :: aninteger, another
! Create a list of integers
WRITE(*,*)' Type in a list of integers - end with -1'
current => head
DO
  READ(*,*) aninteger
  IF(aninteger < 0)EXIT
  ALLOCATE(new)
  new%data=aninteger
  new%previous => current
  current%next => new
  current => current%next
ENDDO
! Write out the list
current => head
DO
  IF(.NOT. ASSOCIATED(current%next))EXIT
  current => current%next
  WRITE(*,*)current%data
ENDDO
! Read another integer and insert in the list
WRITE(*,*)'Type in the integer to be inserted'
READ(*,*) another
call insert(another, head)
! Write out the list
WRITE(*,*) ' The new list is:'
current => head
DO
  IF(.NOT. ASSOCIATED(current%next))EXIT
  current => current%next
```

```
  WRITE(*,*)current%data
ENDDO

CONTAINS
SUBROUTINE insert(i, head)
  TYPE(list), TARGET :: head
  TYPE(list), POINTER :: current, new, temp
  INTEGER :: i
  current => head%next
  DO
    WRITE(*,*)'current list item',current%data
    IF(i <= current%data )EXIT
    IF(.NOT.ASSOCIATED(current%next))THEN
      WRITE(*,*)' couldn''t insert item'
      RETURN
    ENDIF
    current => current%next
  ENDDO
  WRITE(*,*)'Inserting new item'
  ALLOCATE(new)
  temp => current%previous! take copy
  current%previous => new
  temp%next => new
  new%next => current
  new%previous => temp
  new%data = i
END SUBROUTINE
END PROGRAM
```

Chapter 10

Exercise 10.1:

```
PROGRAM Exercise10_1
CHARACTER(LEN=20) :: name
REAL :: mark1, mark2, mark3, mark4
OPEN(UNIT=4,FILE='MARKS.DAT')
DO
  READ(*,*) name, mark1, mark2, mark3, mark4
  IF(name == 'END')EXIT
  WRITE(UNIT=4,FMT=*) name, mark1, mark2, mark3, mark4
  WRITE(UNIT=*,FMT=*) name, mark1, mark2, mark3, mark4
ENDDO
CLOSE(UNIT=4)
END PROGRAM
```

Sample data for the above program:

'Bowles' 54. 67. 87. 34.
'Major' 78. 76. 56. 45.
'Thorp' 89. 98. 87. 76.

'END'   0. 0. 0. 0.

Exercise 10.2:

```
PROGRAM Exercise10_2
CHARACTER(LEN=20) :: name
REAL :: mark1, mark2, mark3, mark4
INTEGER :: error=0
OPEN(UNIT=4,FILE='MARKS.DAT')
DO
  READ(UNIT=4,FMT=*, IOSTAT=error) name, mark1, mark2,
mark3, mark4
  IF(error < 0)EXIT    ! end of file test
  average = (mark1 + mark2 + mark3 + mark4)/4.0
  WRITE(*,*) name, average
ENDDO
CLOSE(UNIT=4)
END PROGRAM
```

Exercise 10.3:

```
PROGRAM Exercise10_3
CHARACTER(LEN=20) :: name
CHARACTER(LEN=6)  :: pos_spec
   REAL :: mark1, mark2, mark3, mark4
! The POSITION parameter can be used to specify that the
file
! should be opened and positioned so that the end-of record
is
! the next record.
READ(*,*) pos_spec
OPEN(UNIT=4,FILE='MARKS.DAT',POSITION=pos_spec)
DO
  READ(*,*) name, mark1, mark2, mark3, mark4
  IF(name=='END')EXIT
  WRITE(UNIT=4,FMT=*) name, mark1, mark2, mark3, mark4
ENDDO
CLOSE(UNIT=4)
END PROGRAM
```

A more sophisticated program might use the statement

```
OPEN(UNIT=4,FILE='MARKS.DAT',POSITION=append_or_not() )
```

where the function `append_or_not` is defined as:

```
FUNCTION  append_or_not()
  CHARACTER(LEN=6) :: append_or_not
  CHARACTER(LEN=1) :: ans
  WRITE(*,*)'Do you want to append to the file?'
  READ(*,*)ans
  append_or_not='REWIND'
```

```
  IF(ans(1:1)=='y')append_or_not='APPEND'
END FUNCTION
```

Exercise 10.4:

A sequential file is written one record after the other and can only be read back in the same order. In order to reach record n it is necessary to read the previous n-1 records in the file. Direct access files are usually also written in sequential order but each record can be accessed randomly by its record number.

Direct access files are thus used when records are to be retrieved in random order from a file.

Exercise 10.5:

```
PROGRAM Exercise10_5
CHARACTER(LEN=30) :: name, address
OPEN(UNIT=4,FILE='people.dat',ACCESS='DIRECT',&
   ACTION='READWRITE',RECL=60,FORM='FORMATTED')
DO I=1,10
  READ(*,*) name, address
  WRITE(UNIT=4,FMT='(2A)',REC=I) name, address
ENDDO
WRITE(*,*)'File written'
REWIND 4
! Read in reverse order
DO I=10,1,-1
  READ(UNIT=4,FMT='(2A)',REC=I) name, address
  WRITE(*,'(2A)') TRIM(name), TRIM(address)
ENDDO
END PROGRAM
```

Exercise 10.6:

See answer to exercise 10.7.

Exercise 10.7:

```
PROGRAM Exercise10_6
CHARACTER(LEN=32) :: fname
CHARACTER(LEN=1)  :: answer
INTEGER :: ierr
LOGICAL :: file_exists
DO
  WRITE(*,*)'Type in the name of a file'
  READ(*,*) fname
! Check file exists
  INQUIRE(FILE=fname,EXIST=file_exists)
  IF(.NOT.file_exists)THEN
    WRITE(*,*)'File does not exist'
    CYCLE
  ENDIF
  OPEN(UNIT=8, FILE=fname, IOSTAT=ierr, ACTION='READ')
```

```
! Check file opened correctly
  IF(ierr == 0)THEN
    WRITE(*,*)'File opened successfully'
    EXIT
  ELSE
    ! note that any positive or negative values of ierr
    ! will have meaning which is installation specific
    WRITE(*,*)'Unable to open ', fname
    WRITE(*,*)'Reason given by IOSTAT number = ', ierr
    WRITE(*,*)'Do you wish to specify another file?'
    IF(answer() == 'n')THEN
      WRITE(*,*)'Program aborted - file not opened'
      EXIT
    ENDIF
  ENDIF
ENDDO
END PROGRAM
FUNCTION answer()
! this function returns either y or n
  CHARACTER(LEN=1) :: answer
  DO
    READ(*,*) answer
    IF(answer == 'y' .OR. answer == 'n')EXIT
    WRITE(*,*)'You must answer ''y'' or ''n'' '
    WRITE(*,*)'Try again'
  ENDDO
END FUNCTION answer
```

Chapter 11

Exercise 11.1:

```
CHARACTER(LEN=12) :: name
INTEGER           :: age
REAL              :: height
LOGICAL           :: married
```

name would contain `LINCOLNbbbbb`

Exercise 11.2:

`A=1.5, B=3.4, C=5.6, I=0, J=0, K=45,arr(1:3)=23.7, arr(4:5)=0.`

Exercise 11.3:

`A=5.3,I=<unchanged>, C1=<unchanged>, C2='Thank you'`

Exercise 11.4:

a) `A=5.34, C='NO',L=.TRUE.`
b) `A=5.34, C='Y ',L=.FALSE.`
c) `A=600000.032, C='11',L=.TRUE.`

d) `A=0.0, C='    ',L=.FALSE.`

Exercise 11.5:

```
(F8.3,A12,I5)
(F8.4,5X,A4,4x,3x,I2)
(F8.5,2X,A4,8X,I2)
(F8.2,8X,A4,2X,I2)
```

The above are not the only answers.

Exercise 11.6:

```
READ(*,'(2I1)') A
```

The format will be re-scanned and a new record read each time the format is exhausted.

Exercise 11.7:

```
PROGRAM Exercise11_7
     CHARACTER(LEN=15) :: name
     INTEGER :: age, tel_no, stat
     REAL :: height
     OPEN(UNIT=8, FILE='personnel.dat')
     WRITE(*,100)
 100 FORMAT(T22,'Height')
     WRITE(*,200)
 200 FORMAT(T4,'Name',T17,'Age',T21,'(metres)',T30,'Tel.
No.')
     WRITE(*,300)
 300 FORMAT(T4,'----',T17,'---',T21,' ------
',T30,'--------')
     DO
       READ(8,*, IOSTAT= stat) name,age,height,tel_no
       IF(stat<0)EXIT   ! Test for end of file
       WRITE(*,400)name,age,height,tel_no
 400   FORMAT(A,T17,I3,T23,F4.1,T32,I5)
     ENDDO
END PROGRAM
```

Exercise 11.8:

```
   PROGRAM Exercise11_8
    CHARACTER(LEN=20) :: format
    REAL :: a,b,c
    REAL :: e
    INTEGER :: d,f
 L1:   DO I=1,2
         READ(*,*) format
         WRITE(*,*) format
 L2:     DO
           IF(I==1)THEN
             READ(*,format) a,b,c,d
```

```
            WRITE(*,*) a,b,c,d
          ENDIF
          IF(I==2)THEN
            READ(*,format) e,f
            WRITE(*,*) e,f
          ENDIF
          IF(a == 99.9 .OR. e == 99.9)EXIT L2
        ENDDO L2
      ENDDO L1
  END PROGRAM
```

Exercise 11.9:
REAL,DIMENSION(10,10) :: arr
WRITE(*,'(5F10.2)') arr

Exercise 11.10:

```
DO I=1,8
  WRITE(*,'(2F10.3)') arr1(I), arr2(I)
ENDDO
```

Appendix C

Fortran 90 Statements

C.1 Core Statements

The statements in this section are those we have covered in the text of Chapters 1 to 12. These are the statements which we believe form a core of the language which will allow the programmer to code new programs in a modern efficient style which takes advantage of the new features introduced in Fortran 90. The text gives a good overall view of the language and should be helpful as a quick reference. The statements given are not a rigorous definition but should be reasonably self-explanatory. The following conventions have been used:

Items in square brackets [] are optional
Items separated by vertical bar(s) | are alternatives
Items in italics should be substituted by Fortran items
Items in capitals are Fortran keywords

Note: We have used the strict convention that all Fortran keywords are always written in capitals although Fortran 90 does not mandate this.

C.1.1 Program Units

PROGRAM [*program-name*]
END [PROGRAM [*program-name*]]
INCLUDE *name*
MODULE *module-name*
END [MODULE [*module-name*]]
USE *module-name* [, *rename-list*]
USE *module-name*, ONLY: [*object-name-list*]
[RECURSIVE] SUBROUTINE *subroutine-name* [([*args*])]
END [SUBROUTINE [*subroutine-name*]]
[*type*] [RECURSIVE] FUNCTION *function-name* ([*args*]) [RESULT(*name*)]
[RECURSIVE] [*type*] FUNCTION *function-name* ([*args*]) [RESULT(*name*)]
END [FUNCTION [*function-name*]]
ENTRY *procedure-name* [([*args*])] [RESULT(*name*)]
CONTAINS
INTERFACE [OPERATOR(*defined-operator*)|ASSIGNMENT(=)|*procedure-name*]
END INTERFACE
MODULE PROCEDURE *module-procedure-list*
BLOCK DATA [*block-data-name*]
END [BLOCK DATA [*block-data-name*]]

C.1.2 Type Declaration Statements

INTEGER [([KIND=]*integer-value*)][[,*attributes*]::] *entity-decl-list*
REAL [([KIND=]*integer-value*)][[,*attributes*]::] *entity-decl-list*
LOGICAL [([KIND=]*integer-value*)][[,*attributes*]::] *entity-decl-list*
COMPLEX [([KIND=]*integer-value*)][[,*attributes*]::] *entity-decl-list*

CHARACTER [(LEN=*integer-value*|*[,KIND=*integer-value*])] &
[[,*attributes*]::] *entity-decl-list*
CHARACTER [(*integer-value*|*,[KIND=]*integer-value*])] &
[[,*attributes*]::] *entity-decl-list*
CHARACTER [(KIND=*integer-value*[,LEN=*integer-value*|*])] &
[[,*attributes*]::] *entity-decl-list*
DOUBLE PRECISION [[,*attributes*]:: *entity-decl-list*
TYPE(type name) [[,*attributes*]:: *entity-decl-list*

where the *attributes* can be:

PARAMETER, PUBLIC, PRIVATE, ALLOCATABLE, DIMENSION(*extent-list*), EXTERNAL, INTENT(IN|OUT|INOUT), INTRINSIC, OPTIONAL, POINTER, SAVE, TARGET

and the *entity-decl-list* is defined as:

object-name [(*array-specification*][* *character-length*][*initialisation-expression*]
OR
function-name [(*array-specification*)][* *character-length*]

C.1.3 Specification statements covered in the text:

IMPLICIT NONE
TYPE [,PUBLIC|PRIVATE] *type-name*
END TYPE [*type-name*]
PRIVATE [[::] list]
PUBLIC [[::] list]

C.1.4 Assignment statement:

variable-name = *expression*

C.1.5 Pointer assignment:

pointer-name => *pointer-name*

C.1.6 WHERE assignment statement:

WHERE (*logical-array-expression*)
ELSEWHERE
END WHERE

WHERE (*logical-array-expression*) *array-name* = *array expression*

C.1.7 Reference to procedures

CALL *subroutine-name* [([*actual-argument-list*])]
function-name-reference([*actual-argument-list*])

C.1.8 Pointer and allocatable array allocation:

ALLOCATE (*pointer-list* | *allocatable-array-list* [,STAT=*status*])
DEALLOCATE (*pointer-list* | *allocatable-array-list* [,STAT=*status*])
NULLIFY (*pointer-list*)

C.1.9 Loop statements:

[*loop-name*:] DO [*variable=integer-value*, *integer-value*[, *integer-value*]]
CYCLE [*loop-name*]
EXIT [*loop-name*]
END DO [*loop-name*]

C.1.10 IF statements:

[*IF-name*:] IF (*logical-value*) THEN
ELSE [IF (*logical-value*) THEN] [*IF-name*]
END IF [*IF-name*]
IF (*logical-value*) *statement*

C.1.11 Select Statement:

[*select-name*:] SELECT CASE (*value*)
CASE (*value-list*) [*select-name*]
CASE DEFAULT [*select-name*]
END SELECT [*select-name*]

C.1.12 Input/Output Operations:

In this section the right-hand column, where appropriate, specifies the value(s) that the keyword parameter can take. Where a character value is appropriate the enclosing quotes have been omitted for readability. A correct example specification of an OPEN with a BLANK= specifier would therefore correctly read OPEN(UNIT=3, BLANK='NULL',...).

OPEN

[UNIT =] *file-unit*	
IOSTAT = *variable*	
ERR = *label*	Go to *label* on error
FILE = *file-name*	*file-name* must appear unless STATUS = SCRATCH
STATUS = *string*	OLD, NEW, SCRATCH, REPLACE or UNKNOWN
ACCESS = *string*	SEQUENTIAL(default) or DIRECT
FORM = *string*	FORMATTED(default for sequential access) or

	UNFORMATTED(default for direct access)
RECL = *value*	Actual record length for direct access, maximum for sequential
BLANK = *string*	NULL(default) or ZERO
POSITION = *string*	ASIS(default), REWIND or APPEND
ACTION = *string*	READ, WRITE or READWRITE(default)
DELIM = *string*	APOSTROPHE, QUOTE or NONE(default)

PAD = *string* YES(default) or NO. Pad input record with blanks. Formatted input only.

CLOSE

[UNIT =] *file-unit*	
IOSTAT = *variable*	
ERR = *label*	Jump to *label* if error occurrs
STATUS = *string*	KEEP(default for named files) or DELETE(default for scratch files)

READ(*input-control-list*) [*input-list*]
WRITE (*output-control-list*) [*output-list*]

where *input-control-list* and *output-control-list* can include any of the following:

[UNIT =] *file-unit* ǀ * ǀ *string*	
[FMT =] *string*	
[NML =] *namelist-group-name*	
REC = *record-number*	
IOSTAT = *variable*	
ERR = *label*	
END = *label*	
ADVANCE = *string*	YES or NO
SIZE = *variable*	
EOR = *label*	

Note: Some combinations of the above statements and options are illegal. For example END=, EOR=, SIZE= are not permitted in write statements.

INQUIRE(*inquiry-list*)

where *inquiry-list* can contain:

[UNIT =] *file-unit*	
FILE = *file-name*	**Note:** Inquiry can be by unit **or** filename, not both.
IOSTAT = *variable*	Host dependent status

ERR = *label*	Go to *label* on error
EXIST = *variable*	true if file exists or unit is connected, otherwise false.
OPENED = *variable*	true if file is connected to a unit or if unit is connected to a file, otherwise false.
NUMBER = *variable*	the unit number attached to the file or -1
NAMED = *variable*	true if the file has a name otherwise false.
NAME = *variable*	name of the file (if named) or it becomes undefined
ACCESS = *variable*	SEQUENTIAL, DIRECT or UNDEFINED
SEQUENTIAL = *variable*	YES, NO or UNKNOWN
DIRECT = *variable*	YES, NO or UNKNOWN
FORM = *variable*	FORMATTED or UNFORMATTED
FORMATTED = *variable*	YES, NO or UNKNOWN
UNFORMATTED = *variable*	Returns YES, NO or UNKNOWN
RECL = *variable*	The maximum record length in characters for a formatted file
NEXTREC = *variable*	In direct access files, n+1, where n is the number of the last record read or written.
BLANK = *variable*	NULL, ZERO or UNDEFINED
POSITION = *variable*	REWIND, APPEND, ASIS or UNDEFINED
ACTION = *variable*	READ, WRITE, READWRITE or UNDEFINED
READ = *variable*	YES, NO or UNKNOWN
WRITE = *variable*	YES, NO or UNKNOWN
READWRITE = *variable*	YES, NO or UNKNOWN
DELIM = *variable*	APOSTROPHE, QUOTE, NONE or UNDEFINED
PAD = *variable*	YES or NO

BACKSPACE([UNIT =] *file-unit*[,IOSTAT = *variable*[,ERR = *label*]])

REWIND(UNIT = *file-unit*[,IOSTAT = *variable*[, ERR = *label*]]

ENDFILE(UNIT = *file-unit* [,IOSTAT = *variable*[,ERR = *label*]])

C.1.13 Input/Output Formatting:

I*w[.m]*	Integer
B*w[.m]*	Integer as binary
O*w[.m]*	Integer as octal
Z*[w.m]*	Integer as hexadecimal
F*w.d*	Real, fixed form
E*w.d[*E*e]*	Real, exponent form
D*w.d*	Real (D used as exponent letter)

EN*w.d[*E*e]*	Engineering notation
ES*w.d[*E*e]*	Scientific notation
G*w.d[*E*e]*	General, used for any intrinsic data type
L*w*	Logical
A*[w]*	Character
*c*H	Hollerith (obsolescent)

C.1.14 Input/output format control descriptors:

r/	r new records
:	terminates format control if there are no more items in the input/output list
*k*P	Set scale factor for E, F and G processing
T*n*	Tab to position n
TL*n*	Tab left n
TR*n*	Tab right n
*n*X	n spaces
S	Restore default of producing + signs
SS	Suppress + signs
SP	Force + signs
BN	Interpret blanks as nulls
BZ	Interpret blanks as zeros

C.2 Deprecated and/or obsolescent

IMPLICIT *type*(*letter - letter*)
SEQUENCE
DATA
NAMELIST */namelist-group-name/namelist-group-object-list*
COMMON [/[*block-name*]/]*variable-list*
EQUIVALENCE (*variable-name*, *variable-name*)

The following are Fortran statements which correspond to attributes used in the type statements covered in the text. We recommend the use of the attribute form but include this list for completeness.

PARAMETER(*constant-name*=*value*[,...])
DIMENSION [::]*array-name*(*array-spec*)

ALLOCATABLE [::] *array-name*[(*array-spec*)]
POINTER [::] *variable-name*[(*array-spec*)]
TARGET [::] *variable-name*[(*extent list*)]
INTENT(IN|OUT|INOUT) [::] *argument-name-list*
OPTIONAL [::] *argument-name-list*
SAVE [[::] *local-variable-list*

The following flow control statements define facilities which were available in Fortran 77 but which we feel are redundant in Fortran 90:

[*loop-name*:] DO [*label*][,][*index*=*integer-value*, *integer-value*[, *integer-value*]]

Note: non-integer DO indices are obsolescent.

GO TO *label*
GO TO (*label*, *label* ...)[,] *integer-value*
STOP [*stop-code*]
CONTINUE

The following WHILE form of the DO-loop is, as explained in the text (Chapter 13), a special form of the conditional exit loop.

[*loop-name*:] DO [*label*][,]WHILE(*logical-expression*)

C.2.1 Obsolescent statements

IF (*integer-value*) *label*, *label*, *label*
RETURN *integer-value*
ASSIGN *label* TO *integer-variable-name*
GO TO *integer-variable-name* [[,](*label*, *label* ...)]
PAUSE

INDEX

Index to Intrinsic Procedures